Perspectives on Fair Housing

THE CITY IN THE TWENTY-FIRST CENTURY

Eugenie L. Birch and Susan M. Wachter, Series Editors

A complete list of books in the series is
available from the publisher.

Perspectives on Fair Housing

EDITED BY

Vincent J. Reina,
Wendell E. Pritchett,
AND
Susan M. Wachter

FOREWORD BY

Marc Morial

PENN

UNIVERSITY OF PENNSYLVANIA PRESS

PHILADELPHIA

Published by
University of Pennsylvania Press
Philadelphia, Pennsylvania 19104-4112
www.upenn.edu/pennpress

Printed in the United States of America on acid-free paper
10 9 8 7 6 5 4 3 2 1

Library of Congress Cataloging-in-Publication Data
Names: Reina, Vincent J., editor. | Pritchett, Wendell E., editor. |
    Wachter, Susan M., editor.
Title: Perspectives on fair housing / edited by Vincent J. Reina,
    Wendell E. Pritchett, and Susan M. Wachter.
Other titles: City in the twenty-first century book series.
Description: 1st edition. | Philadelphia : University of Pennsylvania
    Press, [2021] | Series: The city in the twenty-first century |
    Includes bibliographical references and index.
Identifiers: LCCN 2020019214 | ISBN 978-0-8122-5275-0 (hardcover)
Subjects: LCSH: United States. Fair Housing Act. | Discrimination
    in housing—United States. | Housing policy—United States. |
Discrimination in housing—Law and legislation—United States.
Classification: LCC HD7288.76.U5 P47 2021 |
    DDC 363.5/5610973—dc23
LC record available at https://lccn.loc.gov/2020019214

CONTENTS

FOREWORD

====

Marc Morial

Let me tell you a story about the city I love.

New Orleans, like all American cities, was segregated in the mid-twentieth century by discriminatory policies like racial zoning and redlining. The Federal Housing Administration (FHA), in particular, was known to insure loans exclusively for white households. In 1954, Mayor deLesseps S. Morrison asked the FHA to make an exception. There was a shortage of housing units where Black households were allowed to live, and Mayor Morrison wasn't about to let them move into white neighborhoods. So he made a deal with the FHA: if the FHA insured a construction loan for a new Black housing development, he would make sure it remained completely segregated from the FHA-insured white development next door.

The NAACP protested the mayor's segregationist plan, but it only made Morrison proud that he had angered them. An FHA spokesman likewise bragged that this segregated project was "the type of thing [the] FHA wanted." He said this *to* African Americans.

The year 1954 was also when my father, Ernest N. Morial, became the first African American graduate of the law school at Louisiana State University. He spent the next twenty years fighting segregationist policies like Mayor Morrison's, and in 1977, my father succeeded in becoming mayor himself. If I learned one thing from his time in the courtroom, it is the lesson that injustice and intolerance do not dissipate without a fight. They hang on, gripping tightly to their power, until the almighty force of law compels them to desist.

It is a lesson I have been reliving in our current political environment.

The chapters in this book tell the story of the Fair Housing Act of 1968: what it is, why it was needed, how it was interpreted, whom it has helped, and where it has failed us—or perhaps more accurately, where *we* have failed *it.* The chapters paint a compelling portrait of a country still at war with the demons that my father's generation set out to vanquish. We have made great progress since those early days. Explicit discrimination is outlawed, and by some measures, segregation has decreased somewhat. But the persistent chasm between the races—in economic opportunity, in social stature, in health and safety, in public opinion—is impossible to deny. The legacy of our nation's sins is on display for all to see.

Where my generation has fallen short, new leaders are beginning to take charge. I am inspired by the young men and women I see protesting, running for office, and demanding equality. I have always believed that a hallmark of leadership is optimism, and I see that hopeful quality in the leaders of tomorrow. But a leader also needs a roadmap. She has to know how we got to where we are, what has worked and what hasn't, and which tools are available to her going forward. This book provides such a road map, and the Fair Housing Act offers one important tool kit.

It may seem, from today's media coverage and political statements, that "housing" ranks low on the list of priorities. Rarely does one hear the word spoken in presidential debates or posted on placards in public demonstrations. But I would argue—and the facts in this book would bear me out—that housing is the foundation that underlies most, if not all, of our current racial divides.

As my friend Raphael Bostic likes to say, housing is a platform. It is the foundation on which we build our lives, our careers, our communities, and our democracy. Housing is a conduit to jobs, to health care, to public safety, and to social interaction. When we segregate our housing, we cut our citizens off from one another. We splinter the bonds that move us forward as one nation. Is it any surprise, after fifty-plus years living in two worlds physically apart from one another, that we seem unable to find common ground, trust collective institutions, or elect politicians with compassion, with empathy, and with respect for all their constituents? The rot of our body politic did not come from the top and work its way down. On the contrary, we instilled it in our homes, and it eroded us from within. Let this be a warning to all who seek to mend the fractures that cleave our land in two: only by living among one another can our spirits truly be joined as one.

I have seen this transformation in my own city in recent years. I am proud to say I lived to see something my father never imagined, when the Civil War monuments erected to subjugate his generation and his father's before him came tumbling down, and the people of New Orleans turned their eyes at long last away from Confederate ghosts of the past toward the diverse opportunity of the future. Though we have not yet vanquished the ghosts of segregation in the same fashion, the progress we have made would make our ancestors proud, and they would advise us to do as they did: turn our eyes toward the future and steel ourselves for the fight ahead, until at long last the almighty force of law compels fairness, justice, and tolerance to triumph.

INTRODUCTION

Vincent J. Reina, Wendell E. Pritchett, and Susan M. Wachter

On April 11, 1968, President Lyndon B. Johnson signed the Civil Rights Act of 1968 into law. Title VIII of the Civil Rights Act of 1968, known as the Fair Housing Act, was the most robust piece of federal legislation aimed at stopping the systemic and severe discriminatory practices that defined the housing market at that time and through the present. This legislation has been crucial to the fight against housing discrimination but has by no means eliminated it. The compounding inequities of historic housing discrimination, and its persistence to this day, present a serious challenge to the future of American society. This book makes the case that fair housing is a critical issue not only for those directly affected by it, but also for society more broadly, and that meaningful government intervention is required to achieve fair housing just as much now as fifty years ago.

The Fair Housing Act, when it was passed in 1968, prohibited discrimination in the sale, rent, and financing of housing based on race, religion, or national origin. Manifold historical and contemporary forces, driven by both governmental and private actors, have segregated these protected classes by denying them access to homeownership or housing options. These forces are all well documented in the first chapter of this book, written by Francesca Russello Ammon and Wendell E. Pritchett. This chapter highlights one of the main themes that runs throughout this book: the fact that residential segregation did not emerge naturally from the benign preferences of the minority. Rather, segregation was forced through legal, economic, social, and even violent measures.

One tool that has been key to discrimination in the housing market is local land use planning. Ritzdorf and Thomas document the many ways land use regulations and zoning were used to further segregation in their

1997 book *Urban Planning and the African American Community: In the Shadows*. The book shows how cities like Atlanta, Richmond, and Baltimore used racial land use and zoning practices in the early 1900s to establish and reinforce racial segregation and how such practices spread across the country. Explicit racial zoning ordinances were ruled illegal in 1917, but they were replaced with land use practices that, though they were less explicitly racist, would prove just as damaging.

Zoning and land use laws decide what can be built and where. They can easily serve as more subtle means to achieve the same goals as explicit racial zoning. As Orfield (2006: 8) notes, "by prohibiting the development of housing that only the better-off can afford, these local policies effectively exclude the poor and people of color from the places that erect those policy fences." The practice of zoning areas exclusively for single-family housing has both reinforced and advanced segregation across the country, from the invention of zoning in the early 1900s to the present day. This fact is borne out by multiple studies. Richard Rothstein's book *The Color of Law* documents how land use and zoning laws, even when not explicitly racial, historically established the foundation for racial segregation in housing markets across the country. Using more recent data, Rothwell and Massey (2009) find a significant relationship between today's low-density zoning and segregation; they argue that antidensity zoning inhibits desegregation over time. Rothwell (2011) also finds that antidensity zoning significantly contributed to both the level and the change in segregation between 1990 and 2000 and that a movement to more liberal zoning could decrease racial segregation by as much as 35 percent.

The exclusionary effects of single-family zoning have been compounded by racially motivated barriers to obtaining the credit necessary to purchase a home. Increased attention is now being paid to redlining and its impact on access to homeownership and neighborhood opportunity for nonwhite households. Redlining is the practice of using race and ethnicity as a primary proxy for risk in lending decisions and color-coding maps based on where minority households live so that lenders can make credit decisions based on those boundaries. The Home Ownership Loan Corporation (HOLC) is widely credited for the advent of redlining in the 1930s and 1940s. However, research shows that the race- and ethnicity-based boundaries explicitly drawn in the HOLC maps largely predated them. The HOLC maps reflected the prevailing discrimination in the market and served to further it, but they should not be viewed as the genesis of this deleterious practice (Hillier 2003). For some time, we have known that redlining created a self-fulfilling prophecy that lending in minority areas was riskier, because redlining effectively chilled investment in those neighborhoods (Guttentag and Wachter 1980). However, new forms of data have allowed for a more detailed and longer-term analysis of this impact of this practice. For example, the Mapping Inequality website led efforts to digitize HOLC maps from across the country and make the data accessible to the general public.

Redlining policies reinforced demographic and economic segregation in American cities, and in many cities, the lines drawn unfortunately still correlate with investment levels (Appel and Nickerson 2016). A recent study by Mikhitarian (2019) shows that median home prices in areas that were redlined remain lower than those rated "best" and that only 1 of the 151 areas analyzed was an exception to this rule. The difference in housing prices is the result of historical discrimination that fueled a cycle of underinvestment in minority neighborhoods on the basis of racially justified credit accessibility (Krimmel 2017). These policies, endorsed and facilitated by the federal government, constrained the physical and economic mobility of minority households in ways that still afflict minority communities today. In fact, the same behavior promoted by the HOLC maps took the form of predatory loan products that targeted minority neighborhoods in the housing boom and bust of the 2000s and is reflected in the barriers to accessing credit that minority households face to this day.

Today's challenges in fair housing are not solely a product of flawed government policies and programs. Sociological dynamics have made segregation a pernicious force that evades reform, as documented by Justin P. Steil and Camille Z. Charles in the second chapter of this book. Steil and Charles discuss the "color line" that has divided cities in every area from job access to public services to social relations; the authors also discuss how this physical separation inculcates mistaken beliefs on both sides, reinforcing the suspicion and prejudice that led to the oppression of minorities in the first place. The themes in Chapter 2 provide an important extension to previous research. For example, Cutler, Glaeser, and Vigdor (1999) found that collective action from whites drove segregation for the first half of twentieth century, but since 1990 more decentralized dynamics, such as whites' willingness to pay more to live near other whites, have driven ongoing segregation. Korver-Glenn (2018) conducted an in-depth qualitative study to identify how and when racial stereotypes and discrimination affect a minority household's housing search process. This research shows that minorities are subject to negative racial stereotypes throughout their housing search process, whereas white households benefit from positive ones. Such realities affect whether, and where, a minority household purchases a home, and aggregate to stereotypes and bias being applied to majority minority neighborhoods. The decentralized racist dynamics highlighted by Cutler and colleagues are rooted in the self-reinforcing divisions that Steil and Charles present in this book and are formalized, consciously or unconsciously, in the housing search process.

The second main assertion of this book is that discrimination in the housing market results in unequal outcomes for minority households and, in aggregate, diminishes economic prosperity in American cities and across the country. As shown by Akira Drake Rodriguez and Rand Quinn in Chapter 3, racial inequity in housing has a powerful effect on access to high-performing and safe schools, investments in schools, and educational outcomes. This effect is particularly concerning when we consider that schools are even more segregated by race and income than their surrounding neighborhoods, since the childless households who do not factor school quality into their location decisions tend to represent the more affluent, nonminority portion of overall low-income minority communities (Jargowsky 2016).

When housing markets are fair, individuals have access to better economic opportunity and the ability to build more wealth, as Vincent J. Reina and Raphael Bostic argue in Chapter 4. Absent fair housing, minorities have greater difficulty becoming homeowners and experience lower house price growth. These experiences translate into minority households having persistently lower homeownership rates and significantly lower levels of housing wealth than white households (Acolin, Lin, and Wachter 2019). These economic realities affect rates of minority entrepreneurship and local investment, and then permeate the broader regional economy. Such forms of income and wealth inequality have severe and important macroeconomic implications. Research demonstrates that, relative to whites, black Americans continue to face substantially lower rates of upward mobility—while also experiencing far higher rates of downward mobility (Chetty 2016). This leads to income disparities that fuel the self-reinforcing nature of inequality.

The importance of fair housing is clear, but the best mechanisms to achieve this goal are harder to ascertain. The third main assertion of this book is that at least one thing is certain: government action is required if we want to meaningfully address fair housing. On the most basic level, government action substantively contributed to the current situation of segregation and unequal access to public amenities and economic opportunities, and it is the duty of the government now to correct for that. Second, the pernicious nature of fair housing and the troubling level of inequity make this an issue that the market will not address on its own. Advantage has multiplied upon advantage and disadvantage upon disadvantage, institutionalizing the gap between races.

Fortunately, the law authorizes the federal government to take up this challenge. The Fair Housing Act of 1968 prohibited discrimination by landlords, lenders, insurance companies, and cities. The law outlawed racial zoning, redlining, and racially restrictive covenants. As highlighted by Nestor M. Davidson and Eduardo M. Peñalver in Chapter 5 of this book, the Fair Housing Act (FHA) also instructed the executive branch to administer all housing-related programs and activities "in a manner affirmatively to further" the dual purpose of the law: to eliminate discrimination and to desegregate communities. Through this law, Congress charged the Department of Housing and Urban Development (HUD) with actively reversing segregation. In recent opinions, the Supreme Court has upheld this mandate in the form of disparate impact liability that allows plaintiffs to sue for discriminatory outcomes in the absence of discriminatory intent. This mandate does not appear to be unlimited, so we must interpret and apply it with prudence. HUD's "affirmatively furthering fair housing" initiative under the Obama administration offers one such application, leveraging newly available data to identify programs and policies that contribute to the dual mandate that legislators approved in April 1968.

Recent scholarship has focused on the importance and meaning of the FHA itself. Its continuing relevance stems from its recognition that housing is important for the groups affected and for the greater good. In this book we argue that the FHA is absolutely necessary, but given the myriad of challenges that confront us, it may not be sufficient on its own. That is not a fault of the FHA itself, but a result of the complexity of the problem at hand. While the FHA is the law of the land, its power lies entirely in meaningful enforcement and in programs that further its goals. Under the Obama administration, the FHA saw renewed support, buoyed by a Supreme Court decision that concluded that the act protected not only against direct discrimination, but also against the "disparate impact" of seemingly neutral policies on protected classes. The Obama administration developed a series of tools and incentives for localities to develop meaningful programs and policies that would reduce segregation and "affirmatively further fair housing." Research shows that this mandate indeed motivated municipalities to produce fair housing plans that were more ambitious, involved more community engagements, and had clearer quantifiable goals than previous plans (Steil and Kelly 2019). This mandate is now the subject of litigation as the Trump administration endeavors to roll back the policies set in place by the Obama administration. This sequence of events highlights how political will can, and does, affect the strength of the FHA. On the one hand, the FHA mandate can be realized through programs and policies aimed at advancing its goals; on the other hand, it can exist solely through litigation meant to protect the progress that has been made. In this book we acknowledge the importance of the FHA but embrace a broader focus on the importance of fair housing itself. Fair housing represents a moral, societal, and economic imperative to address the intentional and *un*intentional oppression that remains ingrained in our system.

The final major point raised in this book is that, though fair housing is often defined as a white-versus-nonwhite phenomenon, discrimination actually goes well beyond race. As Amy Hillier and Devin Michelle Bunten argue in Chapter 6 of this book, discrimination based on sexual identity and orientation is also well documented. When the Fair Housing Act was passed, it protected people based on race, religion, national origin. The act was then amended in 1974 to include gender and again in 1988 to include families with children and people with disabilities. The list of those who fall within the legal category of a protected class must continue to change as our society evolves if our goal is to ensure true equality of opportunity and outcomes for all.

In this volume, we offer distinct perspectives on the topic of fair housing—from historical, sociological, economic, and legal points of view—and show how the importance of fair housing permeates every aspect of our society. We also demonstrate that while we have tools in place to address housing discrimination, we have a long way to go. Fair housing's continuing relevance is driven by the same issues that necessitated the passing of the Fair Housing Act in 1968: a recognition that the structural prevention of discrimination in housing is necessary to further the greater good in our communities. It may seem, in hindsight, that fifty years is too long to wait for true fairness and integration. Indeed, any time is too long to live with such inequities.

References

Acolin, Arthur, Desen Lin, and Susan Wachter. "Endowments and Minority Homeownership." *Cityscape: A Journal of Policy Development and Research* 21, no. 1 (2019): 5–62.

Appel, Ian, and Jordan Nickerson. "Pockets of Poverty: The Long-Term Effects of Redlining." 2016. SSRN: https://dx.doi.org/10.2139/ssrn.2852856.

Chetty, Raj. "Socioeconomic Mobility in the United States: New Evidence and Policy Lessons." In *Shared Prosperity in America's Communities*, edited by Lei Ding and Susan M. Wachter. Philadelphia: University of Pennsylvania Press, 2016.

Cutler, David M., Edward L. Glaeser, and Jacob L. Vigdor. "The Rise and Decline of the American Ghetto." *Journal of Political Economy* 107, no. 3 (1999): 455–506.

Guttentag, J. M., and Susan M. Wachter. 1980. *Redlining and Public Policy.* New York University, Graduate School of Business Administration, Salomon Brothers Center for the Study of Financial Institutions.

Hillier, Amy E. "Redlining and the Home Owners' Loan Corporation." *Journal of Urban History* 29, no. 4 (2003): 394–420.

Hsieh, Chang-Tai, and Enrico Moretti. "Housing Constraints and Spatial Misallocation." National Bureau of Economic Research, 2015.

Jargowsky, Paul. "Neighborhoods and Segregation." In *Shared Prosperity in America's Communities*, edited by Lei Ding and Susan M. Wachter. Philadelphia: University of Pennsylvania Press, 2016.

Korver-Glenn, Elizabeth. "Compounding Inequalities: How Racial Stereotypes and Discrimination Accumulate Across the Stages of Housing Exchange." *American Sociological Review* 83, no. 4 (2018): 627–56.

Krimmel, Jacob. "Persistence of Prejudice: Estimating the Long Term Effects of Redlining." Wharton Business Economic and Public Policy, 2017.

Mikhitarian, Sarah. "Home Values Remain Low in Vast Majority of Formerly Redlined Neighborhoods." Accessed August 21, 2019. https://www.zillow.com/research/home-values-redlined-areas-19674/.

Nelson, Robert K., LaDale Winling, Richard Marciano, Nathan Connolly, et al. "Mapping Inequality." In *American Panorama*, edited by Robert K. Nelson and Edward L. Ayers. Accessed August 21, 2019. https://dsl.richmond.edu/panorama/redlining/.

Orfield, Myron. "Land Use and Housing Policies to Reduce Concentrated Poverty and Racial Segregation." *Fordham Urban Law Journal* 33 (2006): 877.

Ritzdorf, Marsha, and June Manning Thomas. *Urban Planning and the African American Community: In the Shadows.* Newbury Park, CA: Sage, 1997.

Rothstein, Richard. *The Color of Law: A Forgotten History of How Our Government Segregated America*. New York: Liveright, 2017.

Rothwell, Jonathan. "Racial Enclaves and Density Zoning: The Institutionalized Segregation of Racial Minorities in the United States." *American Law and Economics Review* 13, no. 1 (2011): 290–358.

Rothwell, Jonathan, and Douglas S. Massey. "The Effect of Density Zoning on Racial Segregation in US Urban Areas." *Urban Affairs Review* 44, no. 6 (2009): 779–806.

Steil, Justin P., and Nicholas Kelly. "Survival of the Fairest: Examining HUD Reviews of Assessments of Fair Housing." *Housing Policy Debate* (2019): 1–16.

CHAPTER 1

The Long History of Unfair Housing

Francesca Russello Ammon and Wendell E. Pritchett

Introduction

When Congress passed the Fair Housing Act of 1968, it was responding most immediately to the civil rights and housing crises of that era. But the roots of this policy reach much further back in time to encompass a long history of housing discrimination and segregation. This chapter traces the federal policies, professional practices, legal decisions, and local actions, from the end of Reconstruction through passage of the Fair Housing Act, through which people of color and African Americans in particular have experienced unequal access to affordable housing and homeownership. This is a story of individual choices grounded in larger structural forces that have shaped the legal, economic, and practical accessibility of indiscriminately available and integrated housing through the postwar decades.

Following World War II, the issues of housing discrimination and residential segregation emerged as important areas of debate among policymakers, politicians, community members, and activists. The Fair Housing Act of 1968 was the culmination of more than twenty years of advocacy and opposition, and marked a major step forward for the country in the promotion of equality. At the same time, as this chapter shows, the political, economic, and social structures that limited the opportunities for people of color to live where they choose created barriers that legal reforms could not, on their own, overcome.

Zoning for Segregation

While federal policies following the Civil War helped safeguard the civil rights of African Americans, those protections were short-lived or relatively ineffectual. Subsection 1982 of the Civil Rights Act of 1866, for example, was the nation's first fair housing law; but the requirement to demonstrate intentional discrimination limited citizens' ability to make use of it (Fennell 2017: 391). Instead, with the end of Reconstruction, a set of state and local policies known as the Jim Crow laws instituted segregation in multiple domains. These laws suppressed African American voting and imposed the myth of "separate but equal" institutions and environments. The 1896 Supreme Court ruling in *Plessy v. Ferguson* further cemented the legality of such practices. Housing segregation took root as part of this legal regime. While the Jim Crow laws were explicit, or de jure, in the South, similar impacts were more commonly achieved in the North through de facto means. In either scenario, African Americans began experiencing a period of protracted discrimination that would not be undone—in the law—until well into the post–World War II years. In practice, however, righting these wrongs would take even longer.

About 90 percent of African Americans resided in the South at the end of the Civil War, but many soon began migrating to northern U.S. cities. As historian Arnold Hirsch has observed, "the upsurge in urban black population in the United States meant, universally, an increase in residential segregation" (Hirsch 1993: 68). In the South, African American communities tended to cluster together within blocks and neighborhoods. This clustering continued into the North as the rise of industrialization and consequent decline of the walking city limited previously necessary intermixing by class, ethnicity, and race. The new, typically poor migrants often settled in existing African American communities, as well as in neighborhoods where speculative development catered to them, such as Chicago's South Side and New York's Harlem. While European immigrant communities also clustered in this way, the resultant white ethnic enclaves were often stopping points on a path to dispersal and "Americanization." Over time, these clustered settlements largely dissipated. But African Americans did not have the same choices as these immigrants, and their clustering proved more permanent (Hirsch 1993).

Some municipalities actively excluded African Americans—and often other minorities as well—from within their borders. While live-in servants could be an exception, these "sundown towns" systematically worked to prevent Blacks from moving in and to expel those who already resided there. Beginning in the 1890s, but continuing through 1940 (and sometimes even today), residents of these towns achieved these goals by deploying violence, passing ordinances that forbade African Americans from remaining in their town after dark, and posting signs at the city limits announcing this policy. Thousands of sundown towns functioned this way, and the vast majority were located in the North, rather than the South. Sundown suburbs began a bit later in time, but they followed the same pattern (Loewen 2005).

Exclusionary zoning emerged at this time as a potent tool for formalizing the color line in increasingly multiracial cities. On its face, zoning may seem largely a mechanism for separating incompatible uses, such as industrial and residential uses. But zoning also produced corollary, and often explicitly, racial impacts. In the 1880s, California cities used their police power to restrict laundries from operating in residential areas. Since Chinese immigrants owned most such businesses, these laws disparately impacted one minority group over others. When New York City introduced restrictions on land uses and heights in 1916, as part of the first municipal zoning code in the country, perceptions of race, ethnicity, and class drove those policies as well. By zoning out garment factories from Fifth Avenue, commercial interests were also attempting to protect against the perceived invasion of immigrant factory workers onto this fashionable street (Fischler 1998; Freund 2007; Hirt 2013, 2014).

While the racial and ethnic impacts of these examples were inexplicit by-products of land use policies, racial zoning named its demographic interests more directly. These explicit policies proliferated in the South, becoming, as historian Christopher Silver has argued, "as much a foundation for overall land use regulations as was regulation of the garment industry in New York City or encroaching industrial use in Los Angeles" (Silver 1997). Beginning with Baltimore in 1910, as illustrated in Figure 1.1, cities passed ordinances restricting Black occupancy on majority-white blocks, and vice versa (Nightingale 2012). The Baltimore ordinance became a model that other cities in Virginia, Georgia, and the Carolinas followed. Multiple common, but specious, justifications underpinned these ordinances around the country. In defending the law in Baltimore, for example, the city's mayor cited concerns over safety, public health, and property values. Through the imposition of racial zoning, he hoped to contain disease and violence and preserve real estate investments for whites (Silver 1997).

Figure 1.1. In 1910, a Black lawyer's purchase of property on an otherwise white-owned block prompted Baltimore to pass an ordinance restricting Black occupancy. As this article suggests, fear of declining property values played a large role in furthering support for this "Jim Crow" measure. ("Baltimore Tries Drastic Plan of Race Segregation," *New York Times*, December 25, 1910)

Racial zoning laws continued to proliferate until 1917, when the Supreme Court ruled them illegal in *Buchanan v. Warley*. In this case from Louisville, Kentucky, the court defended the right of an African American to purchase property on an integrated block. The rationale behind the decision, however, was not to support African American opportunity but rather to ensure white property owners' ability to sell to African American buyers (Whittemore 2017). In any event, this judicial decision did not mark the end of these practices, and neither did various other court cases and laws over time; proponents of segregation often found ways to achieve their intended outcomes through alternative means.

In the face of legal opposition to official race-based zoning, Southern cities turned to "race-based planning processes" (Silver 1997). Here they met with mixed success. Atlanta's 1922 plan designated zones for Black residential expansion but was successfully challenged in court (Bayor 1996). In 1923, New Orleans prohibited Black occupancy of houses in white areas unless a majority of white block residents approved. The Supreme Court struck down this provision in 1927. Charleston, South Carolina, embedded racial exclusion into its designation of the nation's first historic district. Without including racial labels in the official documents, the city's plan designated separate Black and white areas. Notably, the Old and Historic District was to become white. As these various cities proposed implicit planning iterations on racial zoning ordinances, other cities, like Birmingham, Alabama, continued to illegally enforce racial zones until at least 1951 (Silver 1997).

Private Real Estate Interventions

With *Buchanan* applying only to the actions of government officials, communities in the North and, increasingly, throughout the country turned to private alternatives to racial zoning. One such mechanism was the restrictive covenant, a deed provision that limited the construction, sale, or rental of property along various dimensions—race among them. Another means was the set of professional practices deployed by the real estate industry. Using both of these methods, developers, real estate agents, homeowners, and communities privately perpetuated housing segregation.

Restrictive covenants have existed since the early 1800s, when they were largely deployed by affluent communities; but their prevalence increased at the end of the nineteenth century as their application spread to other classes.

Figure 1.2. J. C. Nichols included restrictive covenants in deeds for houses in his "1000 Acres Restricted" Country Club District development, located in Kansas City, Missouri, 1912. (The State Historical Society of Missouri–Kansas City)

Developers and homeowner associations wrote covenants into deeds to limit nuisances (such as undesirable businesses and land uses), residents of certain races (including African Americans, Asian Americans, and Jews), and building types and styles. In many ways, restrictive covenants presaged zoning rules (Fogelson 2005).

Beginning in 1910, the impact of restrictive covenants increased in scale as community builders incorporated them into new residential subdivisions. In these cases, the existence of covenants could even become marketing devices. Prominent among these builders was J. C. Nichols, a Kansas City developer who included in his deeds that "none of the lots hereby restricted may be conveyed to, used, owned, nor occupied by Negroes as owners or tenants." One of his promotional billboards for Country Club District appears in Figure 1.2. Restrictive covenants gradually spread from higher-end developments like Country Club District in Kansas City and Palos Verdes Estates in Los Angeles to new middle-class and older urban neighborhoods. Homeowner associations, for example, applied covenants to existing white neighborhoods that bordered Black areas (Gotham 2000: 625). In 1926, following race riots in several cities in the post–World War I years, the Supreme Court endorsed the legality of restrictive covenants in *Corrigan v. Buckley*. It would not be until the

WHAT HOUSING SEGREGATION MEANS TO THE CAPITAL'S NEGROES

Figure 1.3. This 1948 report on Washington, D.C., illustrates the impact of the professional real estate Code of Ethics on the enclosure of African American residents. (National Committee on Segregation in the Nation's Capital, *Segregation in Washington: A Report* [Chicago, 1948])

1948 Supreme Court case of *Shelley v. Kraemer*—which will be discussed later—that these covenants lost their legal legitimacy (Gonda 2015). Yet, by that time, scholars estimate that roughly half of newly built subdivisions contained racially restrictive covenants (Gotham 2000). Throughout their existence, these contracts particularly targeted African Americans. As just one example, 99 percent of St. Louis's covenants pertained to Blacks (Hirsch 1993).

The very practice of restricting residences by race also became an informal part of real estate practices, enforced by both real estate agents and residents—even without the presence of covenants themselves. Realtors would steer prospective home buyers away from some neighborhoods and toward others, thereby preserving the color line even when it was not written down (Hornstein 2005). They were bolstered in these efforts by the official Code of Ethics of the National Association of Real Estate Boards, which stated that agents should "never be instrumental in introducing into a neighborhood a character of property or occupancy, members of any race or nationality, or any industry whose presence will be clearly detrimental to real estate values." If agents broke these codes, they risked losing access to listings or facing boycotts by white customers (Sugrue 1996: 46). Figure 1.3 reproduces a graphic from a report on segregation in the nation's capital, which equated the housing treatment of African Americans with racial enclosure.

The Segregation of Financing

Despite these many obstacles, African Americans still found a place in the suburbs—albeit in limited numbers. During the Great Migration, for example, Black southerners relocated to both northern and eastern cities and their outskirts (Wiese 2004). But homeownership required financing through favorable mortgage terms—which were often impossible for people of color to obtain. Such financial obstacles were often bank policy, with the result that lending became another mechanism for segregating residential space. During the New Deal, the federal government took a more active role in supporting homeownership. But government-sponsored financial institutions distributed the benefits of that support in uneven ways.

The Home Owners' Loan Corporation (HOLC), created in 1933 during the Depression, offered amortized, low-interest mortgages to prevent foreclosure among existing homeowners. But HOLC limited these mortgages to properties that met the corporation's criteria for risk. Local real estate agents assessed hundreds of U.S. cities to grade neighborhoods on a scale from A to D, or green to red, as they were designated on the maps that HOLC subsequently produced (Nelson et al. n.d.). Figure 1.4 shows one example of such a map, for Atlanta. These assessments were subjective and in keeping with real estate ethics codes that supported racial segregation. The mere presence of African Americans superseded socioeconomic characteristics, resulting in a low rating. In turn, these ratings limited the ability of current and future homeowners to obtain loans for properties in areas with low ratings. Scholars continue to assess the long-term impacts of these redlining practices on diminished levels of neighborhood investment over time and diminished family wealth for people of color (Hillier 2003; Jackson 1985; Rothstein 2017).

In parallel, the formation of the Federal Housing Administration (FHA) in 1934 aimed to expand the reach of middle-class homeownership through amortized, long-term mortgages with low down payment rates. FHA property appraisals restricted the reach of these loans, however, making the racial bias explicit. The FHA *Underwriting Manual* instructed appraisers to rate properties highly when they protected against the "infiltration of inharmonious racial or nationality groups." Such infiltration could already be present or simply exist as an adjacent threat. The limitations on mortgage guarantees applied both to properties being purchased by African Americans and to those owned by whites but planned for African American rental. Further,

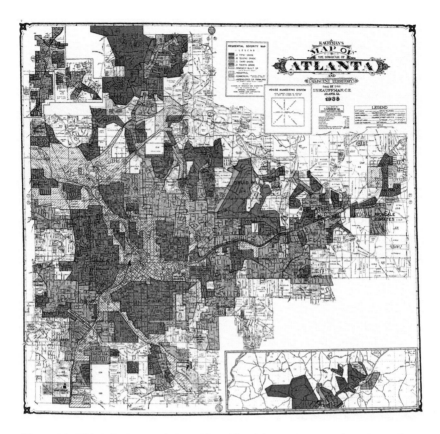

Figure 1.4. This HOLC-commissioned "Residential Security Map" for Atlanta, from 1938, assesses the risks associated with various neighborhoods. A (Green) is Best, B (Blue) is Still Desirable, C (Yellow) is Definitely Declining, and D (Red) is Hazardous. In this grayscale reproduction, D (red) appears as the dark gray nearest the center city. Assessors "redlined" most African American neighborhoods with a D rating. (National Archives II, College Park, Maryland, via *Mapping Inequality*, https://dsl .richmond.edu/panorama/redlining/#loc=11/33.754/-84.356&city=atlanta-ga [accessed May 15, 2018])

the FHA encouraged banks to make loans to new suburbs, rather than existing urban housing. When the G.I. Bill of Rights of 1944 introduced home loans for veterans, it extended these discriminatory lending practices even further. Although African Americans had fought alongside whites during World War II, they could not fully partake of the postwar benefits of low-interest home loans. Veterans Administration (VA) appraisers also adopted the appraisal guidelines of the FHA (Rothstein 2017). While banks could have bucked these trends and given loans to credit-worthy, middle-income Blacks, racial conservatism characterized banks' lending practices. This deprived most African Americans of access to the capital necessary for home purchases. Discrimination in the labor market only exacerbated these trends by limiting African Americans' ability to improve their economic circumstances through employment as well (Sugrue 1996; Highsmith 2015).

Housing Segregation Through Community Institutions

In addition to land use controls, real estate restrictions, and limits to financial funding for African American residence and homeownership, a fourth set of practices also shaped spatial segregation. Municipal leaders and businesspeople exercised their own influence over housing opportunities by limiting related access to community institutions. These included public parks, pools, and schools—all of which were segregated not only in the South, but in the North as well. Decisions around public schools played a significant role in shaping neighborhood composition. Of course, segregated neighborhoods led to segregated schools. But historians have increasingly shown how segregated schools—legal until the 1954 Supreme Court ruling in *Brown v. Board of Education*—drove housing segregation as well (Lassiter 2012). To understand residential segregation, then, requires that we also examine intersecting real estate markets and public institutions.

The city of Austin, Texas, offers one illustrative example. While Austin was unable to implement explicit racial zoning in its 1928 master plan, it used the siting of various services to nudge the city's African Americans into one area: the East Side neighborhood. These inducements included both carrots and sticks. The city closed schools and parks outside of the East Side, while building new segregated institutions—including a library, a park, and a high school—within it. In 1938, the city sited a major African American public housing project there as well. Although some of these new investments in the area could have potentially boded well for the future, municipal services in the area declined over time—from street repairs to bus services and zoning enforcement (Rothstein 2017). As a result, racial and economic segregation in Austin was entrenched in these areas.

Particularly in the South, where school segregation was most prevalent, the siting of white and Black public schools immediately affected the racial composition of surrounding neighborhoods. These educational changes could involve new school construction or the conversion of existing schools from one racial designation to another. Such educational decisions could also undo successfully integrated—or at least scattered—areas of racial diversity. If families wished to send their children to the newest schools, they had little choice but to follow these institutions to implicitly race-designated sections of the city. In Raleigh, North Carolina, in the 1920s, for example, the school board relocated or constructed most white public schools in the city's annexed northwest suburbs, whereas it confined all newly constructed Black schools to the southeast quadrant of the city (Benjamin 2012). These distinct educational geographies restructured housing markets. Similarly, whereas the courts had denied Atlanta's racial zoning ordinance in 1924, the city subsequently achieved the desired racial realignment of its master plan in part through a series of school openings and closings that were guided by the earlier segregation maps (Rothstein 2017). Thus, even when cities were unable to zone a neighborhood for a single race, they could achieve the same outcome through their public schools.

Such practices continued even after *Brown v. Board of Education* forbade school segregation. In cities like Nashville, Tennessee, members of the planning commission and school board worked together to construct new schools on developer-donated land in segregated suburban areas. Then developers could market the full package of neighborhood schools with their home sales. Such collaborations lay bare the myth of de facto segregation: the reality is that, across the country, public and private entities overtly collaborated in planning residential and educational real estate (Erickson 2016).

Postwar Housing Policies and Practices

After World War II, the confluence of a variety of factors—including pent-up housing demand, growth of a consumer culture, expansion of the automobile and highway networks, favorable mortgage terms through housing policies like the G.I. Bill, and the rise of mass builders—spurred rapid suburbanization. African Americans struggled to participate in this phenomenon. The FHA perpetuated racial segregation in housing through its financing of new suburban subdivisions—with the proviso that they be all-white. By guaranteeing bank loans for master builders, the FHA enabled these

Figure 1.5. In 1957, a large crowd of protestors gathered in front of the house of
Bill and Daisy Myers, the first African American family to move into Levittown,
Pennsylvania. (George D. McDowell Philadelphia Evening Bulletin Collection,
Special Collections Research Center, Temple University Libraries, Philadelphia,
Pennsylvania)

developers to proceed with the enormous costs of land acquisition and construction. Without these loans, such large-scale undertakings would not have
been as possible. Further, with these guarantees in place, home buyers for
these properties were preapproved for their own individual mortgages.
Thus, the FHA facilitated the ease, speed, and scale of homeownership. But
by racially limiting the types of subdivisions it would support, the FHA
created massive new segregated enclaves. From Oak Forest in Houston,
Texas, to Lakewood, California; Levittown, New York; and scores of developments in between, homeownership in the suburbs remained exclusive
and restricted (Rothstein 2017).

African Americans had more luck making limited homeownership
inroads in older, more inner-ring suburbs (Wiese 2004). Gradually, how-

Figure 1.6. At Concord Park, located in suburban Philadelphia, developer Morris Milgram achieved an integrated residential counterpart to nearby Levittown. This image shows some of the roughly three hundred children who resided in the community in 1957. ("An Example of Open Housing," *Ebony*, February 1957, Morris Milgram Papers, Historical Society of Pennsylvania)

ever, some pioneering residents broke the color line even in new postwar suburbs—albeit at significant personal costs. In 1957, for example, when Daisy and Bill Myers and their three children moved into Levittown, Pennsylvania, existing residents met the arrival of their new African American neighbors with rioting. Figure 1.5 depicts some of these crowds, some members of which threw rocks at the Myerses' house, burned crosses, blared loud music, and harassed their supporters in the neighborhood. Four years later, the Myerses moved out of the area (Sugrue 2010; Myers 2010). Such stories were not uncommon. Two years earlier, the

Wilson family had crossed an invisible color line when they purchased a house in a predominantly white section of Detroit's Northeast Side. Their harassment began early, with vandalism damaging the house before the Wilsons could even move in. Once they were in residence, neighbors picketed and chanted in front of the Wilsons' house and threw rocks, eggs, bricks, and paint at the structure. When their young son's health began to suffer as a result, the family moved out. The effects of such harassment were enduring; by 1960, less than 3 percent of area residents were Black (Sugrue 1996). The failure of police to fully protect African American residents from these abuses only abetted their suffering. Richard Rothstein has gone so far as to label this inaction as "state-sponsored violence" (Rothstein 2017).

But some progressive developers, like Morris Milgram, constructed new suburban housing with African American residents specifically in mind. As depicted in Figure 1.6, his Concord Park project, built in suburban Philadelphia in 1954—only miles from Pennsylvania's Levittown—targeted not only African Americans, but also integration. Demand for Concord Park's 139 houses was so strong that Milgram had to give preference to whites in order to maintain that integration. Nationwide, during his lifetime, Milgram built roughly twenty thousand such housing units. The further growth of such integrated projects was more strongly limited by access to financing than by any lack of interested Black residents (Hurley 2017; Sugrue 2008).

Although African Americans ultimately purchased only 2 to 3 percent of the new owner-occupied postwar suburban housing units across the country, a distinct Black middle class grew, in part, as a result (Ammon 2016). Its very existence, despite its relatively small size, counters the notion that Blacks lacked either the means or the desire to live in the suburbs. But African Americans' relatively limited participation in the equity opportunities embedded in home purchasing furthered patterns of spatial and economic inequality that have compounding and enduring legacies today.

African Americans could also gain access to homeownership—in urban or suburban areas—through a more insidious real estate practice known as blockbusting. After the Supreme Court outlawed the enforcement of restrictive covenants with *Shelley v. Kraemer* in 1948, real estate agents who had previously steered Blacks away from white neighborhoods could purposefully point them in that direction with the goal of profiting from enduring anxieties over racial mixing. These agents began by selling a house on a white block to a Black family and then advertising that sale widely. Or they would just make a show of walking prospective Black buyers around the neighborhood. Having thereby stoked fears of a Black takeover, the agents actively encouraged whites to sell their houses—often at below-market prices—before it was too late. These agents would then resell the house—at a markup—to an African American family with otherwise limited housing options. In the absence of available financing, speculators would sometimes assist these new home purchasers with contract loans. Through these predatory practices, new homeowners paid high interest rates, albeit without accruing any equity until they had paid off the loan in full. In the case of default, the home buyer lost all they had paid, and the speculator resold the house to a new African American buyer (Seligman 2005; Sugrue 1996; Satter 2009). Some municipalities tried to stop blockbusting by banning "For Sale" signs or restricting door-to-door solicitation. But the practice was not outlawed until the eventual passage of the Fair Housing Act.

Most postwar people of color lived not in suburban houses, however, but in urban rental units—which existed in increasingly dense and dilapidated conditions. Urban physical and economic decline helped spur passage of the Housing Act of 1949, the objective of which was to provide "a decent home and suitable living environment for every American family" (von Hoffman 2000). Title I of the act introduced urban renewal, under which the federal government covered two-thirds of the cost of acquiring and clearing land for redevelopment. City governments were responsible for the remaining expenses, and policy-makers envisioned that public-private partnerships would help realize new, modern construction on those same sites. Title III of the act allocated funding for public housing, which would in part provide a home for some of those low-income residents displaced by urban renewal. While it appeared on the surface that these large-scale housing policies could have addressed African Americans' segregated housing challenges, in many cases the policies only served to worsen the problem.

Urban renewal quickly became known as "Negro removal," given its disproportionate displacement of African American urban residents. By 1970, roughly 60 percent of those displaced by urban renewal were non-white (U.S. Department of Housing and Urban Development 1971). Clearance for highway construction, including especially projects instigated by the Interstate Highway Act of 1956, only added to the toll. Sociologists found that, while those residents whose destinations could be tracked often

Figure 1.7. Protestors marched outside of Philadelphia's City Hall, in 1968, in
opposition to the proposed Crosstown Expressway. In order to connect
interstates to the east and west of Center City, the expressway would have
wiped out a large swath of the city, including a historically African American
neighborhood. (George D. McDowell Philadelphia Evening Bulletin Collection,
Special Collections Research Center, Temple University Libraries, Philadelphia,
Pennsylvania)

relocated to physically improved housing in other parts of the city, this material advancement could not compensate for the corollary destruction of
long-standing communal ties (Ammon 2016). The resultant psychosocial
impacts, which psychiatrist Mindy Fullilove has termed "root shock," were
great (Fullilove 2004). Moreover, as wrecking companies demolished the
former homes of these displaced residents, construction crews typically replaced them with luxury high-rises, downtown shopping malls, and office
buildings—none of which catered to the original population (Ammon 2016).

Over time, residents standing in the way of the bulldozer increasingly protested to stop this displacement. As depicted in Figure 1.7, freeway revolts

Figure 1.8. The family of Mr. Edward Vaughn appears here inside the living room of their housing unit at the Ida B. Wells Homes, in Chicago, in 1942. The Vaughns were typical of the "worthy poor" who inhabited many prewar public housing projects. Mr. Vaughn worked for the War Department. (Jack Delano, Farm Security Administration/Office of War Information Black-and-White Negatives, Library of Congress Prints and Photographs Division, Washington, D.C.)

were at the forefront of this opposition, but organized urban renewal protests also followed. In cities around the country, these efforts met with mixed results (Mohl 2004).

The new postwar public housing that was simultaneously developed differed from that which had characterized the start of the public housing program, during the New Deal. In that earlier iteration, housing authorities targeted the so-called "worthy poor," who were working their way up to home ownership. Figure 1.8 depicts one such family. These developments were often low- to mid-rise in nature and included high-quality design and rich community amenities. As made clear by the sign protesting Black occupancy in one such project (in Figure 1.9), they were also segregated by race. Yet the example of now landmarked communities like the Harlem

Figure 1.9. In Detroit, Michigan, in 1942, white residents erected this sign across from the Sojourner Truth Homes, in opposition to occupancy by African American residents. (Arthur Siegel, Farm Security Administration / Office of War Information Black-and-White Negatives, Library of Congress Prints and Photographs Division, Washington, D.C.)

River Houses, which were designed explicitly for African Americans, testified to the appeal of the infrastructure, even in these uneven circumstances (Radford 1996).

Postwar public housing, however, largely broke with this tradition. These later projects often consisted of high-rise towers, with much more limited amenities. With some noteworthy exceptions, a combination of poor construction quality, insufficient maintenance, and declining social and economic conditions in the cities around them caused many of these projects to quickly fall into disrepair (Bloom 2008). Despite the postwar promise of racial integration, African Americans alone increasingly populated their units. These households were often very low-income and led by single female parents. Postwar projects were also often distantly located within the city, cut off by highways or railroad tracks, and isolated from their immediate surroundings by a sea of asphalt (Hunt 2009; Heathcott 2012). While scholars have also shown how some residents found in public housing opportunities for activism, entrepreneurialism, and community formation, the dominant outcome was the creation of new urban ghettos (Williams 2004; Venkatesh 2000). The utter failure of these developments came to be symbolized by the implosion of many of these high-rise projects only a few decades after their construction (Hirsch 1983; Vale 2013).

Thus, while civil rights activists had been attacking segregation laws and agreements for decades, the early postwar years were a time of increasing attention to the problems of Blacks in Northern cities. They were also a period of great debate over housing policy in the United States. With passage of the Housing Act of 1949, activists were particularly concerned that the nation's housing effort provide shelter on an equal basis to all Americans, and they decided to organize an expanded effort to combat the problem of housing discrimination. Nearly simultaneously, just one year earlier, the 1948 Supreme Court opinion in *Shelley v. Kraemer* had declared that government enforcement of restrictive covenants was unconstitutional, eliciting additional attention for this topic.

Shelley was at best a mixed victory for civil rights. While the court declared it unconstitutional for states to enforce restrictive covenants, the court also specifically declared that nothing in the Constitution forbade individuals from entering into such agreements. Implicit in the holding was that private parties retained the right to deny housing to persons on the basis of race. Hence, the previously discussed discriminatory practices endured at many subdivisions and smaller-scale properties around the county. *Shelley* reinforced other precedents declaring the Constitution powerless against housing discrimination. These challenges shaped the efforts and strategies of postwar activists fighting discrimination in housing.

The "fair housing movement" (as it came to be called) reveals the multifaceted nature of civil rights activism in the 1950s. In contrast to the battle against school segregation, which mainly took place in courtrooms, the fair housing movement aimed at changing public opinion and lobbying legislatures to ban housing discrimination. The coalitions these fair housing activists created were important institutions that provided models for the emerging civil rights movement.

The 1950s: The Fair Housing Movement and the Federal Approach

After World War II, racial segregation emerged as a national issue and the subject of much debate. Civil rights advocates argued that the nation could not truly reflect the ideals of equality while people of color experienced exclusion from major parts of American society. While all of the civil rights efforts were contentious, none was more so than the debate over residential integration. The battle for fair housing brought together several groups to create a permanent organization to fight housing discrimination. These groups began locally, and New York was at the forefront of such efforts. The New York State Committee Against Discrimination in Housing (NYSCDH) formed in 1949. Its primary purpose was to secure local and state legislation banning discrimination in housing. In a resolution adopted December 2, 1949, at the organization's founding meeting, the group stated that "residential segregation is bad planning. It is inconsistent with the tenets of our democratic society." The committee called on the New York State Legislature to "take effective action to prevent racial and religious discrimination and segregation in all housing constructed in this state with public assistance." The NYSCDH drew its strength from the coalition of groups that supported fair housing. Most active among its constituent members were the National Association for the Advancement of Colored People (NAACP) and the American Jewish Congress. Both organizations provided staff resources and legal assistance to the NYSCDH (Pritchett 2003).

The committee's intellectual leader was a Harvard-educated African American economist named Robert Weaver. Scion of an elite family in Washington, D.C., who would in 1966 become the first African American cabinet secretary (of the Department of Housing and Urban Development), Weaver was a founding member of President Franklin Roosevelt's "Negro Cabinet" and had been a leader of the movement against housing discrimination for two decades. In 1948, Weaver published *The Negro Ghetto*, a study of racial change in Northern cities that quickly became required reading for students of urban policy. *The Negro Ghetto* was a historical, sociological, and economic analysis of the Black ghetto. The work was also a vigorous critique of the system of restrictive covenants and of the government's role in supporting segregation. NAACP lawyers relied heavily on Weaver's work in their brief in the *Shelley* case. By the late 1940s, Weaver was widely acknowledged to be among the foremost authorities on housing discrimination (Pritchett 2008).

In *The Negro Ghetto*, Weaver declared that urban renewal could be an "opportunity or threat" depending on how it was implemented. Weaver argued that only "sound city planning," without segregation, would enable urban redevelopment to succeed. He worried that urban renewal "carried a triple threat to minorities and good housing," because it might displace Blacks from desirable areas, be used to break up integrated neighborhoods, and result in a decrease in housing. Appropriately implemented, however, urban redevelopment could also be, Weaver argued, a chance to create "new patterns of living" for Blacks (Weaver 1948).

Influenced by his concern about the impact of the program, housing advocates decided at the 1949 conference that it was necessary to establish an organization to focus on the national problem of housing discrimination. The conferees voted to create the National Committee Against Discrimination in Housing (NCDH), and they elected Weaver president. The stated purpose of the NCDH was to conduct research on the housing situation of minorities in cities across the country and to work with grassroots groups interested in achieving equal access in housing. But the NCDH quickly became involved in advocacy for fair housing efforts. During the group's first decade, NCDH leaders undertook numerous campaigns, particularly at the federal level, to secure equal access to housing for all individuals. The committee's publications sought to influence public opinion to support legislation against discrimination. "One fact is starkly clear: Discrimination in housing is the keystone of all forms of discrimination," stated one such pamphlet (Pritchett 2003: 415).

While the NCDH was a coalition of many groups with strong ideas about civil rights, Weaver's perspective on these issues was very influential. Weaver had written frequently about the unfairness of the exclusion Blacks, particularly higher-income Blacks, experienced in the housing market. "No less ironic is the fact that when, at long last, an appreciable number of colored Americans have sufficient incomes to afford decent housing, those who want to better their home surroundings are forced to pay through the nose." Throughout the late 1940s and 1950s, Weaver argued that there was a growing number of

Black families able to pay for suburban housing and that builders and policy-makers were wrongly preventing them from participating. "Under a free economy," he asserted, "the purchaser is supposed to have access to the total supply (within his price range) at the same time that the seller is supposed to have access to the total effective demand." In his economic analysis, the housing market failed to meet this standard. "Nowhere is the repudiation of the promise of a free, private enterprise economy better illustrated than in the development of postwar communities like Levittowns and Park Forest, where colored families regardless of income and cultural attainments, are systematically excluded" (Pritchett 2003: 415–16).

To build their case, fair housing advocates employed the rhetoric of property. Through conferences, pamphlets, and other efforts, activists worked to convince the country that denying property rights to minorities was un-American. Property ownership, the activists claimed, was so crucial to the political economy of the country that its denial amounted to a denial of full citizenship. Advocates argued that it was time that the country follow the principles established in the Civil Rights Act of 1866, which stated, "All citizens of the United States shall have the same right in every State and territory, as is enjoyed by white citizens thereof to inherit, lease, sell, hold, and convey real and personal property." Advocates further argued that segregation was wrong, that it had negative social and economic effects, and that America would be a truly democratic society when all races lived in one community. In the postwar era, when Blacks, Jews, and other minorities constantly pointed to the sacrifices they had made for their country, the demand for equal access to property and the right to full participation was a powerful argument. But these claims contradicted the widely accepted principle that property ownership included the full right of disposal. Implicit in this right was the "privilege to choose one's neighbors" (Pritchett 2003).

Throughout the 1950s, opponents continued to prevent reform at the national level. The Truman administration often professed support for anti-discrimination measures but offered tepid proposals that made little impact. Housing officials in the Eisenhower administration generally fell back on philosophical statements about "local control" in response to demands for federal action. As a result, in the context of urban renewal, public housing, and (racially exclusive) suburbanization, housing segregation in most urban areas intensified during the 1950s. By the end of the decade, northern cities faced significant racial challenges (Hirsch 1983).

At the same time, as a result of the efforts of fair housing activists, many cities and states passed laws prohibiting housing discrimination during the decade. New York City and New York State were among the first to pass such laws and create regulatory systems for victims of discrimination to file claims against property owners. These systems were fairly weak and did not provide much recompense to families suffering racial exclusion, but they did serve as templates for stronger measures in the 1960s and were the forerunners to the national Fair Housing Act of 1968.

The 1960s: The Civil Rights Movement and the Fair Housing Act

The Fair Housing Act of 1968 was the last of the major civil rights laws of the 1960s. This is appropriate, as it was the most hotly contested. Even more than the battles over the right to vote, the right to equal employment, and the right to equal treatment in public accommodations, the battle against housing discrimination laid bare the fundamental structures of American society and the deep antipathy toward racial integration. As suggested by the protesters depicted in Figure 1.10, throughout the 1960s, civil rights advocates argued that America could not truly call itself a democracy until racial barriers fell. In the area of residential segregation, even efforts to secure basic equality of treatment for Blacks in the housing market proved difficult. By the end of the decade, however, with the passage of the Fair Housing Act, the country did acknowledge that the law should, at the least, state clearly the principle of equal treatment in housing.

The 1960s opened with a flourishing of civil rights activities and the dawn of President John Kennedy's "New Frontier." During the 1960 campaign, Kennedy did not make civil rights a major issue, but he made several statements to establish his support for the cause. One issue that candidate Kennedy chose to highlight his support for equal rights was housing. In August 1960, Kennedy held a news conference to criticize the Eisenhower administration and its approach to civil rights, focusing in particular on the administration's intransigence in dealing with housing discrimination. Calling on the president to issue an executive order banning discrimination in federal housing programs—a demand of fair housing activists for two decades—Kennedy said, "If he does not do it, a new Democratic Administration will." Later, in October, Kennedy repeated this critique, stating "one stroke of the pen would

Figure 1.10. As depicted on signage carried during the Civil Rights March on Washington in 1963, decent housing was just one among many rights that activists were demanding. (Warren K. Leffler, *U.S. News & World Report* Magazine Photograph Collection, Library of Congress Prints and Photographs Division, Washington, D.C.)

have worked wonders for millions of Negroes who want their children to grow up in decency." Campaign aides made sure that the remarks were widely reported in the Black press (Pritchett 2008: 212–13).

After his election, however, the president delayed acting on his commitments for more than two years. The president's political calculus was complicated by opposition to the reforms from many in Congress. The majority of congressional opponents were southern, but others also asked the administration to reconsider. Congresswoman Martha Griffiths (D-MI) argued that "there is not time enough left before election for the white areas to understand the full implications of this order. . . . Most white people have resigned themselves to the fact of integration, but the suburbs of Detroit believe it will be years before it applies to their exact area." She presciently argued that the issuance of the order would have serious implications for Democrats representing suburban districts. "If such an order is to be issued, it should not be issued immediately preceding an election because it will be interpreted as political and as an attempt to buy votes" (Pritchett 2008: 238).

On November 20, 1962, more than two years after he first raised the issue, Kennedy signed an executive order banning discrimination in federal housing programs. He made the announcement in the most low-key manner possible, telling the press after announcing that the Soviets had agreed to remove all their bombers from Cuba and confirming that the Soviet missile silos had been dismantled. Kennedy stated that he was "directing Federal departments to take every proper and legal action to prevent discrimination" in housing owned, operated, funded, or insured by the federal government. Under the order, each agency would be responsible for securing compliance with its programs. The order also established the President's Committee on Equal Opportunity in Housing, composed of government officials and public members, to oversee federal activities and recommend policy changes to the president (Bryant 2006).

The order was more limited than that proposed by fair housing advocates. While it covered all federal housing programs, it did not regulate the financial institutions that funded housing development, and it did not apply retroactively. The order directed agencies to use their "good offices" (in other words, persuasion) to get existing projects to comply. Exempting the sale of homes by individuals, the order applied solely to commercial builders.

Fair housing activists were disappointed that the order was not as expansive as they desired. However, NCDH director Frances Levinson stated, it was "an important gain in practice as well as principle." To assuage civil rights leaders, Weaver publicly noted that broadening the order in the near future was a "possibility." The order did have an immediate impact on the real estate industry, which changed its code of ethics to state for the first time that real estate agents who sold homes to Blacks in previously all-white neighborhoods did not violate association rules (Pritchett 2003).

Two years after President Kennedy made history by prohibiting discrimination in some federal programs, administration and fair housing activists admitted that the order had had little impact in improving access of racial minorities to housing. At the same time as the federal government continued to fund segregated housing, the movement expanded dramatically. NCDH officials reported that there were at least a thousand fair housing groups in the country. Through their efforts, seventeen states and twenty-eight cities had passed fair housing laws.

Activists continued to demand greater federal involvement, but they were frustrated by the Johnson administration's weak response. In the spring of 1965, the President's Committee on Equal Opportunity in Housing issued a report recommending that federal antidiscrimination regulations be expanded to all housing financed by federally regulated banks, but the committee did not propose making the rule apply to housing already financed, as fair housing activists had requested. NCDH chair Algernon Black called the recommendations "totally inadequate." But many in the administration had reservations about even this limited proposal. Like those on Kennedy's staff, many of Johnson's advisers believed that the president did not have the legal authority to expand the executive order. After several weeks of discussion in October and November, all of the president's White House aides agreed to pursue legislation instead of expanding the executive order (Pritchett 2003).

After significant pressure by civil rights leaders, in 1966 President Johnson began to take action. In his State of the Union address, Johnson gave his civil rights legislation prominent placement, stating, "Justice means a man's hope should not be limited by the color of his skin." The president's 1966 Civil Rights bill included provisions protecting civil rights workers and increasing federal power over discrimination in the judicial system and education. The last section, which immediately became the focus of debate on a bill that otherwise received strong bipartisan support, prohibited discrimination by "property owners, real estate brokers, and others engaged in the sale, rental or financing of housing." Noting that 1966 was the hundredth anniversary of the 1866 Civil Rights Act (which declared that "all citizens of the United States shall have the same right, in every State and territory, as is enjoyed by white citizens thereof, to inherit, purchase, lease, sell, hold and convey real and personal property"), Johnson argued that not enough had been done to "guarantee that *all* Americans shall benefit from the expanding housing market Congress has made possible." The time had come, he asserted, "for the Congress to declare resoundingly that discrimination in housing and all the evils it breeds are a denial of justice and a threat to the development of our growing urban areas" ("Text of President's Special Message to Congress Urging New Civil Rights Legislation" 1963).

Liberals and conservatives both criticized Johnson's plan. Fair housing advocates continued to argue that the president could eliminate discrimination immediately through the issuance of an executive order. Republicans and southern Democrats assailed the bill for exceeding federal authority. Senate

Republican leader Everett Dirksen (R-IL) called it "absolutely unconstitutional." He argued that housing purchases were an inherently local issue. "If you can tell me what interstate commerce is involved in selling or renting a house fixed to the soil, or where there is federal jurisdiction, I'll go out and eat the chimney off the house," Dirksen told reporters ("Dirksen Assails Fair Housing Plan" 1966). Alabama Senator John Sparkman argued that the bill "clearly violates the right to free use and disposal of property" ("I'll Eat the Chimney" 1966).

Not surprisingly, real estate agents were vigorously opposed to the bill, arguing that it would "destroy the American tradition of freedom of contract." Realtor James Lynch argued that "if this act is passed, we may as well repeal the Bill of Rights." As a result of lack of excitement on the part of liberals, strong opposition by conservatives, as well as election-year concerns for moderates, few pundits gave the bill much chance for passage (Stern 1992).

Conservative opposition to such legislation was long-standing, but the battle for fair housing was complicated by a growing conflict within the civil rights movement. By 1966, the latent tensions among activists over philosophy and strategy had grown into a rift that would not be repaired. Many Blacks, frustrated by the continuing attacks on civil rights workers in the South and the hypocrisy of northern leaders who professed support for civil rights but watched as discrimination continued, gravitated away from a focus on racial integration toward nationalist ideologies (Ralph 1993).

The president's task of managing the violently diverging opinions on the nation's race relations was made more difficult by the continued racial conflict in many American cities. No city exemplified the increasing tension between Blacks and whites more than Chicago, where the battle over housing discrimination hit the streets in a long summer of confrontation. At the center of the conflict were Martin Luther King Jr., and the Chicago Freedom Movement. In 1965, King chose to bring the Southern Christian Leadership Conference (SCLC) campaign to Chicago. Together with local activists, they decided to focus their attention on the housing discrimination that made the Windy City among the nations most segregated. Arguing that housing discrimination was "a moral transgression, an offense against the dignity of human beings and the American creed of equal opportunity," activists organized marches through all-white communities to dramatize the injustice of housing residential segregation (Ralph 1993).

The reaction to these protests by white residents of working-class neighborhoods, such as Gage Park and Marquette Park, was swift and violent. In Marquette Park, whites threw rocks, bottles, and cherry bombs at the marchers and yelled, "Go home niggers." When the protesters returned to their cars, they found that many had been set on fire and dozens had their tires slashed. When King himself led a march through Marquette Park, he was almost immediately hit in the head by a rock "as large as a fist," and a knife thrown at the civil rights leader barely missed him. King remarked that he had "never seen anything like it. . . . I've been in many demonstrations all across the South, but I can say that I have never seen—even in Mississippi and Alabama—mobs as hostile and hate-filled as I've seen in Chicago." After a summer of violence, the activists reached a weak agreement with Mayor Richard Daley and real estate leaders to promote open housing in the city (Ralph 1993: 120–23).

Historian James Ralph argues that the open housing battles in Chicago "dramatically exposed the limits of the civil rights consensus," and they clearly influenced the debate over the Civil Rights Act. But unlike earlier protests in Selma and Birmingham and other southern cities in 1964 that galvanized support for federal legislation, the Chicago conflicts had, if anything, the opposite effect: hardening opponents of fair housing without bringing together followers (Ralph 1993).

Realizing the extent of the opposition to the fair housing proposal, the administration quickly began to take conciliatory positions. Just days after the bill was introduced, Attorney General Katzenbach agreed to exempt owner-occupied houses from the law. Called the "Mrs. Murphy exemption," the proposal was advanced by several representatives who argued it would be unfair to regulate "little old ladies" who rented parts of their homes for "companionship." However, because of strong opposition to the housing section, it became clear that the bill would not be approved by the House without significant changes. In the end, Johnson decided to support the amendment, which passed the House by one vote (Stern 1992).

Johnson acknowledged that it was not everything he wanted, but he argued that the bill's significance was "large in both practical and symbolic terms." Civil rights leaders were disheartened. "I don't think the bill is worth passing like it is," Dr. Martin Luther King Jr., told reporters. Approving the amended bill would only "add to the tensions and violence in our Northern cities," he claimed. Lincoln Lynch, associate director of the Congress of Racial Equality (CORE), stated that "in essence the black man is being told by Congress that he only has constitutional rights in 40% of the nation's housing; in the other 60% he is not equal" (Pritchett 2008: 293).

But most observers thought that even the watered-down version would not pass the Senate. The reason was not that there were not enough votes—a majority appeared to support the bill. The reason was the Senate's voting rules. Southern Democrats would certainly oppose the legislation, and supporters would need a two-thirds vote to overcome the delaying tactic. After working for more than a month to break a filibuster, administration officials gave up and declared the bill dead.

The president continued to pursue fair housing legislation during 1967, but this time his strategy was even more measured than the year before. After much internal discussion over the administration's civil rights agenda, Johnson decided to introduce another bill that banned discrimination in housing. The major difference in the proposal was that it would require compliance gradually over two years, applying first to larger projects and then to individual homes. Administration officials hoped that this process would show the public that the law would not cause drastic changes in neighborhoods. The president called his proposal the "next and more profound stage of the battle for civil rights," but he was slow to engage in this struggle, and his staff did not actively pursue it. Most administration officials remained pessimistic about the proposal's chances in 1968 (Stern 1992).

Soon thereafter, though, Senator Walter Mondale (D-MN) introduced the administration's fair housing bill, beginning a debate that would last almost five weeks. Senator Edward Brooke (R-MA), a cosponsor of the bill, argued that fair housing was crucial to ending urban violence. "No other solution will work," he asserted. As activists had done for years, the bill's promoters focused on the desires of middle-class Blacks in making their case. Senator Mondale argued that "it is impossible to gauge the degradation and humiliation suffered by a man in the presence of his wife and children when he is told that despite his university degrees, despite his income level, despite his profession, he is just not good enough to live in a white neighborhood." The bill, he argued, would enable the private market to work as it should. The only people who would move would be upstanding middle-class families who would contribute positively to their new neighborhoods. These people deserved to live the American dream just like their white counterparts (U.S. Congress 1968).

Throughout the month of February, the opponents of the bill engaged in a filibuster, presenting long speeches listing the bill's defects. But by the end of February, civil rights advocates had become confident that they would be able to pass a fair housing measure. The passage of the bill was aided by the March 1 release of the report of the president's riot commission. Chaired by Illinois governor Otto Kerner, the commission conducted hearings around the country throughout the fall and spring and spent over a million dollars on more than a dozen studies of conditions within Black urban areas and the causes of racial tensions. The final document, which was more than four hundred pages long, blamed white racism for the riots and argued that the nation was "moving toward two societies, one black, one white—separate and unequal." The report called for a massive program of housing, education, and employment costing several billion dollars. The commission also recommended the passage of a "national, comprehensive, and enforceable open occupancy law" (Stern 1992).

On March 5, the Senate finally broke the filibuster and, on March 11, an exhausted Senate approved the civil rights bill, the only legislation it had considered for two months. Attention then shifted to the House, where Minority Leader Gerald Ford (R-MI) objected to many of the Senate bill's provisions. Given the opposition of southern Democrats, a large number of Republican votes was necessary if the bill was going to succeed. Many observers believed that the bill faced a long delay, if not defeat.

Then, on the afternoon of April 4, James Earl Ray shot Martin Luther King Jr. in Memphis, Tennessee. The assassination sent the nation into chaos—riots erupted in 125 cities, and at least thirty-nine people were killed. The next day, as depicted in Figure 1.11, Johnson organized a meeting of civil rights leaders. The gathering was more a chance for the activists to vent their frustrations, but when it was over they agreed to work for the passage of the civil rights bill as a testimonial to King. Less than a week later, the House passed the bill. At the bill signing, the president stated, "In the Civil Rights Act of 1968 America moves forward and the bell of freedom rings out a little louder" (Stern 1992).

The passage of the Fair Housing Act was the culmination of decades of effort by civil rights activists, and many celebrated the achievement. NAACP leaders forecast that the law would be extremely valuable in combating discrimination and opening up the suburbs. But others were more skeptical. By this time, many Blacks were beginning to join more radical activists in questioning the philosophical framework that had driven the movement for several decades. Interviewed in the Chicago *Defender*, self-described militant Russell Meek called the law "nothing more than a miserable gesture. . . .

Figure 1.11. President Lyndon B. Johnson met with civil rights leaders at the White House on the day following the assassination of Martin Luther King Jr. Less than a week later, Johnson signed the Fair Housing Act. (A6016-19, LBJ Library photo by Yoichi Okamoto, White House Photo Collection)

If we have to wait for the assassination of one of our black leaders before Congress will even serve up a bill such as the one in question, then the graveyards will be full of black leaders and we'll still be in slavery" (Pritchett 2008: 316–17).

Columnist William Raspberry, writing in the *Washington Post*, celebrated the bill's passage as a symbolic victory, but concluded that the law "doesn't begin to get down to where the problem is." Like most civil rights laws, Raspberry argued, this one would benefit primarily the middle class. "Don't expect much dancing in the ghetto streets," Raspberry advised. Weaver later described the bill as "just about as good an act as we could have gotten. . . . If it had been any better and more teeth in it as some wanted to see, we wouldn't have had a chance of getting it through." The fact was, he had concluded, that most Americans still did not support open occupancy (Pritchett 2008: 317).

By 1968, many activists were tiring of the traditional legal approach to equality. Increasingly, they were focusing on economic issues and disregarding the goal of racial integration. Soon after Johnson signed the bill, Rev.

Ralph Abernathy, King's successor in the Southern Christian Leadership Conference, arrived in Washington to lead the "Poor People's Campaign." The group, which King had organized before his death, planned a series of protests to demand greater federal assistance to the poor in housing, education, and job training. For weeks, hundreds of protestors from around the country lived in a "tent city" near the Capitol to bring attention to the needs of the poor. Abernathy told congressional leaders that their requests were more important than laws providing theoretical access to neighborhoods that the poor could not afford.

During any other year, the passage of the Fair Housing Act would have been seen as a dramatic step forward in the nation's race relations. After all, only seven years earlier, President Kennedy had concluded that issuing a limited directive prohibiting discrimination in a small part of federal housing programs—a regulation covering a fraction of the housing covered by the 1968 law—was not possible. The act provided powers of a magnitude many times what was considered feasible at the beginning of the decade, and it signified that the federal government was strongly behind African Americans in their efforts to live wherever they chose. However, 1968 was not any year. By the time the bill was passed, many questioned whether it provided much of an answer to the racial problems that beset the nation.

Conclusion

Between Reconstruction and the post–World War II decades, African Americans had been the victims of a long history of unfair housing. By the postwar years, while racial zoning and restrictive covenants were no longer legal, real estate agents, lenders, and white homeowners could still achieve similar outcomes through alternative means. Less explicit planning practices, such as the siting of schools, furthered segregation in even more subtle ways. All of these mechanisms restricted African American access to homeownership in both cities and suburbs. Within the context of these limited options, urban renewal and highway construction disproportionately burdened this community with displacement. New public housing often offered only a hollow solution. Just as government policies had been critical to the imposition of segregated housing, during the 1950s and 1960s, a growing constituency of civil rights activists looked to the federal government to provide a policy solution to these injustices.

Early fair housing laws became models for the expanded movement in the 1960s and led to passage of the federal Fair Housing Act. The laws in New York and in other cities had relied on the initiative of individuals to pursue claims of discrimination, and they established new institutions to oversee the system. These bureaucracies were limited in scope, however, and struggled to secure adequate funding for the job. Critics of the Fair Housing Act have argued that the law provides limited protection because poor minorities do not have the means to secure legal assistance to bring a claim. The class-based limitations of the fair housing strategy were present from its inception.

An analysis of the movement against housing discrimination highlights the contradictions of rights-based ideology as a means for furthering social improvement. Fair housing advocates argued that race should be removed from the consideration of housing opportunities—that all persons should have equal access. At the same time, activists sought to achieve an integrated society. Advocates thought that these goals were complementary, but even as discrimination seemed to subside, segregation remained the norm.

In using the dominant discourse of property rights, which had long been used to substantiate discriminatory practices like racial zoning and restrictive covenants, advocates revealed the class-based nature of the fair housing movement. Fair housing advocates were certainly concerned about shelter for the poor—they were active in lobbying for increased public housing and other affordable housing programs—but their political arguments focused on the impropriety of denying an individual the right to *buy a house* on the basis of race. Fair housing advocates hoped to open up opportunities for middle-class Blacks who would lead the way to an integrated society. By shaping their strategy in this manner, advocates narrowed the scope of debate on the responsibility of government to provide meaningful access to housing for all America.

References

Ammon, Francesca Russello. *Bulldozer: Demolition and Clearance of the Postwar Landscape.* New Haven, CT: Yale University Press, 2016.

Bayor, Ronald H. *Race and the Shaping of Twentieth-Century Atlanta.* Chapel Hill: University of North Carolina Press, 1996.

Benjamin, Karen. "Suburbanizing Jim Crow: The Impact of School Policy on Residential Segregation in Raleigh." *Journal of Urban History* 38, no. 2 (2012): 225–46.

Berry, Brian. *The Open Housing Question: Race and Housing in Chicago, 1966–1976*. Cambridge, MA: Ballinger Publishing Co, 1979.

Bloom, Nicholas Dagen. *Public Housing That Worked: New York in the Twentieth Century*. Philadelphia: University of Pennsylvania Press, 2008.

Bryant, Nick. *The Bystander: John F. Kennedy and the Struggle for Black Equality*. New York: Basic Books, 2006.

"Dirksen Assails Fair Housing Plan." *New York Times*, May 3, 1966.

Erickson, Ansley T. *Making the Unequal Metropolis: School Desegregation and Its Limits*. Chicago: University of Chicago Press, 2016.

Fennell, Lee Anne. "Searching for Fair Housing." *Boston University Law Review* 97, no. 2 (2017): 349–424.

Fischler, Raphaël. "Health, Safety, and the General Welfare: Markets, Politics, and Social Science in Early Land-Use Regulation and Community Design." *Journal of Urban History* 24, no. 6 (1998): 675–719.

Fogelson, Robert M. *Bourgeois Nightmares: Suburbia, 1870–1930*. New Haven, CT: Yale University Press, 2005.

Freund, David M. *Colored Property: State Policy and White Racial Politics in Suburban America*. Chicago: University of Chicago Press, 2007.

Fullilove, Mindy Thompson. *Root Shock: How Tearing up City Neighborhoods Hurts America, and What We Can Do About It*. New York: One World/Ballantine Books, 2004.

Gonda, Jeffrey D. *Unjust Deeds: The Restrictive Covenant Cases and the Making of the Civil Rights Movement*. Chapel Hill: University of North Carolina Press, 2015.

Gotham, Kevin Fox. "Urban Space, Restrictive Covenants and the Origins of Racial Residential Segregation in a US City, 1900–50." *International Journal of Urban and Regional Research* 24, no. 3 (2000): 616–33.

Heathcott, Joseph. "The Strange Career of Public Housing." *Journal of the American Planning Association* 78, no. 4 (2012): 360–75.

Highsmith, Andrew R. *Demolition Means Progress: Flint, Michigan, and the Fate of the American Metropolis*. Chicago: University of Chicago Press, 2015.

Hillier, Amy. "Redlining and the Home Owners' Loan Corporation." *Journal of Urban History* 29, no. 4 (2003): 394–420.

Hirsch, Arnold R. *Making the Second Ghetto: Race and Housing in Chicago, 1940–1960*. Cambridge: Cambridge University Press, 1983.

———. "With or without Jim Crow: Black Residential Segregation in the United States." In *Urban Policy in Twentieth-Century America*, edited by Arnold R. Hirsch and Raymond A. Mohl, 65–99. New Brunswick, NJ: Rutgers University Press, 1993.

Hirt, Sonia. "Home, Sweet Home: American Residential Zoning in Comparative Perspective." *Journal of Planning Education and Research* 33, no. 3 (2013): 292–309.

———. *Zoned in the USA: The Origins and Implications of American Land-Use Regulation*. Ithaca, NY: Cornell University Press, 2014.

Hornstein, Jeffrey M. *A Nation of Realtors: A Cultural History of the Twentieth-Century American Middle Class*. Durham, NC: Duke University Press, 2005.

Hunt, D. Bradford. *Blueprint for Disaster: The Unraveling of Chicago Public Housing*. Chicago: University of Chicago Press, 2009.

Hurley, Amanda Kolson. 2017. "'Housing Is Everybody's Problem': The Forgotten Crusade of Morris Milgram." *Places Journal* (October 2017). https://doi.org/10.22269/171010.

"I'll Eat the Chimney." *Newsweek*, May 13, 1966.

Jackson, Kenneth T. *Crabgrass Frontier: The Suburbanization of the United States*. New York: Oxford University Press, 1985.

Lassiter, Matthew D. "Schools and Housing in Metropolitan History: An Introduction." *Journal of Urban History* 38, no. 2 (2012): 195–204.

Loewen, James W. *Sundown Towns: A Hidden Dimension of American Racism*. New York: New Press, 2005.

Mohl, Raymond A. "Stop the Road." *Journal of Urban History* 30, no. 5 (2004): 674–706.

Myers, Daisy D. "Reflections on Levittown." In *Second Suburb: Levittown, Pennsylvania*, edited by Dianne Harris, 41–59. Pittsburgh: University of Pittsburgh Press, 2010.

Nelson, Robert K., Ladale Winling, Richard Marciano, and Nathan Connolly. *Mapping Inequality: Redlining in New Deal America*, n.d. Accessed July 3, 2017. https://dsl.richmond.edu/panorama/redlining/#loc=5/39.105/-94.583.

Nightingale, Carl H. *Segregation: A Global History of Divided Cities*. Chicago: University of Chicago Press, 2012.

Pritchett, Wendell E. *Robert Clifton Weaver and the American City: The Life and Times of an Urban Reformer*. Chicago: University of Chicago Press, 2008.

———. "Where Shall We Live? Class and the Limitations of Fair Housing Law." *Urban Lawyer* 35, no. 3 (2003): 399–470.

Radford, Gail. *Modern Housing for America: Policy Struggles in the New Deal Era*. Chicago: University of Chicago Press, 1996.

Ralph, James, Jr. *Northern Protest: Martin Luther King, Jr., Chicago, and the Civil Rights Movement*. Cambridge, MA: Harvard University Press, 1993.

Rothstein, Richard. *The Color of Law: A Forgotten History of How Our Government Segregated America*. New York: Liveright, 2017.

Satter, Beryl. *Family Properties: Race, Real Estate, and the Exploitation of Black Urban America*. New York: Metropolitan Books, 2009.

Seligman, Amanda I. *Block by Block: Neighborhoods and Public Policy on Chicago's West Side*. Chicago: University of Chicago Press, 2005.

Silver, Christopher. "The Racial Origins of Zoning in American Cities." In *Urban Planning and the African American Community: In the Shadows*, edited by June Manning Thomas and Marsha Ritzdorf, 23–42. Thousand Oaks, CA: Sage Publications, 1997.

Stern, Mark. *Calculating Visions: Kennedy and Johnson's Civil Rights*. New Brunswick, NJ: Rutgers University Press, 1992.

Sugrue, Thomas J. "Jim Crow's Last Stand: The Struggle to Integrate Levittown." In *Second Suburb: Levittown, Pennsylvania*, edited by Dianne Harris, 175–99. Pittsburgh: University of Pittsburgh Press, 2010.

———. *The Origins of the Urban Crisis: Race and Inequality in Postwar Detroit*. Princeton, NJ: Princeton University Press, 1996.

———. *Sweet Land of Liberty: The Forgotten Struggle for Civil Rights in the North*. New York: Random House, 2008.

"Text of President's Special Message to Congress Urging New Civil Rights Legislation." *New York Times*, April 29, 1966.

U.S. Congress. *Congressional Record*. 90th Cong., 2d Sess., 114 CONG. REC. 2270 (1968).

U.S. Department of Housing and Urban Development. *1970 HUD Statistical Yearbook*. Washington, D.C.: Government Printing Office, 1971.

Vale, Lawrence J. *Purging the Poorest: Public Housing and the Design Politics of Twice-Cleared Communities*. Chicago: University of Chicago Press, 2013.

Venkatesh, Sudhir. *American Project: The Rise and Fall of a Modern Ghetto*. Cambridge, MA: Harvard University Press, 2000.

von Hoffman, Alexander. "A Study in Contradictions: The Origins and Legacy of the Housing Act of 1949." *Housing Policy Debate* 11, no. 2 (2000): 299–326.

Weaver, Robert Clifton. *The Negro Ghetto*. New York: Harcourt, Brace, 1948.

Whittemore, Andrew H. "The Experience of Racial and Ethnic Minorities with Zoning in the United States." *Journal of Planning Literature* 32, no. 1 (2017): 16–27.

Wiese, Andrew. *Places of Their Own: African American Suburbanization in the Twentieth Century*. Chicago: University of Chicago Press, 2004.

Williams, Rhonda Y. *The Politics of Public Housing: Black Women's Struggles Against Urban Inequality*. New York: Oxford University Press, 2004.

CHAPTER 2

Sociology, Segregation, and the Fair Housing Act

Justin P. Steil and Camille Z. Charles

Introduction

The sociological study of urban life in the United States over the past century and the study of residential segregation are inextricably intertwined. From W. E. B. Du Bois (1903) to St. Clair Drake and Horace Cayton (1945), efforts to understand the causes and consequences of segregation were central to urban sociology in the first half of the twentieth century. These authors challenged contemporaneous sociological and legal arguments about the naturalness of segregation and established that segregation was not just an example of physical separation in dwelling places, but actually part of a systemic structure of racial subordination. At the same time, Drake and Cayton noted that Black Chicagoans took pride in "*their city within a city*" and "remain ambivalent about residential segregation: they see a gain in political strength and group solidarity, but they resent being compelled to live in a Black Belt" (1945: 115). This sociological research on segregation helped lay an academic foundation for the civil rights struggles that ultimately led to the passage of the Fair Housing Act in 1968. In this chapter, we review this stream of sociological scholarship and add contemporary assessments of the Fair Housing Act's contributions. More than a century of sociological scholarship has repeatedly found that residential segregation is one mechanism through which socioeconomic inequalities are reproduced. Although the Fair Housing Act has made progress toward eliminating intentional discrimination in access to housing, the act has been much less effective in achieving the broader reformation of the institutions and practices that reproduce the subordinate social status of historically oppressed groups through unequal access to place-based opportunities. At the same time, conceptions of fair housing defined primarily by access to high-income suburban neighborhoods are becoming outdated, as investment and jobs flow again into many central cities. In low-income communities of color within high-cost cities, displacement and resegregation are emerging as the most pressing concerns as the struggle for urban space intensifies.

W. E. B. Du Bois and the Sociology of Segregation

The first rigorous, empirical sociological studies in the United States were conducted by W. E. B. Du Bois in the late 1890s and early 1900s (see Morris 2015). From careful inductive analysis of the social life of Black residents of Philadelphia, Pennsylvania, and then Atlanta, Georgia, Du Bois began to formulate a theory of social stratification and organization, with attention to the role that race plays in the social order of the United States. In Philadelphia in 1896, Du Bois went from house to house in the city's Seventh Ward to conduct more than 2,500 surveys and supplemented those surveys with interviews and participant observation. In *The Philadelphia Negro* (1899), Du Bois painstakingly described the complexity of the African American community in Philadelphia, analyzing the geographical distribution, daily life, organizations, and social relations of Philadelphia's Black residents. He critiqued in particular the segregation that so many at the time took for granted. He wrote: "Here is a large group of people—perhaps forty-five thousand, a city within a city—who do not form an integral part of the larger social group. This in itself is not altogether unusual; . . . and yet in the case of the Negroes the segregation is more conspicuous, more patent to the eye, and so intertwined with a long historic evolution, with peculiarly pressing social problems of poverty, ignorance, crime and labor, that the Negro problem far surpasses in scientific interest and social gravity most of the other race or class questions" (1899: 5).

Du Bois pointed out that the segregation of African Americans is related to the segregation of other groups in the city, and yet is distinct, shaped by the unique history of slavery, emancipation, and a rigid white supremacist caste system. In an article for the *Annals of the Association of Political and Social Science*, Du Bois (1898: 8) similarly noted how the challenges of poverty faced by African Americans are universal ones and yet distinct because of the "peculiar environment" in cities in the United States characterized by "a widespread conviction among Americans that no persons of Negro descent should become constituent members of the social body." It is this experience of the "definitely segregated mass of eight millions of Americans [who] do not wholly share the national life of the people" and "the points at which they fail to be incorporated into this group life" that constitute social problems, Du Bois argued (1898: 7). In both of these turn-of-the-century writings, Du Bois set a penetrating agenda for sociological research in the United States at the time—to understand the broad processes of social stratification through the experiences of African Americans. Central to that stratification, Du Bois recognized, were the lines of residential segregation that were being drawn ever more starkly at the moment he was writing.

In *The Souls of Black Folk,* just a few years later, Du Bois started by famously pronouncing that "the problem of the Twentieth Century is the problem of the color-line." He noted the significance of patterning in "dwelling-places, the way in which neighborhoods group themselves" and described the ease with which a physical color line can be drawn on the map, "on the one side of which whites dwell and on the other Negroes" (Du Bois 1903). Du Bois (1903) wrote that an observer in the South finds that "the world about flows by him in two great streams: they ripple on in the same sunshine, they approach and mingle their waters in seeming carelessness—then they divide and flow wide apart. It is done quietly; no mistakes are made, or if one occurs, the swift arm of the law and of public opinion swings down."

Even as Du Bois analogized the separate lives of Black and white residents of the South to the waters in two flowing streams, he emphasized how this was all set in motion and enforced by human action and institutions, in particular state and collective action to enforce white supremacy through the arm of the law and through norms of social control (Muhammad 2011). He continued: "Between these two worlds, despite much physical contact and daily intermingling, there is almost no community of intellectual life or point of transference where the thoughts and feelings of one race can come into direct contact and sympathy with

the thoughts and feelings of the other" (Du Bois 1903). Du Bois here suc-
cinctly identified segregation as an effective mechanism for enforcing
social distance and, as a result, racial inequality. As profoundly, he highlighted the dangers that a lack of a shared intellectual life create for a
divided society.

From these works, Du Bois (1905/2000) moved to consider the direction of the field of sociology as a whole in investigating "the vast and be-
wildering activities of men and lines of rhythm that coordinate certain of
these actions." Du Bois, in 1903, alluded to ways in which the field of sociology was implicated in racializing and sexualizing poverty and inequality,
writing in *The Souls of Black Folk* (1903: 9), "while sociologists gleefully
count his bastards and his prostitutes, the very soul of the toiling, sweating black man is darkened by the shadow of a vast despair." One can see
Du Bois in this turn-of-the-century scholarship challenging other sociologists to use this new social science to understand how the social order
subjugates African Americans and privileges whites, as a specific example
of broader processes of stratification in which "a combination of social
problems is far more than a matter of mere addition" (Du Bois 1899: 385).
The color line that residential segregation made visible was for Du Bois so
problematic because it was a cornerstone in the creation of durable racial
inequality.

Segregation was so pernicious not because of the mere fact of separation
but because of the discrimination it represented and the inequality it created. As Du Bois later wrote, "Theoretically, the Negro needs neither segregated schools nor mixed schools. What he needs is Education" (1935: 335).
He continued: "Other things being equal, the mixed school is the broader,
more natural basis for the education of all youth. . . . But other things sel-
dom are equal" and being "treated like human beings . . . is infinitely better
than making our boys and girls doormats to be spit and trampled upon and
lied to" by white classmates, teachers, and administrators in integrated
schools (1935: 335). Du Bois's leadership in the Niagara Movement and the
National Association for Colored People in the following decades made segregation a central target of African American collective action, particularly
resistance to the municipal segregation ordinances and white supremacist collective violence that spread through U.S. cities in the first decades of the twentieth century. "The opposition to segregation," he wrote, "is not or should not
be any distaste or unwillingness of colored people to work with each other, to
live with each other. The opposition to segregation is an opposition to discrim-

ination. The experience in the United States has been that usually when there is racial segregation, there is also racial discrimination" (Du Bois 1934: 20).

The Chicago School of Urban Sociology

Despite Du Bois's groundbreaking scholarship at Atlanta University, the department of sociology at the University of Chicago is often seen as the foundation of sociology in the United States and, in particular, of urban sociology. Robert Park's 1915 article, "The City: Suggestions for the Investigation of Human Behavior in the City Environment," described the city as an institution that manifests "the habits and customs of the people who inhabit it" (1915: 578); Park proposed conceiving of "the city as a laboratory or clinic in which human nature and social processes may be most conveniently and profitably studied" (1915: 612). Park had studied with John Dewey, William James, and Georg Simmel and worked with Booker T. Washington at the Tuskegee Institute before joining the University of Chicago in 1914. Park was particularly interested in neighborhoods, processes of segregation, and "the forces which tend to break up the tensions, interests, and sentiments which give neighborhoods their individual character" (1915: 581).

Perhaps the best-known publication of the Chicago School was Ernest Burgess's 1924 essay theorizing the growth of a city in terms of a model of concentric zones. This model conceptualized urban growth through an analogy to processes of invasion and succession borrowed from plant ecology, and it conceived of the incorporation of individuals into communities through an analogy to "the anabolic and katabolic processes of metabolism" borrowed from human biology (1924: 51). Relying on these analogies to the natural sciences, Burgess suggested that "a process of distribution takes place which sifts and sorts and relocates individuals and groups by residence" (1924: 54) and that this "differentiation into natural economic and cultural groupings gives form and character to the city . . . for segregation offers the group, and thereby the individuals who compose the group, a place and a role in the total organization of city life" (1924: 56). "The life of the community," Park (1926: 5) later wrote, "involves a kind of metabolism . . . constantly assimilating new individuals, and just as steadily, by death or otherwise, eliminating older ones."

Park's and Burgess's analyses of urban neighborhoods and processes of segregation were flawed in many ways, but perhaps most importantly by naturalizing processes of segregation as part of inevitable, almost biological processes of invasion, succession, and assimilation. Their analyses also conceived of the inequality so visible in Chicago as a largely temporary condition for all, with little attention to the processes of racialization and the institutional structures that made inequality, especially Black-white inequality, so durable.

At the same time, Park and the Chicago School documented a foundational insight into the relationship between social and spatial stratification. Park began exploring the concept of social distance in the context of racial prejudice (1924) and then developed a theory of the intertwining of social and spatial distance (1926) in the concept of "position." Park (1926: 1, 9) noted that "changes in social and economic status and degrees of personal success or failure are registered in changes of location of residence" and that "location, position, and mobility" are fundamental to understanding social phenomena (see also extensive subsequent scholarship about spatial assimilation and place stratification, e.g., Charles 2003; Tienda and Fuentes 2014). Sociology cannot be reduced to laws of physics or geometry, Park observed, because the foundation of social life is communication, and transformation of the individual as a result of that communication. Thus, spatial distance is significant for sociology because it defines the "conditions under which communication and social life are actually maintained" (Park 1926: 11).

With this emphasis on the interrelationship between social and spatial distance, the Chicago School educated generations of urban sociologists. One of its early graduates was Charles S. Johnson, who studied under Robert Park and received his Ph.D. in 1917. After Chicago's infamous "race riot" in July 1919, Johnson was named as the principal researcher for the Chicago Commission on Race Relations and in 1922 published *The Negro in Chicago*, which emphasized the poor housing conditions faced by Chicago's African American residents and resistance to the denial of social, political, and economic opportunity they faced. The community self-survey that Johnson led was one of many ethnographic studies of various occupational roles, groups, and neighborhoods that the Chicago School inspired and supported. One of the most influential of those ethnographies was St. Clair Drake and Horace Cayton's 1945 masterwork of social research, *Black Metropolis: A Study of Negro Life in a Northern City*.

Black Metropolis

In *Black Metropolis*, Drake and Cayton asked, "To what degree is the Negro subordinated and excluded in relation to white people in society, what are the mechanisms by which the system is maintained, and how do the lives of Negroes reflect this subordination and exclusion?" (1945: 776). To answer these questions, they coordinated the work of more than two hundred researchers who conducted studies of Black businesses, churches, unions, newspapers, and other aspects of African American life in Chicago. Drake and Cayton (1945: 101) focused in large part on the "color-line which marks Negroes off as a segregated group deemed undesirable for free association with white people in many types of relationships." They noted that "the color-line . . . serves to subordinate Negroes by denying them the right to compete as individuals, on equal terms with white people for economic and political power" (1945: 101).

Drake and Cayton carefully documented the ways in which segregation in Chicago was not the product of any organic process of city growth, but was instead produced by private violence, institutional policies, political decisions, and state action. They documented the white violence, the refusal of services, and the police action used to keep beaches, parks, restaurants, and other public accommodations racially segregated. They also clarified the way in which racially restrictive property covenants both segregated and subordinated Black Chicagoans into the most rundown areas of the city. They squarely placed the responsibility for this subordination on white racism. "Segregation," Drake and Cayton wrote, "is fundamentally a reaction against the specter of social equality," combined with a white "economic interest that results in the concentration of Negroes within the Black Belt" (1945: 127–28).

But Drake and Cayton simultaneously recognized the agency of Black Chicagoans in transforming a "Black Ghetto" into a "Black Metropolis," in forging a vibrant community in the face of pervasive discrimination (see also Pattillo 2015). Chronicling the strength of Black newspapers, churches, unions, and other institutions, Drake and Cayton noted that Black Chicagoans took pride in "*their* city within a city" and "remain ambivalent about residential segregation: they see a gain in political strength and group solidarity, but they resent being compelled to live in a Black Belt" (1945: 115).

Ultimately, Drake and Cayton argued, like Du Bois, that racial segregation and subordination were not just local or regional issues but issues of national and global importance: "The fate of the people of Black Metropolis— whether they will remain the marginal workers to be called in only at times of great economic activity, or will become an integral part of the American economy and thus lay the basis for complete social and political integration—depends not so much on what happens locally as on what happens in America and the world" (Drake and Cayton 1945: 767).

The Road to the Fair Housing Act

In the two decades following the initial publication of *Black Metropolis*, Black migration to Northern and Western cities continued, while the construction of federal highways and the mortgage assistance provided by the G.I. Bill spurred white suburbanization. African American homeseekers were largely shut out of these federal housing benefits because of racially restrictive covenants and redlining. Many new suburbs used racially restrictive covenants, encouraged by the Federal Housing Administration, to bar sales to Black home buyers (Satter 2010; Brooks and Rose 2013). Even without these covenants, federally encouraged race-based grading of neighborhoods for mortgage underwriting meant that residents of predominantly nonwhite and racially integrated neighborhoods would have to pay significantly more for private mortgage financing, if they could obtain it at all (Jackson 1987; Sugrue 1996; Rothstein 2017). Even as the U.S. economy grew rapidly, those gains were not evenly distributed; and as the civil rights movement gained momentum in the South, Black residents of increasingly segregated and disinvested inner cities began to revolt against racial subordination.

The NAACP continued to challenge policies enforcing residential segregation, especially the racially restrictive covenants that had become so common. At a 1945 NAACP conference in Chicago, Charles Hamilton Houston described the strategy of using "the court as a forum for the purpose of educating the public on the question of restrictive covenants because, after all, the covenants reflect a community pattern" (Vose 1959: 60). As part of that education, Houston proposed always beginning litigation by challenging accepted conceptions of race altogether, by "deny[ing] that the plaintiffs are white and the defendants are Negroes.... Every time you drag these plaintiffs in and deny that they are white, you begin to make them think about it" (Vose 1959: 61). Just as the NAACP lawyers could challenge conceptions of race itself, so too could they challenge conceptions of segregation. "Play whites on their own prejudices," Houston suggested—"what degree of penetration changes a neighborhood from white to colored? One drop makes you colored, but one family in a block doesn't make the block colored?" (Vose 1959: 61). A crucial part of the NAACP's strategy for using these segregation cases as a form of public education was the incorporation of sociological and psychological research on the effects of segregation, as in the well-known Kenneth B. Clark (1950) study of the "Effect of Prejudice and Discrimination on Personality Development" and Gunnar Myrdal's *An American Dilemma: The Negro Problem and Modern Democracy* (1944) (see also Ralph Ellison's [1964a] contemporaneous review) that the Supreme Court referenced in *Brown v. Board of Education* (1954).

Consistent with this emphasis on more quantitative analyses of segregation, scholars from the Chicago School continued to study segregation extensively, but moved in a demographic direction, rather than the more ethnographic one that Drake and Cayton represented (Taeuber and Taeuber 1964; Taeuber and Taeuber 1965). Karl Taeuber, a well-known sociological scholar of segregation at the time, together with his co-authors Alma Taeuber, Evelyn Kitagawa, and others, played a central role in popularizing commonly used measures of segregation in sociology operationalized as measures of population dispersion (Duncan and Duncan 1955; Kitagawa and Taeuber 1963; Taeuber and Taeuber 1976; James and Taeuber 1985; Massey and Denton 1988). These and other sociological studies played an important role in measuring and documenting segregation and continuing to set the stage for civil rights legislation like the Fair Housing Act.

After the passage of the Voting Rights Act in 1965, Martin Luther King Jr. and the Southern Christian Leadership Conference turned their focus to housing segregation in Northern cities. In January 1966, they announced a partnership with the Coordinating Council of Community Organizations and launched the Chicago Freedom Movement to "eradicate a vicious system" of housing discrimination and residential segregation "which seeks to further colonize thousands of Negroes within a slum environment" (King 1966a). The struggle to create truly equal access to housing and to neighborhoods was one of the most complex and challenging of all the difficult struggles that King faced (Ralph 1993).

At a march near Marquette Park on August 5, 1966, white residents hurled rocks, bottles, and firecrackers at the marchers. King was struck in the head by a rock and knocked to the ground. Catching his breath, he said, "I have seen many demonstrations in the South, but I have never seen anything so hostile and so hateful as I've seen here today" ("Rock Thrown from Crowd" 1966). Against this hostility to neighborhood integration, however, King had little concrete progress to show even after seven months of marches, protests, and meetings. King and the movement struggled to effectively organize Chicago's culturally and economically diverse Black residents and faced mounting opposition from many white residents. King eventually moved on to the Poor People's Campaign.

The Black Power movement simultaneously began to question whether integration was a worthwhile goal at all. Stokely Carmichael in a 1966 speech argued that "we were never fighting for the right to integrate, we were fighting against white supremacy" (Carmichael 1966: 6). With Charles Hamilton, Carmichael articulated the Black Power call for "black people in this country to unite, to recognize their heritage, to build a sense of community. It is a call for black people to begin to define their own goals, to lead their own organizations and to support those organizations" (Carmichael and Hamilton 1967: 44). Carmichael and Hamilton (1967: 55) challenged a conception of integration "based on complete acceptance of the fact that in order to have a decent house or education, black people must move into a white neighborhood or send their children to a white school." They described how this emphasis on integration "reinforces, among both black and white, the idea that 'white' is automatically superior and 'black' is by definition inferior" (1967: 55). "Integration," they argued, then, "is a subterfuge for the maintenance of white supremacy" (1967: 55).

Urban uprisings across the country in 1967 led President Johnson to convene a commission to study civil disorders, led by Illinois governor Kerner. In language not dissimilar to that of Du Bois and of Drake and Cayton, the Kerner Commission's report, released in February 1968, stated that "what white Americans have never fully understood—but what the Negro can never forget is that white society is deeply implicated in the ghetto. White institutions created it, white institutions maintain it, and white society condones it" (National Advisory Commission on Civil Disorders, 1968: 1). The Commission famously described the nation as "moving toward two societies, one black, one white—separate and unequal" (1968: 1).

The report recommended, among other prescriptions, that the federal government "enact a comprehensive and enforceable open housing law to cover the sale or rental of all housing," and that it "reorient federal housing programs to place more low and moderate income housing outside of ghetto areas" (National Advisory Commission on Civil Disorders, 1968: 28). Whether the highly publicized report would actually lead to legislative change was unclear, however. Civil rights legislation that included antidiscrimination provisions in housing had failed repeatedly even as bills regarding voting rights and segregation in public accommodations had passed. As Senator Mondale noted, the focus on housing nationwide, instead of Southern segregation, "was civil rights getting personal" for Northern voters and their representatives (in Hannah-Jones 2015).

Then, on April 4, 1968, Martin Luther King Jr. was assassinated, and the threat of racial conflict consumed the country. One week after King's assassination, in the midst of continuing unrest, Congress finally passed the Fair Housing Act, "to provide, within constitutional limitations, for fair housing throughout the United States" (42 U.S.C. § 3601 [1968]). Speaking in support of the act, Senator Javits cautioned that "the crisis of the cities . . . is equal to the crisis which we face in Vietnam" (114 Congressional Record 1968: 2703). Senator Mondale warned that "our failure to abolish the ghetto will reinforce the growing alienation of white and black America. It will ensure two separate Americas constantly at war with one another" (1968: 2274). He emphasized that citywide problems are "directly traceable to the existing patterns of racially segregated housing" (1968: 2276). The Fair Housing Act therefore aimed, in Mondale's words, to replace segregated ghettos with "truly integrated neighborhoods" (1968: 3422). The primary operative provisions of the act prohibited discrimination on the basis of race, religion, national origin, or sex, in the sale, rental, or financing of a home. The Fair Housing Act also required that federal housing and community development funding "affirmatively further" fair housing; however, as discussed later, this provision was largely ignored for nearly a half century. The Fair Housing Act was amended in 1988 to, among other things, prohibit discrimination on the basis of disability or family status.

Sociology and Segregation After the Fair Housing Act

Despite the protections of the Fair Housing Act, discrimination in the rental, sale, and financing of homes persisted. Community organizers and civil rights activists pressed for additional protections against pervasive lending discrimination and succeeded in winning the passage of the Equal Credit Opportunity Act in 1974, the Home Mortgage Disclosure Act in 1975, and the Community Reinvestment Act in 1977 (Squires 2003). Combined with the Fair Housing Act, these laws provided some middle-class Black families greater choice in their housing and financing options.

Economic Restructuring and Enduring Segregation

But as these laws were raising the costs of discrimination, economic shifts were undermining hopes of social mobility for many urban Black residents. As William Julius Wilson documented (1987, 1996), the process of deindustrialization—the shift from a goods-producing to a service-producing economy—beginning in the late 1960s precipitated a dramatic decline in the number of decently paid manufacturing jobs available to non-college-educated urban job seekers. Those job sectors that were growing were often characterized by a mismatch in either skills or location for poor and working-class inner-city residents. As jobs left, some Black middle-class households also departed central city neighborhoods, intensifying the social isolation, concentration of poverty, and lack of access to job networks for many of those who remained in inner-city communities.

In *American Apartheid*, Douglas Massey and Nancy Denton (1993) emphasized the central role of residential segregation in making the declining access to jobs that Wilson had chronicled so significant. They argued that structural changes in the economy "would not have produced the disastrous social and economic outcomes observed in inner cities" if not for "segregation that confined the increased deprivation to a small number of densely settled, tightly packed, and geographically isolated areas" (1993: 8). Documenting the public and private actions that contributed to the rise in residential segregation by race during the first half of the twentieth century and its persistence in the second half, Massey and Denton focused in depth on the role that residential segregation has played in "mediating, exacerbating, and ultimately amplifying the harmful economic and social processes" associated with the shift from a manufacturing to a service economy and the shift in the location of production to suburbs, the Sunbelt, and offshore (1993: 7).

Numerous other scholars have extended upon, innovated from, and critiqued this work, focusing on the intersection of race, class, and residential segregation (South and Crowder 1998; Iceland and Wilkes 2006); on multiethnic dimensions of segregation (Frey and Farley 1996; Charles 2003; Iceland 2004; South, Crowder, and Pais 2008); on the segregation of immigrants (Iceland and Scopilliti 2008); on the significance of metropolitan level characteristics (South, Crowder, and Pais 2011); on change in segregation over time (Logan, Stults, and Farley 2004); and critiques of the focus on racial as compared to class disparities (Reed and Chowkwanyun 2012; Reed 2016), among other topics. Other scholars, such as Rhonda Williams (2004), have used extensive qualitative interviews and archival research to document Black women's interactions with public housing and their politicization and activism in relation to the neighborhood transformations that public policy changes and economic restructuring wreaked on their communities.

Neighborhood Effects

Attention to both differences in neighborhood characteristics and the effects that neighborhoods might have on outcomes grew significantly in the 1990s and 2000s (see, e.g., Ellen and Turner 1997; Sharkey and Faber 2014). One branch of that scholarship focused on the stability of neighborhood inequality and how that differentiation by residential location is part of "a durable spatial logic [that] organizes or mediates social life" (Sampson 2012: 21). Indeed many of the social problems on which sociologists often focus, from educational attainment to crime to mortality, have persistent spatial arrangements despite relatively high levels of individual geographic mobility. In that context, Robert Sampson investigated "how residential mobility, organizational ties, and elite social networks differentially connect neighborhoods to the cross-cutting institutions and resources that organize much of contemporary economic, political, and social life" (Sampson 2012: 61). This attention to neighborhood differences and the effects of those differences is intertwined with segregation by both race and class.

Relatedly, scholars such as Mario Small highlighted the heterogeneity of poor, Black neighborhoods and the complexity of contemporary Black residential patterns (Small 2008). Small observed that while Black households' locational decisions were not wholly predetermined, they continue to be shaped by constrained choice sets and made in a context in which local governments are increasingly significant for the lives of poor and working-class households as federal economic and social supports are diminished (Small 2008; Small and McDermott 2006). This attention by Sampson, Small, and others to neighborhood differences and their effects illustrates how residential segregation has become both an object of study in sociology (for example, research on what drives household locational decisions and continuing segregation) and simultaneously a tool for understanding social stratification more broadly (for example, research on what differences in neighborhood characteristics most powerfully affect individual outcomes).

The spatial dynamics of intergenerational socioeconomic mobility have become a focus of more recent research in both sociology and economics. Scholars such as Patrick Sharkey have suggested that racial inequality can be accurately understood only from a multigenerational perspective and that the neighborhood must be conceptualized as an independent dimension of that stratification—in other words, that we should examine the "trajectories of individual families in combination with the trajectories of the places they occupy" (Sharkey 2013: 6). Sharkey writes that "to understand why the children of the civil rights era have made such minimal progress toward racial equality, we need to consider what has happened to the communities and cities in which they have lived over the past four decades" (Sharkey 2013: 5). He chronicles changes in predominantly African American neighborhoods characterized by "severe disinvestment and persistent, rigid segregation; where the employment base that supported a middle-class urban population has migrated away, contracted, or collapsed; and where the impact of punitive criminal justice policies has been concentrated" (Sharkey 2013: 6).

Racially segregated residential patterns continue to be associated with unequal access by race to basic goods and services, such as the provision of financial services (Faber 2013, 2019) or health care (Figueroa 2019), and the targeting of predominantly Black and Latino neighborhoods for high-cost, high-risk products (Hwang, Hankinson, and Brown 2014; Steil et al. 2018) that strip these communities of already limited assets. Like wealth, "neighborhood environments, along with all of the advantages and disadvantages that go with them, tend to be passed on from parents to children" and "African Americans have remained tied to places where poverty has become increasingly concentrated, where opportunities for economic advancement have declined, and where the risk of going to prison has become more prevalent than the hope of going to college" (Sharkey 2013: 44, 49). Sharkey identifies effects of neighborhood disadvantage experienced during childhood that continue to have an impact into adulthood and that cumulate over generations. This work has taken place as scholars in economics have noted similar trends, including the significance of metropolitan areas in shaping intergenerational socioeconomic mobility (Chetty et al. 2014) and the negative effects of childhood exposure to higher neighborhood poverty rates on future college graduation and earnings (Chetty et al. 2016).

While much of the literature on segregation focused on the effects of neighborhood characteristics on the Black poor (e.g., Wilson 1987) or "underclass" (e.g., Massey and Denton 1993), segregated living patterns continued to characterize the experience of much of the Black middle class as well (Pattillo 2005; Sharkey 2014). Evoking Drake and Cayton's *Black Metropolis*, Mary Pattillo (1999: 4) notes that "the black middle class has not outmigrated to unnamed neighborhoods outside of the black community" but instead "are an overlooked population still rooted in the contemporary 'Black Belts' of cities across the country." Pattillo's rich ethnography explores how continuing racial segregation meant that Black middle-class neighborhoods "are characterized by more poverty, higher crime, worse schools, and fewer services than white middle-class neighborhoods," contributing to economic fragility and downward economic mobility (1999: 3). Indeed, the average African American or Latino household with an income over $75,000 lives in a census tract with a higher poverty rate than the average white household that earns less than $40,000 (Logan 2011).

Although African Americans have historically been far more segregated than other nonwhite groups, Latino-white and Black-white segregation levels converged between 1980 and 2010 (Iceland and Nelson 2008).[1] The growth of the U.S. Latino population is provoking a transformation in twenty-first-century metropolitan areas similar to the Great Migration of the twentieth century (Tienda and Fuentes 2014). As the Latino population continues to grow, Latinos are inheriting the segregated urban structures still experienced by African Americans. Although there is substantial heterogeneity among Latino groups of different ancestry, residential segregation is associated on average with significant negative educational and employment outcomes for native-born Latino young adults (De la Roca, Ellen, and Steil 2018). These negative effects for Latinos are as, or more, significant than the negative effects of segregation for African American young adults.

Drivers of Continuing Segregation

Although there is increasing recognition of the significance of residential location for access to opportunity, whites' preferences for living in

predominantly white neighborhoods continue to reinforce residential segregation by race today. Whites tend to favor predominately white neighborhoods (estimated at less than 20 percent Black) and are often reluctant to
move into neighborhoods with more than a few nonwhite households
(Charles 2006). Black homeseekers, however, prefer significantly more integrated neighborhoods (Krysan and Farley 2002). Research on neighborhood
preferences has also found the existence of a racial hierarchy in preferred
neighborhood composition, with whites as the most-preferred "out-group"—a
race different from the homeseeker—and Blacks consistently the least preferred of out-group neighbors, and Asians and Latinos usually in the middle
of the hierarchy (Charles 2003).

The strongest evidence that racial composition matters independently of
class or other neighborhood characteristics when whites make housing
decisions comes from studies employing experimental methods to test the
independent effects of race and class characteristics on neighborhood preference. For example, in one study, researchers showed a video of the exact same
neighborhood scene but changed the race of visible neighborhood residents
or the class valence of their activities. White homeseekers consistently rated
all-white neighborhoods as the most desirable. The effect of race was smaller
for Black homeseekers, who identified racially mixed neighborhoods as the
most desirable (Krysan et al. 2009).

In addition to differences by race in preferred neighborhood racial composition and neighborhood perception, segregation is exacerbated by the
"mismatch" between whites' desired neighborhood racial composition and
the composition of neighborhoods in which they perform their housing
search. While Black and Latino homeseekers conduct their search in neighborhoods that correspond to their stated preferences, whites search in neighborhoods with even higher percentages of whites than they say they would
prefer (Havekes, Bader, and Krysan 2016).

Schelling (1971) demonstrated that the interactive dynamics of discriminatory individual choices mean that extreme segregation can arise from
relatively small differences in preferences. The interactions between individual choices can generate a nonlinear response, so that when the share of
nonwhites in a neighborhood passes a certain tipping point, white flight or
white avoidance quickly leads to near-total isolation (Krysan and Crowder
2018). Given both Schelling's insights and the reality that society continues
to be structured by substantial divergence in preferred neighborhood compo-

sition, it is not surprising that residential segregation continues to be so pervasive (Charles 2006; Card, Mas, and Rothstein 2008; Krysan, Carter, and van Londen 2017).

Residential segregation is also enabled in part by the decentralized structure of government in the United States, which leaves the provision of many goods and services, and the raising of a substantial share of government revenue, to municipal governments (Briffault 1990; Frug 2001; Massey and Hajnal 1995). This metropolitan fragmentation facilitates processes that sociologist Charles Tilly (1998) and others have called opportunity hoarding (Reeves 2017; Freemark, Thelen, and Steil 2020). Tilly suggests that durable inequalities, such as racial inequalities, arise "because people who control access to value-producing resources solve pressing organizational problems by means of categorical distinctions" (1998: 7–8). The structure of local governance in the United States is predicated upon competition and inequality among local governments, upon some municipalities touting their high property values, low tax rates, and high-performing school systems to attract wealthy businesses and residents and to differentiate themselves from municipalities with lower property values, higher tax rates, and schools with lower test scores. In metropolitan areas in the United States, valuable resources, such as access to high-performing schools, well-maintained parks, and other amenities have been and continue to be valuable resources guarded by wealthier, whiter households against those seen as threatening or encroaching upon them (Oliver and Shapiro 1995; Conley 1999). Through these processes of opportunity hoarding and the intergenerational transfer of unequally resourced neighborhoods, residential segregation serves as the "structural linchpin" of racial stratification (Massey 2016; Pettigrew 1979; Bobo 1989).

Gentrification and Displacement

Despite most whites' preferences for living in predominantly white neighborhoods, there is growing public concern about the extent and significance of neighborhood change through gentrification. Cities in the United States have become increasingly popular for young professionals over the past two decades, and housing costs, especially median rents, have increased faster than median incomes for renters in many cities. Many historically Black and

Latino neighborhoods near the centers of growing cities have witnessed the displacement or departure of poor and working-class Black and Latino households and their replacement by higher-income, often white, households. Looking across the past half-century, Lawrence Vale (2013: xiii) has described how urban development policies, as political acts operationalized through urban design, created "twice-cleared communities"—working-class neighborhoods razed once to construct public housing and again to demolish it, with repeated purges of "the poorest citizens from suddenly desirable land," often driven at least in part by racial or ethnic prejudice. While some have suggested that these recent neighborhood changes associated with gentrification could lead to more racially and economically integrated neighborhoods (Byrne 2002; Godsil 2013), it seems more likely that these shifts will drive a process of resegregation in which Black and Latino households are dispossessed of desirable neighborhood locations (Powell and Spencer 2002).

Scholars have debated the extent to which gentrification causes displacement directly and the extent to which it leads to neighborhood demographic change (e.g., Freeman and Braconi 2004; Freeman 2005; Newman and Wyly 2006; Lees, Slater, and Wyly 2008; Ellen and O'Regan 2011; Hwang 2016). In theory, an increasing tax base and residents with more political and economic power could help improve neighborhood infrastructure and amenities (such as schools or parks) for all residents. Mary Pattillo suggests, however, that "in practice such a redistribution of resources often takes a backseat to feeding the demands of the new gentry for more public art, smoother streets, and support for more high-end housing, recreational, and commercial activity" (Pattillo 2007: 107). Gentrification may also further subordinate nonwhite or nonwealthy residents in spaces that were once seen as their own (Chaskin and Joseph 2013). For example, new middle-class residents often attempt to control the use of public spaces by low-income neighbors, sometimes through the "progressive criminalization of 'quality of life issues'" (Pattillo 2007: 264). Lance Freeman (2006: 107) gives the example of drinking outside in gentrifying neighborhoods: "certain activities, such as drinking in public, are proscribed unless they conform to the gentry's idea of what is acceptable. . . . What difference should it make whether someone is standing on a corner or sitting behind a restaurant cordon?" Any stability of multiracial, mixed-income neighborhoods created through gentrification is precarious, as pressures for shorter commutes and rising rents can lead to rapid changes in neighborhood residents in some highly valued locations, even as investment and upgrading seem as distant as ever in others (Hwang and Sampson 2014; Edlund, Machado, and Sviatschi 2015).

Conclusion

Through more than a century of sociological scholarship, research has suggested that residential segregation is one mechanism through which socioeconomic inequalities are reproduced. Levels of Black-white residential segregation have decreased from their 1968 levels but remain high, and levels of Latino-white segregation have remained relatively consistent over the same period. Research suggests that residential segregation by race continues to produce separate and unequal access to resources, such as schools or jobs, and exposure to hazards, such as violence or environmental risks (Steil, De la Roca, and Ellen, 2015).

The Fair Housing Act has been a crucial tool in the fight against discrimination in housing. Enforcement has been limited, however, by a combination of lack of awareness by victims of discrimination, low levels of enforcement by the government agencies empowered to implement the act, and relatively weak penalties for lawbreakers (Schill 2007). Nevertheless, audit studies have suggested that explicit discrimination in housing has decreased and taken somewhat more subtle forms, such as nonwhite homeseekers being shown fewer units or offered fewer financing options (Turner et al. 2013; Pager and Shepherd 2008). More fundamentally, however, the Fair Housing Act has been less effective in reducing segregation and inequalities in access to place-based resources overall because the structures that encourage and perpetuate segregation are entrenched in our local government boundaries and home ownership structures (Steil 2011). Continuing asymmetrical preferences for neighborhood racial composition combine with metropolitan fragmentation, exclusionary zoning, and regressive local financing structures to generate neighborhoods that remain separate and unequal (Freemark, Thelen, and Steil 2020). As Du Bois, Drake and Cayton, and others noted a century ago, the intersection of residential segregation and neighborhood inequality continue to generate racial disparities in educational outcomes, wealth, health, and well-being, while obscuring their causes. Continuing segregation also decreases the likelihood of being able to shift racial attitudes.

Data from the General Social Survey on changing attitudes is illuminating. In the 1976 General Social Survey, 63 percent of white respondents nationwide, or nearly two out of every three, believed that homeowners should be allowed to discriminate on the basis of race when selling their home (Smith et al. 2017). In 2016, that share had fallen dramatically, but still included more than 14 percent of white respondents, or nearly one out of every seven (Smith et al. 2017). These results suggest that a sizable minority of white Americans today still openly oppose the protections enshrined in the Fair Housing Act. There have been sweeping changes in white attitudes regarding de jure segregation, mixed-race marriages, and the categorical inferiority of nonwhites (Bobo et al. 2012). Yet, despite growing acceptance of the general principle of integration in social life, whites still express strong preferences for social distance from non-white people, particularly African Americans (Bobo et al. 2012). Support for government action to reduce both segregation and inequality remains limited among whites and is declining among African American respondents as well (Bobo et al. 2012). While whites have moved away from biological explanations of racial inequality, they have moved toward cultural ones, and African American respondents have moved from structural explanations toward cultural explanations as well (Bobo et al. 2012; see also O'Connor 2001). This naturalization of inequality through cultural narratives is consistent with the ways in which segregation reinforces inequality by making its origins less visible. These shifts in attitudes among both white and African American respondents toward cultural explanations, and African American shifts away from support for government intervention, present challenges for the future of fair housing.

Simultaneously, conceptions of fair housing as defined primarily by the fight to access high-income suburban neighborhoods are becoming outdated as investment and jobs flow again into many central cities. In low-income communities of color within high-cost cities, displacement and resegregation seem to be the most pressing concerns as the struggle for urban space intensifies. The suburbanization of poverty generally makes crucial supports, such as employment services or affordable housing programs, harder for lower-income households in suburbs to access than these supports were in cities, where there is a greater density of supportive institutions (Allard 2009). The dispersal of low-income households and of communities of color may also make political organizing and electoral power more challenging to mobilize. Beyond the tangible effect of further isolating low-income households from growing central city resources, gentrification also sometimes has the less tangible consequence of cultural dispossession, again marking African

Americans as the "displaced persons" of American democracy (Ellison 1964b: 287, 300; Rhodes-Pitts 2011: 117).

Concerns about displacement are consistent with the Fair Housing Act's priorities of confronting the durable structural inequalities embedded in our metropolitan areas. Addressing the ways in which our local governance structures and housing policies continue to re-create inequality will require innovative policy-making focused simultaneously on affordability and equity. Tackling the fragmented and exclusionary structures of local government is essential, if vexingly challenging. Some potential approaches could include creating financial incentives for inclusionary zoning changes and affordable housing development through federal block grant programs or through allowing affordable housing developers whose planning and zoning permits are denied by local governments to appeal to state courts if that locality does not already have some set percentage of units designated as affordable (see, e.g., Massachusetts General Laws Chapter 40[b]). A revitalized "affirmatively furthering fair housing" rule that requires state and local governments to create their own locally tailored plans to address racial disparities in access to opportunity will also be crucial for the promise of the Fair Housing Act to be realized (Steil and Kelly 2019a; Steil and Kelly 2019b; O'Regan 2019).

Basic steps—such as fully funding the Housing Choice Voucher program to eliminate its long waiting lists and requiring housing authorities to calculate small-area fair market rents—would help households escape crushing rent burdens and have broader sets of choices about where to live. Investing in the nation's public housing stock as part of comprehensive community investments is an essential part of preserving valuable islands of affordability for future generations, especially in high-cost cities (Lens and Reina 2016). Federal financial support for local efforts to make housing in resource-rich neighborhoods permanently affordable by removing it from the speculative market through community land trusts is one way to address affordability and homeownership simultaneously. Congress should also update the Fair Housing Act and related civil rights protections to reflect the societal developments of the past fifty years. Amending the Fair Housing Act to prohibit discrimination on the basis of source of income as well as sexual orientation and gender identity would update the act to meet contemporary policy challenges and values.

If the goal of the Fair Housing Act is the elimination of intentional discrimination, audit studies suggest the Fair Housing Act has made progress, even if intentional segregation does continue (Turner et al. 2013; Freiberg 2013). If the goal of the Fair Housing Act is the broader reformation of the institutions and practices that reproduce the subordinate social status of historically oppressed groups through unequal access to place-based opportunities (Steil and Delgado 2019), however, the Fair Housing Act has not been nearly as effective and needs amendments to both widen and strengthen its protections. In terms of creating real housing choice and meaningful equality of neighborhood resources, the distance remaining is large.

As the geographer Katherine McKittrick (2011: 948) has written, white supremacy in the United States has repeatedly "marked black working bodies as those 'without'—without legible-Eurocentric history narratives, without land or home, without ownership of self—as this system forcibly secured black peoples to the geographic mechanics" of the plantation economy or other modes of accumulation. In order to change this representation, fair housing and civil rights advocates must take a clear-eyed view of the long-term consequences of gentrification for racial equity. Across all potential policy innovations, policy-makers should adopt an antisubordination approach that foregrounds attention to disparities in access to opportunity across durable categories of inequality, that recognizes institutionalized asymmetries of power and unconscious biases that perpetuate those disparities, and that prioritizes policies that reduce inequality even if they may have higher costs than policies that exacerbate it (Steil 2018).

Notes

The authors thank Mary Pattillo, Wendell Pritchett, Vincent Reina, and Susan Wachter for their helpful comments.

1. Black-white dissimilarity declined consistently between 1980 and 2010 (from 0.73 to 0.60), while Latino-white (0.52 in 1980 and 0.50 in 2010) and Asian-white dissimilarity (0.41 in 1980 and 0.42 in 2010) remained relatively steady (De la Roca, Ellen, and O'Regan 2014). Although Latino isolation (that is, the share of Latino residents in the neighborhood where the average Latino lives) has risen less rapidly than Latinos' quickly rising share of the population, average levels of Latino isolation have still risen substantially and matched average levels of African American isolation in 2010. Over this time period, African American isolation declined from 0.61 to 0.46 while Latino isolation rose from 0.38 to 0.46 (De la Roca, Ellen, and O'Regan 2014).

References

114 Congressional Record 2703 (1968) (statement of Sen. Jacob Javits).
114 Congressional Record 2274-2276 (1968) (statement of Sen. Walter Mondale).

114 Congressional Record 3422 (1968) (statement of Sen. Walter Mondale).

Allard, Scott W. *Out of Reach: Place, Poverty, and the New American Welfare State*. New Haven, CT: Yale University Press, 2009.

Bobo, Lawrence D. "Keeping the Linchpin in Place: Testing the Multiple Sources of Opposition to Residential Integration." *International Review of Social Psychology* 2, no. 3 (1989): 305–23.

Bobo, Lawrence D., Camille Z. Charles, Maria Krysan, and Alicia Simmons. "The Real Record on Racial Attitudes." In *Social Trends in American Life: Findings from the General Social Survey Since 1972*, edited by Peter V. Marsden, 38–93. Princeton, NJ: Princeton University Press, 2012.

Briffault, Richard. "Our Localism: Part I—The Structure of Local Government Law." *Columbia Law Review* 90, no. 1 (1990): 1–115.

Brooks, Richard R. W., and Carol M. Rose. *Saving the Neighborhood: Racially Restrictive Covenants, Law, and Social Norms*. Cambridge, MA: Harvard University Press, 2013.

Burgess, Ernest Watson. "The Growth of the City: An Introduction to a Research Project." In *The City: Suggestions for Investigation of Human Behavior in the Urban Environment*, edited by Robert Ezra Park, Ernest Watson Burgess, and Roderick D. McKenzie. The Heritage of Sociology. Chicago: University of Chicago Press, 2010.

Byrne, J. Peter. "Two Cheers for Gentrification." *Howard Law Journal* 46 (2003): 405–32.

Card, David, Alexandre Mas, and Jesse Rothstein. "Tipping and the Dynamics of Segregation." *Quarterly Journal of Economics* 123, no. 1 (February 2008): 177–218.

Carmichael, Stokely. "Black Power" speech. October 29, 1966. http://voicesofdemocracy.umd .edu/carmichael-black-power-speech-text/.

Carmichael, Stokely, and Charles V. Hamilton. *Black Power: The Politics of Liberation in America*. New York: Vintage Books, 1967.

Charles, Camille Zubrinsky. "The Dynamics of Racial Residential Segregation." *Annual Review of Sociology* 29, no. 1 (August 2003): 167–207.

———. *Won't You Be My Neighbor? Race, Class, and Residence in Los Angeles*. New York: Russell Sage Foundation, 2006.

Chaskin, Robert J., and Mark L. Joseph. "'Positive' Gentrification, Social Control and the 'Right to the City' in Mixed-Income Communities: Uses and Expectations of Space and Place." *International Journal of Urban and Regional Research* 37, no. 2 (2013): 480–502.

Chetty, Raj, Nathaniel Hendren, and Lawrence F. Katz. "The Effects of Exposure to Better Neighborhoods on Children: New Evidence from the Moving to Opportunity Experiment." *American Economic Review* 106, no. 4 (2016): 855–902.

Chetty, Raj, Nathaniel Hendren, Patrick Kline, and Emmanuel Saez. "Where Is the Land of Opportunity? The Geography of Intergenerational Mobility in the United States." *Quarterly Journal of Economics* 129, no. 4 (November 2014): 1553–623.

Clark, Kenneth B. "Effect of Prejudice and Discrimination on Personality Development." Paper presented at the Mid-century White House Conference on Children and Youth, Washington, D.C., 1950.

Conley, Dalton. *Being Black, Living in the Red: Race, Wealth, and Social Policy in America*. Berkeley: University of California Press, 1999.

De la Roca, Jorge, Ingrid Gould Ellen, and Katherine M. O'Regan. "Race and Neighborhoods in the 21st Century: What Does Segregation Mean Today?" *Regional Science and Urban Economics*, SI: Tribute to John Quigley, 47 (July 2014): 138–51.

De la Roca, Jorge, Ingrid Gould Ellen, and Justin Steil. "Does Segregation Matter for Latinos?" *Journal of Housing Economics* 40 (June 2018): 129–41. https://doi.org/10.1016/j.jhe.2017.10.003.

Drake, St. Clair, and Horace R. Cayton. *Black Metropolis: A Study of Negro Life in a Northern City*. Chicago: University of Chicago Press, 2015.

Du Bois, William Edward Burghardt. "Does the Negro Need Separate Schools?" *Journal of Negro Education* 4, no. 3 (1935): 328–35.

———. *The Philadelphia Negro: A Social Study*. New York: Oxford University Press, 1899.

———. "Segregation." *The Crisis* 41, no. 1 (January 1934).

———. "Sociology Hesitant." *Boundary 2: An International Journal of Literature and Culture* 27, no. 3 (1905/2000): 37–44.

———. *The Souls of Black Folk*. New York: Dover, 1903.

———. "The Study of the Negro Problems." *Annals of the American Academy of Political and Social Science* 11 (1898): 1–23.

Duncan, Otis Dudley, and Beverly Duncan. "A Methodological Analysis of Segregation Indexes." *American Sociological Review* 20, no. 2 (1955): 210–17.

Edlund, Lena, Cecilia Machado, and Maria Micaela Sviatschi. "Bright Minds, Big Rent: Gentrification and the Rising Returns to Skill." Working paper. National Bureau of Economic Research, November 2015.

Ellen, Ingrid Gould, and Katherine M. O'Regan. "How Low Income Neighborhoods Change: Entry, Exit, and Enhancement." *Regional Science and Urban Economics* 41, no. 2 (March 2011): 89–97.

Ellen, Ingrid Gould, Justin P. Steil, and Jorge De la Roca. "The Significance of Segregation in the 21st Century." *City & Community* 15, no. 1 (March 1, 2016): 8–13.

Ellen, Ingrid Gould, and Margery Austin Turner. "Does Neighborhood Matter? Assessing Recent Evidence." *Housing Policy Debate* 8, no. 4 (January 1, 1997): 833–66.

Ellison, Ralph. "An American Dilemma: A Review." In *Shadow and Act*. New York: Random House, 1964a, 303–17.

———. "Harlem Is Nowhere." In *Shadow and Act*. New York: Random House, 1964b, 294–302.

Faber, Jacob W. "Racial Dynamics of Subprime Mortgage Lending at the Peak." *Housing Policy Debate* 23, no. 2 (April 1, 2013): 328–49.

———. "Segregation and the Cost of Money: Race, Poverty, and the Prevalence of Alternative Financial Institutions." *Social Forces* 98, no. 2 (December 2019): 819–48.

Figueroa, Jose. "Segregated Health Systems." In *The Dream Revisited: Contemporary Debates about Housing, Segregation, and Opportunity*, edited by Ingrid Gould Ellen and Justin Peter Steil. New York: Columbia University Press, 2019.

Freeman, Lance. "Displacement or Succession?: Residential Mobility in Gentrifying Neighborhoods." *Urban Affairs Review* 40, no. 4 (March 1, 2005): 463–91.

———. *There Goes the 'Hood: Views of Gentrification from the Ground Up*. Philadelphia, PA: Temple University Press, 2006.

Freeman, Lance, and Frank Braconi. "Gentrification and Displacement: New York City in the 1990s." *Journal of the American Planning Association* 70, no. 1 (March 31, 2004): 39–52.

Freemark, Yonah, Justin Steil, and Kathleen Thelen. "Varieties of Urbanism: A Comparative View of Inequality and the Dual Dimensions of Metropolitan Fragmentation." *Politics & Society* (2020). https://doi.org/10.1177/0032329220908966.

Freiberg, Fred. 2013. "Ground Truths About Housing Discrimination." *Poverty and Race* 22, no. 5 (September 2013): 1–16.

Frey, William H., and Reynolds Farley. "Latino, Asian, and Black Segregation in U.S. Metropolitan Areas: Are Multiethnic Metros Different." *Demography* 33, no. 1 (February 1, 1996): 35–50.

Frug, Gerald E. *City Making: Building Communities Without Building Walls.* Princeton, NJ: Princeton University Press, 2001.

Godsil, Rachel D. "The Gentrification Trigger: Autonomy, Mobility, and Affirmatively Furthering Fair Housing Symposium: Post-zoning: Alternative Forms of Public Land Use Controls." *Brooklyn Law Review* 78 (2013): 319–38.

Hannah-Jones, Nikole. "Living Apart: How the Government Betrayed a Landmark Civil Rights Law." *ProPublica*, June 25, 2015. https://www.propublica.org/article/living-apart-how-the-government-betrayed-a-landmark-civil-rights-law.

Havekes, Esther, Michael Bader, and Maria Krysan. "Realizing Racial and Ethnic Neighborhood Preferences? Exploring the Mismatches Between What People Want, Where They Search, and Where They Live." *Population Research and Policy Review* 35, no. 1 (February 1, 2016): 101–26.

Hwang, Jackelyn. "Pioneers of Gentrification: Transformation in Global Neighborhoods in Urban America in the Late Twentieth Century." *Demography* 53, no. 1 (February 1, 2016): 189–213.

Hwang, Jackelyn, Michael Hankinson, and Kreg Steven Brown. "Racial and Spatial Targeting: Segregation and Subprime Lending Within and Across Metropolitan Areas." *Social Forces* 93, no. 3 (2014): 1081–108.

Hwang, Jackelyn, and Robert J. Sampson. "Divergent Pathways of Gentrification: Racial Inequality and the Social Order of Renewal in Chicago Neighborhoods." *American Sociological Review* 79, no. 4 (2014): 726–51.

Iceland, John. "Beyond Black and White: Metropolitan Residential Segregation in Multi-Ethnic America." *Social Science Research* 33, no. 2 (June 1, 2004): 248–71.

Iceland, John, and Kyle Anne Nelson. "Hispanic Segregation in Metropolitan America: Exploring the Multiple Forms of Spatial Assimilation." *American Sociological Review* 73, no. 5 (October 1, 2008): 741–65.

Iceland, John, and Melissa Scopilliti. "Immigrant Residential Segregation in U.S. Metropolitan Areas, 1990–2000." *Demography* 45, no. 1 (February 1, 2008): 79–94.

Iceland, John, and Rima Wilkes. "Does Socioeconomic Status Matter? Race, Class, and Residential Segregation." *Social Problems* 53, no. 2 (February 1, 2006): 248–73.

Jackson, Kenneth T. *Crabgrass Frontier: The Suburbanization of the United States.* New York: Oxford University Press, 1987.

James, David R., and Karl E. Taeuber. "Measures of Segregation." *Sociological Methodology* 15 (1985): 1–32.

King, Martin Luther, Jr. "King Encyclopedia." March 18, 1966a. http://mlk-kpp01.stanford.edu /index.php/encyclopedia/encyclopedia/enc_chicago_campaign.

———. "King Encyclopedia." August 5, 1966b. http://mlk-kpp01.stanford.edu/index.php /encyclopedia/encyclopedia/enc_chicago_campaign.

Kitagawa, Evelyn Mae, and Karl E. Taeuber, eds. *Local Community Fact Book: Chicago Metro-politan Area*. Chicago Community Inventory. Chicago: University of Chicago, 1963.

Krysan, Maria, Courtney Carter, and Marieke van Londen. "The Diversity of Integration in a Multiethnic Metropolis: Exploring What Whites, African Americans, and Latinos Imag-ine." *Du Bois Review* 14, no. 1 (2017): 35–71.

Krysan, Maria, Mick P. Couper, Reynolds Farley, and Tyrone Forman. "Does Race Matter in Neighborhood Preferences? Results from a Video Experiment." *American Journal of Sociology* 115, no. 2 (September 2009): 527–59.

Krysan, Maria, and Kyle Crowder. *Cycle of Segregation*. New York: Russell Sage, 2018.

Krysan, Maria, and Reynolds Farley. "The Residential Preferences of Blacks: Do They Explain Persistent Segregation?" *Social Forces* 80, no. 3 (March 2002): 937–80.

Lees, Loretta, Tom Slater, and Elvin K. Wyly. *Gentrification*. New York: Routledge, 2008.

Lens, Michael C., and Vincent Reina. "Preserving Neighborhood Opportunity: Where Fed-eral Housing Subsidies Expire." *Housing Policy Debate* 26, nos. 4–5 (2016): 714–32.

Lewis, Valerie A., Michael O. Emerson, and Stephen L. Klineberg. "Who We'll Live With: Neighborhood Racial Composition Preferences of Whites, Blacks and Latinos." *Social Forces* 89, no. 4 (June 1, 2011): 1385–407.

Logan, John R. "Separate and Unequal: The Neighborhood Gap for Blacks, Hispanics and Asians in Metropolitan America." *Project US2010 Report*. New York: Russell Sage Foundation.

Logan, John R., Brian J. Stults, and Reynolds Farley. "Segregation of Minorities in the Metropo-lis: Two Decades of Change." *Demography* 41, no. 1 (February 1, 2004): 1–22.

Massey, Douglas S. "Residential Segregation Is the Linchpin of Racial Stratification." *City & Community* 15, no. 1 (March 1, 2016): 4–7.

Massey, Douglas S., and Nancy A. Denton. *American Apartheid: Segregation and the Making of the Underclass*. Cambridge, MA: Harvard University Press, 1993.

———. "The Dimensions of Residential Segregation." *Social Forces* 67, no. 2 (December 1, 1988): 281–315.

Massey, Douglas S., and Zoltan J. Hajnal. "The Changing Geographic Structure of Black-White Segregation in the United States." *Social Science Quarterly* 76, no. 3 (September 1995): 527–42.

McKittrick, Katherine. "On Plantations, Prisons, and a Black Sense of Place." *Social & Cul-tural Geography* 12, no. 8 (2011): 947–63.

Morris, Aldon D. *The Scholar Denied: W. E. B. Du Bois and the Birth of Modern Sociology*. Oak-land: University of California Press, 2015.

Muhammad, Khalil Gibran. 2011. *The Condemnation of Blackness: Race, Crime, and the Making of Modern Urban America*. Cambridge, MA: Harvard University Press.

Myrdal, Gunnar. *An American Dilemma: The Negro Problem and Modern Democracy*. New York: Harper & Row Publishers, 1944.

National Advisory Commission on Civil Disorders. *Report of the National Advisory Commis-sion on Civil Disorders*, 1968.

Newman, Kathe, and Elvin K. Wyly. "The Right to Stay Put, Revisited: Gentrification and Resistance to Displacement in New York City." *Urban Studies* 43, no. 1 (January 1, 2006): 23–57.

Oates, Stephen B. *Let the Trumpet Sound: The Life of Martin Luther King, Jr.* New York: Mentor, 1985.

O'Connor, Alice. *Poverty Knowledge: Social Science, Social Policy, and the Poor in Twentieth-Century U.S. History.* Princeton, NJ: Princeton University Press, 2001.

Oliver, Melvin L., and Thomas M. Shapiro. *Black Wealth, White Wealth: A New Perspective on Racial Inequality.* New York: Routledge, 1995.

O'Regan, Katherine M. "The Fair Housing Act Today: Current Context and Challenges at 50." *Housing Policy Debate* 29, no. 5 (2019): 704–13.

Pager, Devah, and Hana Shepherd. "The Sociology of Discrimination: Racial Discrimination in Employment, Housing, Credit, and Consumer Markets." *Annual Review of Sociology* 34, no. 1 (2008): 181–209.

Park, Robert E. "The City: Suggestions for the Investigation of Human Behavior in the City Environment." *American Journal of Sociology* 20, no. 5 (1915): 577–612.

———. "The Concept of Position in Sociology." *Papers and Proceedings of the American Sociological Society* 20 (1926): 1–14.

———. "The Concept of Social Distance as Applied to the Study of Racial Attitudes and Racial Relations." *Journal of Applied Sociology* 8 (1924): 339–44.

Pattillo, Mary. "Black Middle-Class Neighborhoods." *Annual Review of Sociology* 31, no. 1 (2005): 305–29.

———. *Black Picket Fences: Privilege and Peril Among the Black Middle Class.* Chicago: University of Chicago Press, 1999.

———. *Black on the Block: The Politics of Race and Class in the City.* Chicago: University of Chicago Press, 2007.

———. Foreword. *Black Metropolis: A Study of Negro Life in a Northern City.* Chicago: University of Chicago Press, 2015.

Pettigrew, Thomas F. "Racial Change and Social Policy." *The ANNALS of the American Academy of Political and Social Science* 441 (1979): 114–31.

Powell, John A., and Marguerite L. Spencer. "Giving Them the Old One-Two: Gentrification and the K.O. of Impoverished Urban Dwellers of Color Urban Poverty & Gentrification: An Exchange." *Howard Law Journal* 46 (2002): 433–90.

Ralph, James R. *Northern Protest: Martin Luther King, Jr., Chicago, and the Civil Rights Movement.* Cambridge, MA: Harvard University Press, 1993.

Reed, Adolph L. "The Post-1965 Trajectory of Race, Class, and Urban Politics in the United States Reconsidered." *Labor Studies Journal* 41, no. 3 (2016): 260–91.

Reed, Adolph L., and Merlin Chowkwanyun. "Race, Class, Crisis: The Discourse of Racial Disparity and Its Analytical Discontents." *Socialist Register* 48 (2012): 149–75.

Reeves, Richard V. *Dream Hoarders: How the American Upper Middle Class Is Leaving Everyone Else in the Dust, Why That Is a Problem, and What to Do About It.* Washington, D.C.: Brookings, 2017.

Rhodes-Pitts, Sharifa. *Harlem Is Nowhere: A Journey to the Mecca of Black America.* New York: Little, Brown, 2011.

"Rock Thrown from Crowd Hits Dr. King." *Baltimore Sun*, August 6, 1966, sec. A.

Rothstein, Richard. *The Color of Law: A Forgotten History of How Our Government Segregated America*. New York: Liveright, 2017.

Sampson, Robert J. *Great American City: Chicago and the Enduring Neighborhood Effect*. Chicago: University of Chicago Press, 2012.

Satter, Beryl. *Family Properties: Race, Real Estate, and the Exploitation of Black Urban America*. New York: Metropolitan Books, 2010.

Schelling, Thomas C. "Dynamic Models of Segregation." *Journal of Mathematical Sociology* 1, no. 2 (July 1971): 143–86.

Schill, Michael H. "Implementing the Federal Fair Housing Act: The Adjudication of Complaints." In *Fragile Rights Within Cities: Government, Housing, and Fairness*, edited by John M. Goering, 143–76. Lanham, MD: Rowman & Littlefield, 2007.

Sharkey, Patrick. "Spatial Segmentation and the Black Middle Class." *American Journal of Sociology* 119, no. 4 (January 1, 2014): 903–54.

———. *Stuck in Place: Urban Neighborhoods and the End of Progress Toward Racial Equality*. Chicago: University of Chicago Press, 2013.

Sharkey, Patrick, and Jacob W. Faber. "Where, When, Why, and for Whom Do Residential Contexts Matter? Moving Away from the Dichotomous Understanding of Neighborhood Effects." *Annual Review of Sociology* 40, no. 1 (2014): 559–79.

Small, Mario Luis. "Four Reasons to Abandon the Idea of 'The Ghetto.'" *City and Community* 7, no. 4 (2008): 389.

Small, Mario Luis, and Monica McDermott. "The Presence of Organizational Resources in Poor Urban Neighborhoods: An Analysis of Average and Contextual Effects." *Social Forces* 84, no. 3 (2006): 1697–724.

Smith, Tom, Peter Marsden, Michael Hout, and Jibum Kim. "General Social Surveys, 1972–2016 [Machine-Readable Data File]." Non-partisan and Objective Research Organization at the University of Chicago (NORC), 2017.

South, Scott J., and Kyle D. Crowder. "Leaving the 'Hood: Residential Mobility Between Black, White, and Integrated Neighborhoods." *American Sociological Review* 63, no. 1 (1998): 17–26.

South, Scott J., Kyle Crowder, and Jeremy Pais. "Inter-neighborhood Migration and Spatial Assimilation in a Multi-ethnic World: Comparing Latinos, Blacks and Anglos." *Social Forces* 87, no. 1 (September 1, 2008): 415–43.

———. "Metropolitan Structure and Neighborhood Attainment: Exploring Intermetropolitan Variation in Racial Residential Segregation." *Demography* 48, no. 4 (November 1, 2011): 1263–92.

Squires, Gregory. *Organizing Access to Capital: Advocacy and the Democratization of Financial Institutions*. Philadelphia, PA: Temple University Press, 2003.

Steil, Justin. "Antisubordination Planning." *Journal of Planning Education and Research* (2018): 0739456X18815739.

———. "Innovative Responses to Foreclosures: Paths to Neighborhood Stability and Housing Opportunity." *Columbia Journal of Race & Law* 1, no. 1 (December 30, 2011): 63–117.

Steil, Justin, Len Albright, Jacob S. Rugh, and Douglas S. Massey. "The Social Structure of Mortgage Discrimination." *Housing Studies* 33, no. 5 (2018): 759–76.

Steil, Justin, Jorge De la Roca, and Ingrid Gould Ellen. "Desvinculado y Desigual: Is Segregation Harmful to Latinos?" *Annals of the American Academy of Political and Social Science* 660, no. 1 (July 1, 2015): 57–76.

Steil, Justin, and Laura Humm Delgado. "Limits of Diversity: Jane Jacobs, the Just City, and Anti-Subordination." *Cities* 91 (2019): 39–48.

Steil, Justin, and Nicholas Kelly. "The Fairest of Them All: Analyzing Affirmatively Furthering Fair Housing Compliance." *Housing Policy Debate* 29, no. 1 (2019a): 85–105.

———. "Survival of the Fairest: Examining HUD Reviews of Assessments of Fair Housing." *Housing Policy Debate* (2019b): 1–16.

Sugrue, Thomas J. *The Origins of the Urban Crisis: Race and Inequality in Postwar Detroit.* Princeton, NJ: Princeton University Press, 1996.

Taeuber, Karl E., and Alma F. Taeuber. *Negroes in Cities: Residential Segregation and Neighborhood Change.* London: Aldine, 1965.

———. "The Negro as an Immigrant Group: Recent Trends in Racial and Ethnic Segregation in Chicago." *American Journal of Sociology* 69, no. 4 (January 1, 1964): 374–82.

———. "A Practitioner's Perspective on the Index of Dissimilarity." *American Sociological Review* 41, no. 5 (1976): 884–89.

Tienda, Marta, and Norma Fuentes. "Hispanics in Metropolitan America: New Realities and Old Debates." *Annual Review of Sociology* 40, no. 1 (2014): 499–520.

Tilly, Charles. *Durable Inequality.* Berkeley: University of California Press, 1998.

Turner, Margery Austin, Rob Santos, Diane Levy, Doug Wissoker, Claudia Aranda, and Rob Pitingolo. *Housing and Discrimination Against Racial and Ethnic Minorities 2012.* Washington, D.C.: Urban Institute, 2013.

Vale, Lawrence. *Purging the Poorest: Public Housing and the Design Politics of Twice-Cleared Communities.* Chicago: University of Chicago Press, 2013.

Vose, Clement E. *Caucasians Only: The Supreme Court, the NAACP, and the Restrictive Covenant Cases.* Berkeley: University of California Press, 1959.

Williams, Rhonda Y. *The Politics of Public Housing: Black Women's Struggles Against Urban Inequality.* Oxford: Oxford University Press, 2004.

Wilson, William J. *The Truly Disadvantaged: The Inner City, the Underclass, and Public Policy.* Chicago: University of Chicago Press, 1987.

———. *When Work Disappears: The World of the New Urban Poor.* New York: Knopf, 1996.

CHAPTER 3

Parallel Pathways of Reform

Fair Public Schooling and Housing for Black Citizens

Akira Drake Rodriguez and Rand Quinn

This chapter explores efforts to secure fair public schooling and fair public housing for Black citizens in the years following *Brown v. Board of Education* and the Fair Housing Act. We hold an inclusive definition of citizenship that extends beyond legal status to encompass all residents of our society. The rights and privileges demanded and won by Black citizens in public schools and public housing were an early acknowledgment and application of the Fourteenth Amendment to the Constitution. Yet just as Black citizens gained access and, in some cases, control over these public goods, urban decline and disinvestment prompted by deindustrialization and depopulation altered the government's ability to provide these goods (Rodriguez 2021). We make the case that the goals of fair housing and fair schooling are linked and that the parallel evolution of reform efforts in public education and in public housing should not be considered apart from one another. School reform efforts designed to provide equal educational opportunity accounted for residential racial segregation, and efforts to eliminate housing discrimination may have had the ancillary effect of reducing racial segregation in schools.

We categorize these parallel equal opportunity reforms into three broad efforts—desegregation, resource distribution, and market-based solutions—that states and districts have used (with varying degrees of success) to remedy historical inequities in public housing and public schools. For each of these reform efforts, we provide a brief history of its effectiveness in order to assess its potential to further the equitable provision of housing and education. We close with a statement on future directions for advocates and scholars committed to fair public housing and fair public schooling.

Desegregation in Public Education and Public Housing

Brown v. Board of Education, the 1954 decision by the U.S. Supreme Court that declared educational opportunity "a right which must be available to all on equal terms," resulted in the largest and most controversial postwar reform effort in public education—school desegregation.[1] Linda Brown was not allowed to enroll in her neighborhood elementary school because it was reserved for white students and she was Black. She lived in Topeka, Kansas, which at the time maintained a dual school system—one for white children and a separate one for Black children, as was allowed by state law. Her lawsuit was combined with similar cases from South Carolina, Virginia, and Delaware. Respondent school districts were operating segregated school systems, but they claimed that resources for Black and white students were equal or undergoing an equalizing process. These segregated school districts were propped up by years of de jure policies that codified the separation of race into space, such as the initial requirement of restrictive covenants in neighborhoods approved for federally guaranteed mortgages and the segregated origins of the nation's first public housing developments (Massey et al. 2013).

Petitioners argued that regardless of these efforts, the "separate but equal" doctrine that had been established decades earlier in fact violated the Fourteenth Amendment by depriving Black students of equal educational opportunities.[2] This argument led the Court to consider racial segregation rather than issues of unequal resources or benefits, as it had in earlier cases. In delivering the Court's opinion, Chief Justice Earl Warren stated: "Does segregation of children in public schools solely on the basis of race, even though the physical facilities and other "tangible" factors may be equal, deprive the children of the minority group of equal educational opportunities? We believe that it does."[3]

School Desegregation in the Wake of *Brown*

Dual systems prevalent in communities throughout the South were declared unconstitutional. But creating unitary systems in their place was a drawn-out and at times violent process. Massive resistance to desegregation by white parents resulted in decades of political and legal action before significant progress was made.

School segregation was not limited to the South. Ostensibly unitary school districts in the North and West were also segregated. Housing discrimination produced dual markets in cities throughout the nation that restricted residential options for Black families. For school districts that were not de jure segregated, neighborhood segregation coupled with school attendance boundaries and student assignment policies often created de facto segregated systems. Proving a constitutional violation for de facto segregated districts was a difficult proposition that required accounting for the various local contextual segregatory factors. As in the South, resistance to desegregation was widespread across districts in the North and West and, in places, was violent.

Brown was just one component of school desegregation. A series of court rulings in the decision's immediate aftermath served to clarify the concept of equal educational opportunity and the appropriate means to desegregate school districts. In addition, the Civil Rights Act of 1964 led the Justice Department to take an active role in school desegregation. Occasionally, districts voluntarily adopted desegregation plans following political pressure from local chapters of the NAACP and other civil rights organizations. Often, however, plans were mandated and overseen by a federal district court following legal action.

In 1968, the Supreme Court considered a "freedom of choice" plan from New Kent County, Virginia.[4] The school board allowed families to choose between the county's two schools, but white families refused to enroll their children in all-Black George W. Watkins School, and, likely because of intimidation and coercion, only a handful of Black families enrolled their children in predominantly white New Kent School. The Court ruled that schools were required to racially mix to a degree greater than what would occur merely as a result of ending discrimination. New Kent County was ordered to consider assigning students based on geographic zones or other measures that would force desegregation. In its opinion, the Court established factors to be considered when determining whether a district was unitary: composition of the student body, faculty, and staff, and equality in transportation, extracurricular activities, and facilities. As a result, the case, *Green v. County School Board of New Kent County*, is recognized as one that helped bring about comparatively rapid desegregation as districts were compelled to develop more effective plans.

In *Milliken v. Bradley,* a 1974 decision concerning an interdistrict busing plan for the Detroit metropolitan area, the Supreme Court limited city-suburban school desegregation. Consequently, in metro areas like Detroit where Black families resided in central cities and white families in the surrounding suburbs, full desegregation became nearly impossible.[5] Observers of desegregation jurisprudence have described the years since *Milliken* as increasingly conservative. On balance, courts determined that segregated schools are acceptable so long as they are not the result of overt discrimination but rather the result of housing or demographic patterns. Most recently, in the 2007 case *Parents Involved in Community Schools v. Seattle School District No. 1,* the Supreme Court determined that while school districts may maintain a goal of racial diversity, the use of racial classifications in student assignment—even as a small part of a voluntary effort by a district to integrate its schools—must be narrowly tailored.[6] This effectively prevents districts from voluntarily desegregating.

As a result of the desegregation requirements imposed by *Green,* Black-white school segregation declined substantially from the 1970s to the 1980s, especially in school districts in the South (Reardon and Owens 2014). But declines in segregation lagged in the North and West, where systems tended to be de facto segregated. This fact has been described by desegregation scholar Gary Orfield and his colleagues as an "ironic historic reality"—de jure segregation has been more easily identified and addressed than de facto segregation (Orfield et al. 2016). From the 1980s to the present, as hundreds of formerly dual systems were declared unitary by the courts, Black-white school segregation *increased* (or at best leveled off, depending on the measure of segregation employed) (Reardon et al. 2012; Reardon and Owens 2014). Resegregation in this most recent period was particularly prevalent in elementary schools in the South (Reardon et al. 2012). This is a troubling trend that may have long-term consequences for Black families. A multitude of studies has shown that school desegregation in prior decades—and the increased resources and higher-quality schooling that came with it—led to a range of positive educational and occupational outcomes for Black students, including increased high school graduation rates, higher earnings, and improved health (Guryan 2004; Johnson 2011; Reber 2010).

Sixty-five years after the historic *Brown* ruling, the goal of equal educational opportunities for all students has yet to be achieved. While the proscription on dual school systems remains, permissible remedies for de facto segregation are limited. Among the factors that derailed efforts to desegregate public schools are housing discrimination and residential segregation.

In the following section we assess the parallel reform effort to desegregate public housing as a means of fostering integrated residential neighborhoods.

Gautreaux and Moving to Opportunity: One Approach to Housing Desegregation

Similar to the slow and uneven implementation following the *Brown* ruling, efforts to desegregate or integrate public housing were equally stymied from lawsuits against localities that failed to comply. President John Kennedy's 1962 Executive Order 11063 mandated public housing, as a federal program, to end racial and ethnic discrimination. Two years later, this executive order was codified in Title VI of the Civil Rights Act, which expanded the prohibition of racial discrimination to all programs and activities that receive federal funding. Nonetheless, local housing authorities were slow to comply, instead either continuing the racialized siting of new public housing developments or refusing to desegregate or integrate existing ones. In addition to giving federal agencies the discretion to stop funding discriminatory local programs, Title VI included language giving individuals the right to file administrative complaints against program administrators and the right to file suit in federal court.

In Chicago, the pattern of residential segregation was acute; the majority of the 21,000 public housing units authorized by the housing acts were concentrated along a long corridor of the Dan Ryan expressway that separated Black and white neighborhoods. Altgeld Gardens resident Dorothy Gautreaux and others directly challenged the laissez-faire policy of the Chicago Housing Authority (CHA) of constructing public housing in all-Black and often low-income neighborhoods. Alexander Polikoff, lead attorney for the plaintiffs, filed a suit against the CHA for failing to comply with Title VI.

The court in the *Gautreaux* ruling divided Cook County, Illinois (of which Chicago is the county seat), into General Areas (less than 30 percent Black) and Limited Areas (more than 30 percent Black) for the purposes of determining where the Chicago Housing Authority could construct new public housing or issue project-based Section 8 leases (Pattillo 2006). Families on a waiting list were assigned units based on their availability and thus were randomly assigned or sorted into the two areas (Rosenbaum and Zuberi 2010). The Gautreaux Assisted Housing Mobility program (GAHM) generated improved outcomes in health, employment, and education, and those who moved into General Areas were more likely to remain in less segregated communities (Keels et al. 2005). Between 1976 and 1998, nearly 7,100 public housing residents took advantage of GAHM, with counselors matching households to available units based on their position on the waiting list. Very few (fewer than 5 percent) residents rejected their initial assignment. The program had two phases (*Gautreaux I* and *Gautreaux II*) that expanded and updated the General Areas, but the program was not replicated in other housing authorities or for newer applicants.

The precedent of *Gautreaux* led to a push to "include mobility remedies in virtually all the other public housing desegregation lawsuits" (Roisman 2007: 348). The shift from the GAHM to the Moving to Opportunity (MTO) program was small but set another precedent. Instead of attempting to disperse low-income Black public housing households into neighborhoods that had both low poverty rates and low proportions of Black residents (GAHM General Areas), MTO focused exclusively on moving to high-opportunity (or middle-to-upper-income) neighborhoods. Shifting the focus from race *and* class to *only* class was an emerging approach to policy-making that de-emphasized the role of race in contemporary social problems.

The MTO program was a true random assignment of nearly seven thousand public housing families across five cities (Baltimore, Boston, Chicago, Los Angeles, and New York) to test the mechanisms that could ensure a family moved and stayed in areas of high opportunity. The program was considered a "weak intervention" in its goal to move low-income nonwhite households into high-opportunity areas to remedy the impacts of residential segregation. Without an emphasis on both race and class, many households chose to not stay in the integrated neighborhoods and often went to areas of higher poverty when given the opportunity to choose (Clampet-Lundquist and Massey 2008).

This shift from race to class as a category to remedy consequently undermined the essence of the Fair Housing Act, particularly the years of congressional reports and testimony that led to its enactment. Much of the debate around fair housing was to what extent the federal government, through the Department of Housing and Urban Development (HUD), was responsible for the *racialized* arrangement of its citizens across space—a nation of Black cities and white suburbs. Scholars argue this role was underscored through the Fair Housing Act's "'affirmatively further' language," which places the responsibility back on the public sector (Roisman 2007: 389).

The MTO program also shifted the means of affirmatively furthering fair housing by increasing the distribution of vouchers from public housing authorities instead of integrating existing public housing developments. With the moratorium on new public housing development construction, residents in highly segregated and disinvested public housing stock in urban areas initiated a series of desegregation lawsuits during the 1990s to force housing authorities to comply. These consent decrees were rulings from state supreme courts to implement mobility programs for local housing authorities that were charged with violating the Fair Housing Act or fair share provisions. Many states used a combination of affordable housing tools (such as vouchers, inclusionary zoning, and housing trust funds) to fulfill the consent decrees (Popkin et al. 2000).

Gautreaux and MTO have mixed educational outcomes for students. Studies on *Gautreaux* residents show that voucher holders in General Areas had grades equal to students in Limited Areas, but the former had increasingly positive attitudes toward school, experienced increased college-track placement and attendance, and felt their teachers had higher expectations for them (Rosenbaum, Kulieke, and Rubinowitz 1988; Rosenbaum 1991; Kaufman and Rosenbaum 1992; Keels 2008). Test scores and ACT scores for General Area students improved (Kaufman and Rosenbaum 1992). However, the burden on individuals to see the integration experiment through impacted school choice across the different cities in the MTO program. Families in Boston and Chicago did not send their children to schools in the new neighborhoods, and incidents in new neighborhood schools often forced Chicago parents to send their children to schools in their old communities (Popkin et al. 2003).

Efforts to desegregate schools and housing through the use of mobility programs such as busing and MTO are effective at moving individuals into more integrated environments, but tend to place the burden on the most vulnerable populations. The inability to address systemic segregation in school districts and public housing developments is a result of this individualized approach to desegregation. The violent resistance to school desegregation efforts across the country parallel initial attempts by public housing authorities to integrate all-white developments (Hirsch 1998). Violence was a useful tool to dissuade individuals (and governing bodies) from pursuing integration efforts. To minimize disruptions, states allowed for school districts and housing authorities to desegregate at their own pace, often to the detriment of overcrowded and underserved Black, Latino, and Asian residents, and to the benefit of white residents. More systemic attempts at desegregation that create more standards and accountability for states and localities to equitably provide public goods and services are discussed in the next section.

Resource Distribution Reforms in Public Education and Public Housing

A second line of school reform emerging in the decades following *Brown v. Board of Education* targets state-level education finance systems. Local governments are partly responsible for generating revenue for public schools, primarily through property taxes. This responsibility leads to cross-district resource disparities as wealthier districts generate more dollars for their schools than poorer districts.[7] From the late 1960s to the present day, legal and legislative school finance reform efforts have sought to ameliorate the unequal and inadequate distribution of resources to local school districts.[8] These efforts aim to decouple property wealth from district spending while maintaining a relationship between local demand for education and local revenue.

Similarly, state governments began to push for more equity and access in the distribution of affordable housing. The contentious process of siting public housing developments began to create large concentrations of low-income populations, often within or adjacent to majority nonwhite communities. In response, state and local governments began implementing their own approaches, from mandatory affordable housing requirements to the outright elimination of exclusionary zoning.

Equity and Adequacy in School Finance Systems

In a 1971 case, *Serrano v. Priest,* California's education finance system was determined to be unconstitutional by the state supreme court. More than half of the state's educational revenue came from local property taxes. Despite a program to help equalize funding across school districts, significant disparities remained. "This funding scheme invidiously discriminates against the poor because it makes the quality of a child's education a function of the wealth of his [*sic*] parents and neighbors," argued Associate Justice Raymond Sullivan in the majority opinion. "Recognizing as we must that the right to an education in our public schools is a fundamental interest which cannot be conditioned on wealth, we can discern no compelling state purpose necessitating the present method of financing."[9] Consequently, the court determined that California's education finance system was in violation of the Fourteenth Amendment. The ruling led advocates to initiate similar equity-based lawsuits in other states built on the constitutional guarantee of equal protection (Enrich 1995; Hanushek and Lindseth 2009; Superfine 2010).

The wave of legal action spurred by *Serrano* was brief. In 1973, the U.S. Supreme Court considered a school equity appeal originating from Texas, *San Antonio v. Rodriguez*.[10] Departing from *Serrano*, the Court determined that education was not a fundamental interest and that the Texas system, despite the disparities it created and maintained, did not run afoul of the Constitution. The ruling effectively ended efforts to reform state finance systems through equity- based claims built upon the equal protection guarantee of the Fourteenth Amendment. Subsequent legal action instead focused on equal protection provisions contained in state constitutions, a strategy that succeeded in some but not most cases (Hanushek and Lindseth 2009).[11]

Eventually, to bolster legal claims, advocates leveraged state constitutional provisions for education in addition to state equal protection requirements. State constitutions require the establishment of a "thorough and efficient" (or similar language) schooling for residents. Holding states to their own constitutional standard resulted in the addition of adequacy-based arguments to the equity-based arguments equal protection claims generated, and it allowed plaintiffs to contend that education was a right that required a level of state support adequate to meet student achievement goals (Enrich 1995; Hanushek and Lindseth 2009; Springer, Liu, and Guthrie 2009). Whereas equity in education finance calls for the "fair" distribution of available resources to students across school districts, adequacy refers to the distribution of resources such that all students, regardless of individual circumstances and across district contexts, have an equal opportunity to achieve academic standards. In a landmark 1989 case, *Rose v. Council for Better Education*, the Kentucky Supreme Court delineated factors constituting educational adequacy.[12] Several states subsequently modeled their own adequacy tests based on the factors identified (Enrich 1995).

The standards and accountability movement in education further facilitated adequacy-based approaches to education finance system reform (Superfine 2010). The 2001 reauthorization of the Elementary and Secondary Education Act (ESEA)—titled No Child Left Behind (NCLB)—was an early attempt to produce stronger state-level accountability systems. More recently, the Race to the Top program, the Common Core State Standards Initiative, and the latest reauthorization of ESEA (the Every Student Succeeds Act of 2015) continued the move toward standards and accountability. In prior decades, courts had difficulty devising an effective test to measure equity and adequacy in state education finance systems (Enrich 1995). With the development of state-level performance standards and accountability systems, this was no longer the case (Rebell 2006). The post-*Rose* wave of court cases—particularly for those cases that occurred in the wake of the standards and accountability movement of the 2000s—has found some success. Several state education finance systems were overturned for failing to provide adequate education (Odden, Picus, and Goetz 2010; Springer, Liu, and Guthrie 2009).[13]

School finance reform can have a significant impact if resources are effectively spent. Recent studies of reform efforts from the past four decades concluded that court-mandated equity-based reform narrowed spending gaps between the highest- and lowest-income districts, and court-mandated adequacy-based reform increased district spending. Increased resources led to improvements in achievement and a host of long-run outcomes (Jackson, Johnson, and Persico 2015; Lafortune, Rothstein, and Schanzenbach 2018). Although under certain conditions increased state aid may lead to a reduction in local tax effort (Steinberg et al. 2016), researchers have found that on average, adequacy-based reform increases spending and leads to higher achievement, particularly for poor districts (Lafortune, Rothstein, and Schanzenbach 2018).

Mt. Laurel: A Push Toward Equity and Redistribution

Just as school finance reform efforts created an opportunity for achieving a more equitable state provision of public education, the case of *Burlington County NAACP v. Mt. Laurel Township* provided another approach to create a more equitable provision of affordable housing. The *Mt. Laurel* case was concerned not just with the exclusion of low-income multifamily housing from white suburban zoning codes, but also with the right of Black residents to stay put in a formerly rural but rapidly suburbanizing township in New Jersey. Under the organizing expertise of Ethel Lawrence, a sixth-generation Mt. Laurel resident, local residents formed the Springville Community Action Committee (SCAC) to develop affordable housing in Mt. Laurel. Ms. Lawrence and the SCAC optioned a thirty-two-acre parcel of land in 1968 to build thirty-six units of affordable housing for low-income families. The township denied the required zoning variances, infrastructure hookups, and local-federal cooperation agreement, triggering a lawsuit from the local NAACP and legal aid chapters on behalf of Ms. Lawrence.

Located just ten miles east of Philadelphia, the Springville community of Mt. Laurel was home to multiple generations of Black tenant farmers and manufacturing workers who often lived in converted industrial and informal housing. In the late 1960s, it was also the site of mass dislocations and evictions of these long-term Black residents. As white residents fled from disinvestment and increasing Black populations in the cities of Philadelphia and Camden, New Jersey, these rural interstitial lands were redeveloped into profitable suburban communities filled with all-white, single-family homes (Massey et al. 2013). The strategy of choice for these emerging suburbs was the use of exclusionary zoning codes that prohibited less desirable land uses, such as affordable multifamily housing. In 1975, the court issued the decision known as *Mt. Laurel I*, which explicitly stated that local land use regulation "cannot foreclose the opportunity of the classes of people mentioned for low- and moderate-income housing and in its regulations must affirmatively afford that opportunity, at least to the extent of the municipality's fair share of the present and prospective regional need thereafter."[14]

Although *Mt. Laurel*'s doctrine is the most famous and successful example of state-level approaches to integrating communities across class lines, other states have also introduced fair-share legislation (Payne 2006). Unlike the constitutional precedent and oversight provided by *Mt. Laurel* (which is perhaps the reason for its success), these other fair-share policies are built into local planning and land use efforts. In California's fair-share housing policy, which predates the *Mt. Laurel* decision by five years, housing needs are determined at the state level, and local governments are financed according to the state allocation of housing affordability. However, the challenges in establishing governance processes that adequately balance the disparity in regional needs with local capacity to provide affordable housing have stymied efforts in the state (Baer 2008). The more aggressive Massachusetts constitutional amendment (Chapter 40B) allows for the state to overrule local zoning decisions about housing projects that contain a minimum affordable share, if the locality has failed to meet affordability criteria. In Montgomery County, Maryland, the oldest inclusionary zoning law attempts to remedy disparities in the provision of affordable housing across the Washington, D.C., metropolitan area, and produced more than ten thousand units of affordable housing. Nonetheless, a tightening housing market in the metro area can severely curtail production, as evidenced in the early 2000s (Brown 2001). In sum, *Mt. Laurel* and other state efforts to compel affordable housing development are effective at increasing affordable housing supply, but overreliance on the private market limits the accountability of the state to meet the needs of all citizens.

Efforts to desegregate neighborhoods and schools through the equitable allocation of funding face similar challenges to the mobility approaches described earlier. Using the power of the state to compel localities to act in an interest beyond the local welfare—what the *Mt. Laurel* court called the general welfare of the state—still burdens under-resourced communities to pursue challenges against resourced communities. The diminishing role of the state in providing equitable housing across race and class lines established by the *Mt. Laurel* precedent produced a worrisome trend that uses the private sector and market logics to design and implement social welfare policy. A similar move toward choice and market-based reform occurred in public education. The next section discusses these reforms.

Market-Based Reforms in Public Education and Public Housing

Over the past several decades, public school and housing reform efforts that make use of private sector concepts and ideals have proliferated. Many of these reforms are built upon the idea that market-based systems and choice can improve school quality and reduce educational inequity.

School Choice: Vouchers, Charters, and Portfolio Models of Reform

Proponents argue that market and choice approaches lead schools to vie for students and their families, which in turn stimulates improvement and expands educational opportunity. In a choice system, students who may otherwise be assigned to under-resourced and underperforming neighborhood schools have an opportunity to select more desirable options. Excellent and innovative schools are rewarded, while substandard schools are weeded out. Opponents, however, question the application of a market logic to public schools and maintain that such approaches result in tiered and segregated systems. While some students may choose better schools, others—often low-income students, immigrant students, and students of color—face systemic barriers that impede their ability to choose better schools.

Among the more controversial reforms of this type is the school voucher (Quinn and Cheuk 2018). In publicly funded voucher systems, parents directly control taxpayer funds allocated for public education, most often for use toward private school tuition. Typically, vouchers worth as much as several thousand dollars are issued to eligible families on behalf of their children. Families can then apply the voucher to a qualified private school of their choosing. The most recent wave of school voucher reforms began in 1990 when Wisconsin enacted a program for low-income families residing in Milwaukee. Publicly funded voucher systems have since launched in cities (including Cleveland and Washington, D.C.) and states (including Florida and Indiana) throughout the nation, some targeting students in low-income households, others targeting students with special needs or students enrolled in low-performing schools. According to EdChoice, a national nonprofit that "promotes state-based educational choice programs," there are currently twenty-six voucher programs operating in fifteen states and the District of Columbia collectively serving approximately 190,000 students (EdChoice 2019).

In recent years, states including Minnesota, Louisiana, and Pennsylvania have created programs that rely on a tax break rather than the issuance of vouchers. Nine states provide families with a tax credit or tax deduction for school expenses, including expenses for private school (EdChoice 2019). A second version offers a tax credit for donations to private organizations that provide private school tuition scholarships to qualifying students. There are twenty-three tax credit scholarship programs operating in eighteen states (EdChoice 2019). In addition, five states offer education savings account programs, which provide public funds to qualified families for use toward certain school expenses, including private school tuition (EdChoice 2019).

To understand the impact of school vouchers, researchers leverage the random lotteries used by programs to determine which of their applicants receive a voucher in a given year. By doing so, researchers are able to compare the outcomes of lottery "winners"—those applicants who received a voucher to a private school—against the outcomes of lottery "losers"—those applicants who did not receive a voucher. The results are mixed. There is limited evidence that school vouchers improve academic achievement, and some studies have even found negative achievement effects (Wolf et al. 2013; Abdulkadiroğlu, Pathak, and Walters 2018; Dynarski et al. 2017; Carnoy 2017). For instance, a recent impact study of Washington, D.C.'s Opportunity Scholarship Program (OSP) found that students who won the voucher lottery had math and language arts test scores statistically equivalent to those of students who lost the lottery (Wolf et al. 2013). School vouchers may improve student graduation rates, however (Wolf et al. 2013). To explain this phenomenon, researchers point to scholarship suggesting that students in private schools benefit from conducive environments and motivated peers in ways that increase the likelihood of graduation (Evans and Schwab 1995; Neal 1997).

CHARTER SCHOOLS

While publicly funded voucher programs occupy a small segment of the education sector, the charter school method of reform is more popular and has rapidly expanded over the years. Charter schools are publicly funded but privately managed schools of choice. In 1991, Minnesota became the first state to permit charter schools. Since then, laws authorizing charter schools have been adopted in forty-three states and the District of Columbia, and charter schools now enroll more than 3.2 million students in approximately seven thousand schools (National Alliance for Public Charter Schools 2019).

The term "charter" refers to the legal agreement between school leaders and the local public school board (or another oversight authority) that establishes the school. A school's charter typically lays out its mission, structure, and pedagogical approach. Schools must renew their charters at regular intervals in order to continue operating. In exchange for this increased level of accountability, charter schools are released from portions of state education law.

Part of the rationale of state charter school laws is that charter schools can stimulate system-wide improvements through innovation, competition, and choice. Because charter schools are not beholden to many of the regulations binding traditional public schools, the argument goes, innovative pedagogical techniques, curricula, and structures that improve student outcomes can be developed and tested before spreading throughout the system—to all schools, charter and noncharter alike—as a result of competitive forces. Some proponents also argue that charter innovations can transfer to traditional public schools through shared professional development opportunities and other collaborations that bring charter and noncharter teachers and administrators together. But the research on such "spillover effects" is mixed, with studies resulting in the identification of small or no benefits of charters on student outcomes in traditional public schools (Cohodes 2018; Mehta 2017).

Aside from spillover effects, researchers are interested in identifying the impact of charter schools on their own students. When considering charter schools overall, there is little difference in academic performance as compared to traditional public schools (Cohodes 2018). Differences emerge when the focus is on particular types of charter schools. In a recent study of the most desirable charter schools in Boston, researchers concluded that every year spent in these charter schools resulted in academic achievement gains (Abdulkadiroğlu et al. 2011; Angrist et al. 2010; Cohodes 2018). Most of the charter schools in the Boston study exhibited elements of a "No Excuses" approach to education, a model that has become popular with urban schools serving low-income students and Black and Latino students—for example, the Promise Academies of the Harlem Children's Zone and KIPP (Knowledge is Power Program) Public Charter Schools (Carter 2000; Whitman 2008). The No Excuses approach emphasizes a rigid and regimented school disciplinary environment designed to maximize academic "time on task." Scholars have increasingly come to the conclusion that enrolling in a No Excuses charter school can produce results in tested subjects. However, the scalability of the approach is a question: No Excuses schools are unique in that they are well-funded, have longer school days, and provide various achievement incentives for both students and teachers.

The ability of No Excuses charter schools to narrow the achievement gap has generated a great deal of interest. But scholars have identified trade-offs and unintended consequences of the "regulated environment" the approach requires (Goodman 2013). While No Excuses charter schools may better prepare students for standardized exams in math and reading, the schools may at the same time undermine the development of skills necessary for college, work, and society—assertiveness, initiative, and independence (Goodman 2013; Golann 2015).

Researchers have also examined whether the choices families make when charter schools are an option have an impact on school segregation. A recent national study compared charter and noncharter public schools within the same district and assessed poverty, achievement, and racial disparities (Logan and Burdick-Will 2016). The authors found that charter schools had higher achievement in high-poverty areas but lower achievement in low-poverty areas. In terms of racial disparities, the authors conclude that within the same district, charter schools tend to be more racially isolated than noncharter public schools, particularly for elementary Black and Native American students.

The charter school method of reform has attracted widespread support from private philanthropy, educational entrepreneurs, and policymakers (Quinn, Tompkins-Stange, and Meyerson 2014). Despite pockets of active opposition—the recent wave of teacher strikes across the country have targeted charter school growth, for example—charter schools are likely here to stay (Will 2019).

PORTFOLIO MANAGEMENT AND INTRADISTRICT CHOICE

In several large urban school districts, including Philadelphia and New Orleans, charters operate as part of a "portfolio" of schools (Bulkley, Henig, and Levin 2010). The traditional district structure of a system of public schools with weak lines of accountability has faced criticism. In response, with the portfolio management model of school reform, a central office "manages a portfolio" of different kinds of schools—both traditional and charter—with different kinds of offerings. Central to the strategy is school choice, the creation of new schools, and mechanisms to close schools that fail to meet accountability standards (Bulkley, Henig, and Levin 2010).

Even with intradistrict choice, better schools tend to be in wealthier and predominantly white neighborhoods, and students relying on public transportation or with after-school work commitments, for instance, will be less able to attend crosstown schools, even if presented with that option (Phillippo 2019). Information about schools may also be unevenly distributed. More advantaged students are the ones best positioned to make and act on informed choices. For instance, a recent study using data from Chicago found that while on average, when given the choice, students opted into higher-achieving schools, the lowest-achieving students transferred at lower rates than high-achieving students, and the schools they transferred into were lower-achieving (Sirer et al. 2015).

The Neoliberal Turn: Housing Choice Vouchers, Low-Income Housing Tax Credits, and HOPE VI

Strategies in the previous sections on the pursuit of fair public housing have focused on the deconcentration and dispersal of public housing families out of existing developments, or the production of new developments in more affluent areas. The reactionary lawsuits and legislation reflect the conditions of most major cities from the 1970s to the 1990s: with declining populations, revenues, and capacity to attract new investment, cities were "dying." All of the opportunities—jobs, new housing stock and schools, well-funded public goods and services—were in the suburbs. This section describes attempts to integrate and improve residential segregation and housing choice for public housing residents in the city, and the shift in urban governance that made such policies possible.

Long after the passage of Title VI in 1964, residential segregation rates remained high in public housing developments, and the government slowly began ceding its role and power in addressing these segregation rates by creating the option of "choice" in the provision of subsidized rental housing. The shift of authority from the public to the private sector is a defining feature of the neoliberal turn in urban policy. Robinson describes its pervasiveness in urban policy: "institutional reformers have embraced a pro-market rhetoric and pushed to downplay the public responsibility to manage social well-being in favor of shifting responsibilities to private individuals and organizations" (Robinson 2016: 1093).

The neoliberal turn in public housing began with the end of public housing construction during the Nixon administration in 1973—a moratorium that was never lifted—and the commencement of the Housing Choice Voucher program, then known as "Section 8" of the 1974 Housing and Community Development Act (Bennett et al. 2006). The neoliberal turn provides demand- and supply-side incentives to increase affordable housing availability to low- and moderate-income residents, while decreasing the fiscal obligation for these goods and services. The neoliberal turn represents an ideological turn as well, in how we approach social welfare policy. Goetz describes this in detail:

> The real effect of neoliberalism, at least as it is related to the widespread redevelopment of state housing in American cities, is in discrediting the welfare state rationale behind the program, delegitimizing the very idea of public housing estates, and clearing the way for their removal and replacement. Single-purpose welfare housing for the very poor is defined as counter-productive—counter-productive to the city (by devaluing the land and neighborhood around it) and to the residents themselves (by trapping them in dangerous and hopeless environments). Mixed-use, mixed-income, and mixed-tenure approaches

that substantially incorporate private investment and management, and that can generate additional investment, have become the substitute. (2012: 338)

These approaches have forever shifted the way the nation provides public goods, including public housing. Housing Choice Vouchers, Low Income Housing Tax Credits, HOPE VI, the CHOICE Neighborhoods Initiative, Moving to Work, and the Rental Assistance Demonstration program are some of the many national affordable housing policies that have increasingly limited the role of the state in directly providing subsidized housing. In reducing the burden on the state, neoliberal policy has also reduced the state's accountability to remedy past wrongs and placed this burden instead on individual voucher holders who must navigate private markets to identify the greatest opportunity for their household. These efforts to retreat the state and roll out private provision are discussed in the following section.

SECTION 8, HOUSING CHOICE VOUCHERS, AND LOW-INCOME HOUSING TAX CREDITS

Section 8 of the 1974 Housing and Community Development Act allows for housing authorities to issue vouchers to public housing applicants to use in the private market with restrictions on geographical location and the fair market rent allowed. The shift toward vouchers reflected the moratorium on public housing construction, growing poverty rates in metropolitan areas, and weak housing markets in cities. Voucher holders pay 30 percent of their income toward rent, with the housing authorities covering the rest. Vouchers were long a tool for mobility programs that assumed households would go to areas of high opportunity and low poverty; however, research shows that voucher holders tend to cluster in areas of equal or greater poverty and residential segregation (Wyly and Defilippis 2010; Zielenbach 2006). Even as some cities gained population and jobs in the late 1990s throughout the 2000s, voucher holders continued to see little to no change in their neighborhood conditions (Wang and Varady 2005).

The program has since adjusted to capture the rising inequality in rents across metropolitan areas and now utilizes small-area fair market rents to maximize the value of the voucher holder (Palm 2018). Residents in project-based Section 8 housing, particularly those with forty-year leases expiring between 2011 and 2020, are in the highest-opportunity neighborhoods compared with participants in any other subsidy program. This opportunity can often translate into precarity and vulnerability for residents in this program; the same study suggested that residents in developments that did not renew their leases (making residents ineligible for government subsidy) are often in neighborhoods that are improving (Lens and Reina 2016). The quality of public goods and services in growing urban areas varies significantly across space as for-profit and not-for-profit service providers form a shadow state and the elected government retreats (Lake and Newman 2002). Therefore, even as voucher holders remain in revitalizing neighborhoods through improvements in how voucher values are calculated or through lease renewals, voucher holders' access to neighborhoods of opportunity remains limited by the neoliberal turn in urban governance.

Important equity outcomes from the Housing Choice Voucher (HCV) program include reductions in rent burdens, overcrowding in housing units, and periods of experiencing homelessness (Ellen 2018). However, educational outcomes are mixed, with studies in Chicago suggesting that the reclustering of voucher holders in areas of equal or worse opportunity produces no difference in child educational achievement (Jacob 2004). More recent findings suggest that voucher holders are located near schools of poorer quality than their non-voucher-holding counterparts (Horn, Ellen, and Schwartz 2014).

Low-Income Housing Tax Credits (LIHTCs) are the supply-side companion to housing vouchers. LIHTCs are aimed at what many researchers felt was the most important limitation of the voucher program: the lack of an affordable housing supply to serve voucher holders (Varady, Walker, and Wang 2001; Turner 1998). LIHTCs, unlike HCVs, are distributed at the state level, using the guidelines from state housing credit agencies' Qualification Allocation Plans (QAPs). These QAPs determine the number of tax credits allocated to qualified developers, who in turn sell these credits to investors, using the proceeds to subsidize affordable housing construction (Williamson, Smith, and Strambi-Kramer 2009). The LIHTC program also attempts to reward disinvested communities by increasing the tax credit allocated to historically disinvested places, while also incentivizing LIHTC developers to build in communities with a well-defined revitalization plan. However, LIHTCs suffer from the same limitations as vouchers: the racialized nature of housing markets and rising NIMBYism creates the conditions for low-income housing segregation to perpetuate itself (Williamson, Smith, and Strambi-Kramer 2009).

Results from LIHTC use are also mixed, with early efforts creating affordable housing in less impoverished neighborhoods, while more recent efforts show the clustering pattern found in HCV spatial analysis. More recent studies suggest that LIHTC units are in neighborhoods with limited opportunity: poverty rates are higher, labor markets weaker, and schools of worse quality compared with non-LIHTC units, yet access to transit is greater. Further, nonwhite and impoverished LIHTC units are in neighborhoods of more severe disadvantage than their more affluent and white counterparts (Ellen, Martens, and Kuai 2018). LIHTC, with its supply-side provision and focus exclusively on class, actually perpetuates inequalities in race and place.

HOPE VI AND CHOICE NEIGHBORHOODS

In 1993, the Atlanta Housing Authority (AHA) began its first demolitions in preparation for Atlanta's 1996 Olympics using funding from the Housing Opportunities for People Everywhere (HOPE VI) program. The AHA piloted an initiative to demolish the first public housing units constructed in the United States and redevelop them as temporary athlete housing before converting to a permanent mixed-income, mixed-use community (Newman 2002). HOPE VI was designed after the National Commission for Distressed Public Housing recommended the complete rehabilitation of the nation's most distressed public housing developments. HOPE VI provided planning, demolition, and redevelopment funding that housing authorities could use to attract and subsidize private investment into affordable housing. HOPE VI was the most direct intervention into residential segregation across class lines, creating mixed-income and mixed-tenure developments for tenants eligible for public housing, market-rate tenants, market-rate homeowners, and subsidized homeowners.

When the program was expanded into the CHOICE Neighborhoods Initiative (CNI), it explicitly included language to improve access to education and employment opportunities (Goetz 2012). Evidence from early HOPE VI pilots suggested that the housing authorities that intentionally worked with the school district and city during the planning and implementation were successful in attracting middle-income families into these developments (Varady et al. 2005). The place-based, community-based approach to CNI was largely a move to continue to attract capital and leverage public subsidy for private investment.

HOPE VI also continued HUD's long tradition of demolishing more housing than what is newly constructed. Public housing tenants who were not evicted following the implementation of welfare reform in 1996 and 1998 were given vouchers or assigned to other developments during demolition

(Keating and Flores 2000). Those who were eligible for admission into the new redevelopments, often following drug tests and background and credit checks, had to compete for a limited number of units in new developments. Congress had repealed legislation in 2005 that required housing authorities using HOPE VI funds to have a one-for-one replacement for public housing units. HOPE VI, and the regressive social welfare policy that enabled it, violated the core of fair housing by excluding so many from the choices and opportunity it afforded (Ewert 2016; Cohen 2009). While exclusionary social policy was the plan, the ability to attract and develop market-rate households resulted in greater numbers of public housing units being constructed than originally forecast (Vale, Shamsuddin, and Kelly 2018). The demolition, dispersal, and rebuilding of the nation's most distressed public housing developments, however, have led to improved educational outcomes for students, largely because the baseline for such improvement was lower than the baseline in other programs (Johnson Jr. 2012).

Conclusion

The parallel paths toward equal opportunity in public schools and public housing have been rocky ones. Gains made in the 1970s and 1980s to desegregate public schools have stalled. And academic achievement and attainment gaps remain. Public housing developments have decreased the number of Black residents, but only as a result of the dispersal, deconcentration, and demolition programs of the neoliberal turn. As of 2018, public housing was 63 percent minority and 37 percent white at the national level, but state and local demographics reflect greater segregation in individual developments (HUD 2019). The public housing redevelopment documented in the previous section has actually created more integrated, or less segregated, neighborhoods of increasing affluence. However, the evidence suggests that this outcome resulted more from the effect of low-income and nonwhite household displacement than from the equitable attraction of middle-income, nonminority households (Tach and Dwyer Emory 2017).

The efforts to address segregation and discrimination in either schools or public housing instead of comprehensively addressing both remains a major obstacle for these efforts. "Education policy is constrained by housing policy: it is not possible to desegregate schools without desegregating both low-income and affluent neighborhoods" (Rothstein 2015: 21). Both fair housing and education advocates agree that the scale of the problem cannot be administered exclusively on the local level, nor financed exclusively at the regional or state level. A Baltimore public housing desegregation case (*Thompson v. HUD*), which strengthened the definition of "affirmatively furthering" fair housing, relied on a regional approach to housing markets and evolving authority from the local to the regional and federal levels.[15] The court's ruling in *Thompson* allows for the responsibility of affirmatively furthering fair housing to come from the federal level, through its regional HUDs, which would use a carrot to incentivize localities to include affordable and multi-family housing in their land use and comprehensive plans, while also employing the stick of withholding federal funding for localities that refused to do so.

We recommend that policy-makers take a long and integrative view of these parallel pathways of reform when designing and implementing new legislation to achieve fair public schooling and fair public housing for Black citizens. The three reform efforts, in sum, have demonstrated, first, that place replicates inequality and that local governments need strong, regional goal-setting with state subsidies and federal enforcement to minimize the role of place in socioeconomic outcomes (for more on this relationship, see Chapter 2 in this volume). Equity reforms that prioritize spatial equality not only prevent the deepening of inequitable outcomes for resource-starved communities, but also minimize the perpetuation of opportunity hoarding by redistributing resources across fragmented and unequal regions. Although relying on local revenue allows for local preferences to guide school spending, it creates resource disparities that disproportionately affect poor communities. To equalize the investment in schools across place would require policies that effectively decouple property wealth and education spending, as recent school finance reforms have sought to accomplish.

Second, the failure of these reform efforts demonstrate that race should remain a central component of housing and school desegregation policy. The shift from race to class in the mobility solutions of early public housing desegregation created deepening racial segregation and minimal economic integration. Similarly, the shift from busing in public school desegregation to vouchers and charters has only produced more segregated school districts with even more disparate educational outcomes across race and place. We thus advocate for policies that are explicit in their goal to reduce segregation across places and schools, and to shift the legislative burden of proof from low-resourced communities and individuals to private developers, landlords, realtors, municipalities, and school districts that engage in explicit or implicit racial discrimination. Legislators must incorporate antiracist language into fair housing and school funding policies in order to reverse decades of racial sorting. Lawmakers must also be intentional about linking housing and school policies to create sustainable desegregation policy. Just as busing provided a means for Black low-income urban students to attend better resourced schools in white upper-income suburbs, legislators need to resource access to opportunity, either through moving individuals across space or equitably and adequately redistributing resources.

Finally, we recommend a moratorium on market-based reforms that continue to drive spatially driven inequality by allowing the private sector to "invest" in worthy social policies that have low (financial) risk and high (financial) return. The role of the state in causing the problem of racial and economic segregation in communities and schools has been well demonstrated by a breadth of social science research. The state must thus be a primary contributor to the end of these segregated places and unequal outcomes. This may require some politically unpopular policy such as federal mandates for local housing and school planning. Such federal intervention has been used only in times of intense racial antagonism and racially regressive policymaking (e.g., post–Civil War and post–civil rights eras). Yet the gains from these eras were necessary to bestow citizenship equally across race, class, and place.

The quest for Black citizenship through the provision of equal opportunity for housing and education has suffered from a lack of cohesion and enforcement at the levels of government best equipped to do so. Legal precedent set the guidelines for much of the equal opportunity programming, and the courts have also been used to reverse it. Lawsuits against busing have resulted in the sanctioning of that policy. In 2019, the *Gautreaux* case was settled: five decades after Dorothy Gautreaux's death, the courts found that the Chicago Housing Authority's aggressive "Plan for Transformation" that was forecast to demolish twenty-five thousand units, replacing them with mixed-income communities and housing vouchers, had remedied the CHA's three decades of discrimination and segregative practices (Kasakove 2019). The rollback of these equal opportunity provisions, and other moves such as the removal of the preclearance Section V clause of the Voting Rights Act, are part and parcel of what Carol Anderson calls "white rage" (Anderson 2016). This rage targets advances in Black citizenship, initially manifesting as violence against Black progress (such as the violent desegregation battles described earlier) and currently as more civilized approaches to voter suppression and Black marginalization. Thus, we call for policies that not only comprehensively tie together the disparate aspects of equal opportunity and Black citizenship, but also are codified so that they cannot easily be rescinded by white supremacist partisanship.

Notes

We thank Laura Ogburn for her research assistance. This was a fully collaborative effort. Akira Drake Rodriguez can be contacted at akirad@upenn.edu; Rand Quinn can be contacted at raq@upenn.edu.

1. *Brown v. Board of Education of Topeka*, 347 U.S. 483 (1954).

2. *Plessy v. Ferguson*, 163 U.S. 537 (1896). The ruling allowed for a "separate but equal" distinction that extended to restaurants, public transportation, restroom facilities, and schools.

3. *Brown*, 347 U.S. at 493.

4. *Green v. County School Board of New Kent County (Virginia)*, 391 U.S. 430 (1968).

5. *Milliken v. Bradley*, 418 U.S. 717 (1974).

6. *Parents Involved in Community Schools v. Seattle School District No. 1*, 551 U.S. 701 (2007).

7. These disparities are further exacerbated by the differential ability of wealthy parents to supplement their schools through the establishment of local education foundations (Reich 2005).

8. For comprehensive overviews, see Hanushek and Lindseth 2009; Superfine 2010.

9. *Serrano v. Priest*, 5 Cal.3d 584 (1971) at 588.

10. *San Antonio v. Rodriguez*, 411 U.S. 1 (1973).

11. Legal action following the *Rodriquez* ruling was only marginally successful. Complainants succeeded in seven of twenty-three court cases from 1973 to 1988 (Enrich 1995; Superfine 2010).

12. *Rose v. Council for Better Education, Inc.*, 790 S.W.2d 186 (1989).

13. However, while the period from 2000 to 2009 may have been the height of success, in the more recent past, from 2009 onward, plaintiffs have been less successful (Rebell 2017).

14. *Southern Burlington County NAACP v Township of Mt. Laurel*, 67 N.J. 151, 336 A.2d 713, 1975 N.J.

15. Hon. Marvin J. Garbis, Memorandum of Decision, *Carmen Thompson et al. vs. U.S. Department of Housing and Urban Development et al.* (January 6, 2005).

References

Abdulkadiroğlu, Atila, Joshua Angrist, Susan Dynarski, Thomas Kane, and Parag Pathak. "Accountability and Flexibility in Public Schools: Evidence from Boston's Charters and Pilots." *Quarterly Journal of Economics* 126, no. 2 (2011): 699–748.

Abdulkadiroğlu, Atila, Parag Pathak, and Christopher Walters. "Free to Choose: Can School Choice Reduce Student Achievement?" *American Economic Journal: Applied Economics* 10, no. 1 (2018): 175–206.

Albright, Len, Elizabeth S. Derickson, and Douglas Massey. "Do Affordable Housing Projects Harm Suburban Communities? Crime, Property Values, and Taxes in Mt. Laurel, NJ." *City & Community* 12, no. 2 (2013): 89–111.

Anderson, Carol A. *White Rage: The Unspoken Truth of Our Racial Divide.* New York: Bloomsbury USA Press, 2016.

Angrist, Joshua D., Susan M. Dynarski, Thomas J. Kane, Parag A. Pathak, and Christopher R. Walters. "Inputs and Impacts in Charter Schools: KIPP Lynn." *American Economic Review* 100, no. 2 (2010): 239–43.

Baer, William C. "California's Fair-Share Housing 1967–2004: The Planning Approach." *Journal of Planning History* 7, no. 1 (2008): 48–71.

Bennett, Larry, Janet L. Smith, and Patricia A. Wright. *Where Are Poor People to Live? Transforming Public Housing Communities.* New York: Routledge, 2006.

Brown, Karen Desterol. *Expanding Affordable Housing Through Inclusionary Zoning: Lessons From the Washington Metropolitan Area.* Washington, D.C.: The Brookings Institution Center on Urban and Metropolitan Policy, 2004.

Bulkley, Katrina E., Jeffrey R. Henig, and Henry M. Levin, eds. *Between Public and Private: Politics, Governance, and the New Portfolio Models for Urban School Reform.* Cambridge, MA: Harvard Education Press, 2010.

Carnoy, M. *School Vouchers Are Not a Proven Strategy for Improving Student Achievement.* Washington, D.C.: Economic Policy Institute, 2017.

Carter, Samuel Casey. *No Excuses: Lessons from 21 High-Performing, High-Poverty Schools.* Washington, D.C.: Heritage Foundation, 2000.

Casciano, Rebecca, and Douglas Massey. "School Context and Educational Outcomes: Results from a Quasi-experimental Study." *Urban Affairs Review* 48, no. 2 (2012): 180–204.

Cheng, Albert, Collin Hitt, Brian Kisida, and Jonathan N. Mills. "'No Excuses' Charter Schools: A Meta-Analysis of the Experimental Evidence on Student Achievement." *Journal of School Choice* 11, no. 2 (2017): 209–38.

Clampet-Lundquist, Susan, and Douglas S. Massey. "Neighborhood Effects on Economic Self-Sufficiency: A Reconsideration of the Moving to Opportunity Experiment." *American Journal of Sociology* 114, no. 1 (2008): 107–43.

Cohen, Melissa A. "Vindicating the Matriarch: A Fair Housing Act Challenge to Federal No-Fault Evictions from Public Housing." *Michigan Journal of Gender and Law* 16, no. 1 (2009): 299–317.

Cohodes, Sarah. "Policy Issue: Charter Schools and the Achievement Gap." In *Charter Schools and the Achievement Gap. The Future of Children*, 1–16. Washington, D.C., and Princeton, NJ: Woodrow Wilson School of Public and International Affairs, Princeton University, and the Brookings Institution, Winter 2018.

Connolly, N. D. B. *The World More Concrete: Real Estate and the Remaking of Jim Crow South Florida.* Chicago: University of Chicago Press, 2014.

Dobbie, Will, and Roland G. Fryer Jr. "Are High-Quality Schools Enough to Increase Achievement Among the Poor? Evidence from the Harlem Children's Zone." *American Economic Journal: Applied Economics* 3, no. 3 (2011): 158–87.

Dynarski, Mark, Ning Rui, Ann Webber, and Babette Gutmann. *Evaluation of the DC Opportunity Scholarship Program: Impacts After One Year.* NCEE 2017-4022. Washington, D.C.: National Center for Education Evaluation and Regional Assistance, 2017.

EdChoice. "Fast Facts on School Choice." May 28, 2019. http://www.edchoice.org/our-resources /fast-facts.

Ellen, Ingrid G. "What Do We Know About Housing Choice Vouchers?" *Regional Science and Urban Economics*, no. 71 (2018): 1–5.

Ellen, Ingrid G., Keren Martens, and Yiwen Kuai. "Gateway to Opportunity? Disparities in Neighborhood Conditions Among Low-Income Housing Tax Credit Residents." *Housing Policy Debate* 28, no. 4 (2018): 572–91.

Enrich, Peter. "Leaving Equality Behind: New Directions in School Finance Reform." *Vanderbilt Law Review* 48 (1995): 100–194.

Evans, William N., and Robert M. Schwab. "Finishing High School and Starting College: Do Catholic Schools Make a Difference?" *Quarterly Journal of Economics* 110, no. 4 (1995): 941–74.

Ewert, Michelle Y. "One Strike and You're Out of Public Housing: How the Intersection of the War on Drugs and Federal Housing Policy Violated Due Process and Fair Housing Principles." *Harvard Journal of Racial and Ethnic Justice* 32 (2016): 57–102.

Ferguson, Charles B. "Hamlets: Expanding the Fair Share Doctrine under Strict Home Rule Constitutions." *Emory Law Journal* 49 (2000): 255–94.

Ferguson, Karen. *Black Politics in New Deal Atlanta.* Durham: University of North Carolina Press, 2002.

Freeman, Lance, and Jenny Schuetz. "Producing Affordable Housing in Rising Markets: What Works?" *Cityscape: A Journal of Policy Development and Research* 19, no. 1 (2017): 217–36.

Goetz, Edward G. "Obsolescence and the Transformation of Public Housing Communities in the US." *International Journal of Housing Policy* 12, no. 3 (2012): 331–45.

———. *The One-Way Street of Integration: Fair Housing and the Pursuit of Racial Justice in American Cities.* Ithaca, NY: Cornell University Press, 2018.

Golann, Joanne W. "The Paradox of Success at a No-Excuses School." *Sociology of Education* 88, no. 2 (2015): 103–19.

Goodman, Joan F. "Charter Management Organizations and the Regulated Environment: Is It Worth the Price?" *Educational Researcher* 42, no. 2 (2013): 89–96.

Guryan, Jonathan. "Desegregation and Black Dropout Rates." *American Economic Review* 94, no. 4 (2004): 919–43.

Hanlon, James. "Fair Housing Policy and the Abandonment of Public Housing Desegregation." *Housing Studies* 30, no. 1 (2015): 78–99.

Hanushek, Eric A., and Alfred A. Lindseth. *Schoolhouses, Courthouses, and Statehouses: Solving the Funding-Achievement Puzzle in America's Public Schools.* Princeton, NJ: Princeton University Press, 2009.

Hirsch, Arnold. *Making the Second Ghetto: Race and Housing in Chicago 1940–1960*. Chicago: University of Chicago Press, 1998.

Hoch, Charles. "How Plan Mandates Work." *Journal of the American Planning Association* 73, no. 1 (2007): 86–99.

Horn, Keren Mertens, Ingrid Gould Ellen, and Amy Ellen Schwartz. "Do Housing Choice Voucher Holders Live Near Good Schools?" *Journal of Housing Economics* 23 (2014): 28–40.

HUD (Department of Housing and Urban Development). Picture of Subsidized Households. Data set. Washington, D.C.: U.S. Department of Housing and Urban Development, 2019.

———. *Qualitative Analysis of the MTO Experience, Final Report*. Washington, D.C.: U.S. Department of Housing and Urban Development, 2002. www.huduser.org/publications/pdf/mtoqualf.pdf.

Jackson, C. Kirabo, Rucker C. Johnson, and Claudia Persico. "The Effects of School Spending on Educational and Economic Outcomes: Evidence from School Finance Reforms." *Quarterly Journal of Economics* 131, no. 1 (2015): 157–218.

Jacob, Brian A. "Public Housing, Housing Vouchers and Student Achievement: Evidence from Public Housing Demolitions in Chicago." *American Economic Review* 94, no. 1 (2004): 233–58.

Johnson, Rucker C. *Long-Run Impacts of School Desegregation & School Quality on Adult Attainments*. No. w16664. Cambridge, MA: National Bureau of Economic Research, 2011.

Johnson Jr., Odis. "Relocation Programs, Opportunities to Learn, and the Complications of Conversion." *Review of Educational Research* 82, no. 2 (2012): 131–78.

Kasakove, Sophie. "A Major Chicago Public Housing Lawsuit Is Wrapping Up." *Pacific Standard*, March 11, 2019.

Kaufman, Julie E., and James E. Rosenbaum. "The Education and Employment of Low-income Black Youth in White Suburbs." *Educational Evaluation and Policy Analysis* 14, no. 3 (1992): 229–40.

Keating, Larry, and Carol Flores. "Sixty and Out: Techwood Homes Transformed by Enemies and Friends." *Journal of Urban History* 26, no. 3 (2000): 275–311.

Keels, Micere. "Neighborhood Effects Examined through the Lens of Residential Mobility Programs." *American Journal of Community Psychology* 42, no. 3–4 (2008): 235–50.

Keels, Micere, Greg J. Duncan, Stefanie DeLuca, Ruby Mendenhall, and James Rosenbaum. "Fifteen Years Later: Can Residential Mobility Programs Provide a Long-Term Escape from Neighborhood Segregation, Crime, and Poverty." *Demography* 42, no. 1 (2005): 51–73.

Lafortune, Julien, Jesse Rothstein, and Diane Whitmore Schanzenbach. "School Finance Reform and the Distribution of Student Achievement." *American Economic Journal: Applied Economics* 10, no. 2 (2018): 1–26.

Lake, Robert W., and Kathe Newman. "Differential Citizenship in the Shadow State." *Geojournal* 58, no. 2/3 (2002): 109–20.

Lens, Michael C., and Vincent Reina. "Preserving Neighborhood Opportunity: Where Federal Housing Subsidies Expire." *Housing Policy Debate* 26, no. 4 (2016): 714–32.

Logan, John R., and Julia Burdick-Will. "School Segregation, Charter Schools, and Access to Quality Education." *Journal of Urban Affairs* 38, no. 3 (2016): 323–43.

Manuel, Tiffany. "Dismantling the Narratives that Constrain Public Support for Fair Housing: The Urgent Need to Reframe the Public Conversation to Build Public Will." *Journal of Affordable Housing and Community Development Law* 27, no. 1 (2018): 87–105.

Massey, Douglas S., Len Albright, Rebecca Casciano, Elizabeth Derickson, and David N. Kinsey. *Climbing Mount Laurel: The Struggle for Affordable Housing and Social Mobility in an American Suburb.* Princeton, NJ: Princeton University Press, 2013.

Mehta, Nirav. "Competition in Public School Districts: Charter School Entry, Student Sorting, and School Input Determination." *International Economic Review* 58, no. 4 (2017): 1089–116.

National Alliance for Public Charter Schools. "About Charter Schools." 2019. https://www.publiccharters.org/about-charter-schools.

Neal, Derek. "The Effects of Catholic Secondary Schooling on Educational Achievement." *Journal of Labor Economics* 15, no. 1, part 1 (1997): 98–123.

Newman, Harvey. "The Atlanta Housing Authority's Olympic Legacy Program: Public Housing Projects to Mixed Income Communities." White paper, Research Atlanta, Inc., Atlanta, 2002.

Odden, Allan R., Lawrence O. Picus, and Michael E. Goetz. "A 50-State Strategy to Achieve School Finance Adequacy." *Educational Policy* 24, no. 4 (2010): 628–54.

Orfield, Gary, Jongyeon Ee, Erica Frankenberg, and Genevieve Siegel-Hawley. *Brown at 62: School Segregation by Race, Poverty and State.* Research brief, Civil Rights Project—Proyecto Derechos Civiles, University of California, Los Angeles, 2016.

Palm, Matthew. "Scale in Housing Policy: A Case Study of the Potential of Small Area Fair Market Rents." *Cityscape: A Journal of Policy Development and Research* 20, no. 1 (2018): 147–66.

Pattillo, Mary. "Making (Fair) Public Housing Claims in a Post-racism Legal Context." *Journal of Affordable Housing and Community Development Law* 18, no. 2 (2009): 215–34.

Payne, John M. "The Paradox of Progress: Three Decades of the *Mount Laurel* Doctrine" *Journal of Planning History* 53, no. 2 (2006): 126–47.

Phillippo, Kate. *A Contest Without Winners. How Students Experience Competitive School Choice.* Minneapolis: University of Minnesota Press, 2019.

Popkin, Susan, J. E. Rosenbaum, and P. M. Meaden. "Labor Market Experiences of Low-Income Black Women in Middle-Class Suburbs: Evidence from a Survey of Gautreaux Program Participants." *Journal of Policy Analysis and Management* 12, no. 3 (1993): 556–73.

Popkin, S. J., L. F. Buron, D. K. Levy, and M. K. Cunningham. "The Gautreaux Legacy: What Might Mixed-Income and Dispersal Strategies Mean for the Poorest Public Housing Tenants?" *Housing Policy Debate* 11, no. 4 (2000): 911–42.

Popkin, Susan J., George C. Galster, Kenneth Temkin, Carla Herbig, Diane K. Levy, and Elise K. Richer. "Obstacles to Desegregating Public Housing: Lessons Learned from Implementing Eight Consent Decrees." *Journal of Policy Analysis and Management* 22, no. 2 (2003): 179–99.

Quinn, Rand, and Tina Cheuk. *School Vouchers in the Trump Era: How Political Ideology and Religion Shape Public Opinion.* Philadelphia: Consortium for Policy Research in Education, 2018.

Quinn, Rand, Megan Tompkins-Stange, and Debra Meyerson. "Beyond Grantmaking: Philanthropic Foundations as Agents of Change and Institutional Entrepreneurs." *Nonprofit and Voluntary Sector Quarterly* 43, no. 6 (2014): 950–68.

Radford, Gail. *Modern Housing for America: Policy Struggles in the New Deal Era.* Chicago: University of Chicago Press, 2008.

Reardon, Sean, and Ann Owens. "60 Years After Brown: Trends and Consequences of School Segregation." *Annual Review of Sociology* 40 (2014): 199–218.

Reardon, Sean, Elena Tej Grewal, Demetra Kalogrides, and Erica Greenberg. "*Brown* Fades: The End of Court-Ordered School Desegregation and the Resegregation of American Public Schools." *Journal of Policy Analysis and Management* 31, no. 4 (2012): 876–904.

Rebell, Michael A. "Adequacy Cost Studies: Perspectives on the State of the Art." *Education Finance and Policy* 1, no. 4 (2006): 465–83.

———. *Courts and Kids: Pursuing Educational Equity through the State Courts* (supplement). Chicago: University of Chicago Press, 2017.

Reber, Sarah J. "School Desegregation and Educational Attainment for Blacks." *Journal of Human Resources* 45, no. 4 (2010): 893–914.

Reich, R. "A Failure of Philanthropy: American Charity Shortchanges the Poor, and Public Policy Is Partly to Blame." *Stanford Social Innovation Review* (Winter 2005): 24–33.

Robinson, John N. "Race, Poverty, and Markets: Urban Inequality After the Neoliberal Turn." *Sociology Compass* 10, no. 12 (2016): 1090–101.

Rodriguez, Akira D. *Diverging Space for Deviants: The Politics of Atlanta's Public Housing.* Athens: University of Georgia Press, 2021.

Roisman, Florence Wagman. "Affirmatively Furthering Fair Housing in Regional Housing Markets: The Baltimore Public Housing Desegregation Litigation." *Wake Forest Law Review* 42, no. 2 (2007): 333–91.

Rosenbaum, James E. "Black Pioneers—Do Their Moves to the Suburbs Increase Economic Opportunity for Mothers and Children?" *Housing Policy Debate* 2, no. 4 (1991): 1179–213.

Rosenbaum, James E., Marilyn J. Kulieke, and Leonard S. Rubinowitz. "White Suburban Schools' Responses to Low-income Black Children: Sources of Successes and Problems." *The Urban Review* 20, no. 1 (1988): 28–41.

Rosenbaum, James, and Anita Zuberi. "Comparing Residential Mobility Programs: Design Elements, Neighborhood Placements, and Outcomes of MTO and *Gautreaux.*" *Housing Policy Debate* 20, no. 1 (2010): 27–41.

Rothstein, Richard. "The Racial Achievement Gap, Segregated Schools, and Segregated Neighborhoods: A Constitutional Insult." *Race and Social Problems* 7 (2015): 21–30.

Schwemm, Robert G. "Segregative-Effect Claims under the Fair Housing Act." *New York University Journal of Legislation and Public Policy* 20 (2017): 709–72.

Sirer, M. Irmak, Spiro Maroulis, Roger Guimera, Uri Wilensky, and Luís A. Nunes Amaral. "The Currents Beneath the 'Rising Tide' of School Choice: An Analysis of Student Enrollment Flows in the Chicago Public Schools." *Journal of Policy Analysis and Management* 34, no. 2 (2015): 358–77.

Springer, Matthew G., Keke Liu, and James W. Guthrie. "The Impact of School Finance Litigation on Resource Distribution: A Comparison of Court-Mandated Equity and Adequacy Reforms." *Education Economics* 17, no. 4 (2009): 421–44.

Steinberg, Matthew, Rand Quinn, Daniel Kreisman, and J. Cameron Anglum. "Did Pennsylvania's Statewide School Finance Reform Increase Education Spending or Provide Tax Relief?" *National Tax Journal* 69, no. 3 (2016): 545–82.

Superfine, Benjamin Michael. "Court-Driven Reform and Equal Educational Opportunity: Centralization, Decentralization, and the Shifting Judicial Role." *Review of Educational Research* 80, no. 1 (2010): 108–37.

Tach, Laura, and Allison Dwyer Emory. "Public Housing Redevelopment, Neighborhood Change, and the Restructuring of Urban Inequality." *American Journal of Sociology* 123, no. 3 (2017): 686–739.

Turner, Margery Austin. "Moving Out of Poverty: Expanding Mobility and Choice Through Tenant-Based Assisted Housing." *Housing Policy Debate* 9, no. 2 (1998): 373–94.

Vale, Lawrence, Shomon Shamsuddin, and Nicholas Kelly. "Broken Promises or Selective Memory Planning? A National Picture of HOPE VI Plans and Realities." *Housing Policy Debate* 28, no. 5 (2018): 746–69.

Varady, David, Jeffrey A. Raffel, Stephanie Sweeney, and Latina Denson. "Attracting Middle Income Families in the HOPE VI Public Housing Revitalization Program." *Journal of Urban Affairs* 27, no. 2 (2005): 149–64.

Varady, David, Carole C. Walker, and Xinhao Wang. "Voucher Recipient Achievement of Improved Housing Conditions in the US: Do Moving Distance and Relocation Services Matter?" *Urban Studies* 38, no. 8 (2001): 1273–304.

Wang, Xinhao, and David Varady. "Using Hot Spot Analysis to Study the Clustering of Section 8 Housing Voucher Families." *Housing Studies* 20, no. 1 (2005): 29–48.

Whitman, David. *Sweating the Small Stuff: Inner-City Schools and the New Paternalism.* Washington, D.C.: Thomas B. Fordham Foundation & Institute, 2008.

Will, Madeline. "Teachers Are Still Striking, but Their Demands Have Changed." *Education Week*, February 20, 2019.

Williamson, Anne R., Marc Smith, and Marta Strambi-Kramer. "Housing Choice Vouchers, the Low-Income Housing Tax Credit, and the Federal Poverty Deconcentration Goal." *Urban Affairs Review* 45, no. 1 (2009): 119–32.

Wolf, Patrick J., Brian Kisida, Babette Gutmann, Michael Puma, Nada Eissa, and Lou Rizzo. "School Vouchers and Student Outcomes: Experimental Evidence from Washington, DC." *Journal of Policy Analysis and Management* 32, no. 2 (2013): 246–70.

Wyly, Elvin, and James Defilippis. "Mapping Public Housing: The Case of New York City." *City & Community* 9, no. 1 (2010): 61–86.

Zielenbach, Sean. "Moving Beyond the Rhetoric: Section 8 Housing Choice Voucher Program and Lower-Income Urban Neighborhoods." *Journal of Affordable Housing and Community Development Law* 16, no. 1 (2006): 9–39.

CHAPTER 4

The Economic Importance of Fair Housing

Vincent J. Reina and Raphael Bostic

While the case for fair housing is often couched in terms of moral principles and arguments for equal opportunity across race and class, the economic arguments in support of fair housing are in many regards equally powerful. In this chapter, we highlight the economic importance and value of fair housing. We begin by detailing the disparities in economic well-being that exist along racial and other protected class dimensions. We then argue that geographic disparities arising from racial segregation and other forces have contributed to these economic disparities and note that fair housing efforts are precisely designed to reduce spatial differentials between protected classes that exist beyond personal preferences.

Next, we point to three economic cases for fair housing, all based on outcomes that arise when geographic disparities are reduced. Two cases are direct: one focuses on individual income and employment outcomes, while the other focuses on wealth and entrepreneurship. A third, more indirect case is neighborhood-focused. When economic attachment and wealth in a community increase, that community is likely to become more resilient and is likely to produce well-being and innovation more sustainably—likelihoods that have positive implications for broader macroeconomic growth. We believe that, combined, these arguments establish a powerful rationale for viewing fair housing as a tool to advance both micro- and macroeconomic interests.

Economic Disparities by Protected Class

The reality that economic outcomes differ widely by protected class is well documented. We highlight here a few dimensions that will be relevant for the discussion that follows and focus on race as demonstrative of the general dynamic.

Racial and ethnic minorities earn less, have less wealth, and are less well attached to labor markets than comparable white people. African American workers have long earned less than white workers. Card and Krueger (1993) show that the median and average African American workers earned about 55 percent of what white workers earned in 1960; this earnings ratio grew to about 70 percent by 1990. The authors point to the provisions of the Civil Rights Act of 1964 as important contributors to this improvement. In separate research, the authors argue that improvements in the relative quality of black schools were another key factor contributing to these gains (Card and Krueger 1992). More recent work that focuses on relative income distributions between white and black males shows that relative improvements in black male earning have stalled since 1970 (Bayer and Charles, 2017). The authors show that earnings for the median male African American worker relative to those for the median white worker have fallen to levels not seen since the 1950s. Interestingly, Bayer and Charles do not observe a similar deterioration in relative earnings for African American workers at the top of the income distribution. Black men at the ninetieth percentile of the black income distribution have instead continued their relative rise, such that their earnings are now at the seventy-fifth percentile of the white male earning distribution. It is worth noting that this does not translate to income parity at the top of the relative income distribution.

Bayer and Charles (2017) argue that a key driver of the income disparities between African American and white workers is labor force attachment. They find that African American men have unemployment rates roughly double those of white men, and that this has been the case since the 1940s.[1] The employment gap has widened since 1970, such that unemployment for African American men was more than two times that for white men in 2000. Official records kept by the Bureau of Labor Statistics show a similar relationship. Table 4.1 shows the evolution of the unemployment rate for African American, Hispanic, and white persons since 1975. One can clearly see

Table 4.1. Historic Quadrennial Unemployment Rate Based on Bureau of
Labor Statistics Data

Year	White	Black	Hispanic	Asian
1970	4.4			
1975	8.4	15.1	14.3	
1980	6.6	14.4	10.1	
1985	6.2	15.2	10.6	
1990	4.6	10.6	7.9	
1995	5.0	10.0	9.8	
2000	3.5	7.7	5.8	
2005	4.4	10.1	6.0	4.2
2010	8.7	15.5	12.0	7.8
2015	4.8	10.3	6.8	4.0
2018[a]	3.5	5.9	4.9	2.1

Note: The unemployment rates are based on May of each year because May 2018 was the
most recent month available when this chapter was written.
[a] We included 2018 because it is the most recent year, even though it does not follow the
quadrennial pattern.

that the unemployment rate for white persons has been consistently lower
than for either African Americans or Hispanics. Interestingly, more recent
statistics show that the gap has been narrowing, with the unemployment rate
for African Americans and Hispanics at historic lows (U.S. Bureau of Labor
Statistics 2018).

Black households also have far less wealth than white families. In 2009,
the median black family had a net worth that was one-tenth that of the median white family; this represents a tripling of the wealth gap since 1984
(Shapiro, Meschede, and Osoro 2013). A more recent study by researchers at
the Board of Governors of the Federal Reserve finds that the median wealth
and the mean wealth of white households in 2016 were $171,000 and
$933,700, respectively, whereas they were only $17,600 and $138,200, for
black households and $20,700 and $191,200 for Hispanic households (Dettling et al. 2017). The wealth gap can vary quite dramatically across regions.
A report by the Urban Institute shows that in 2013 and 2014 in Washington,
D.C., the typical white household had a net worth of $284,000, whereas the
typical black household had a net worth of $3,500 (Kijakazi et al. 2016).

The black-white wealth gap has significant ties to homeownership. Because of historic inequities in access to credit, and factors such as residential segregation, the homeownership rate for white families has always greatly exceeded that for black families. In 2018, the white homeownership rate was roughly 29 percentage points higher than the homeownership rate for black families (U.S. Department of Housing and Urban Development 2018). This represents a widening of the homeownership gap from about 22 percentage points in 2007 (U.S. Department of Housing and Urban Development 2018). The decade of the 2000s was particularly rough for black homeowners. The black homeownership rate increased by 0.8 percentage points between 2001 and 2006, but this was the smallest increase among all racial and ethnic groups during that time, with whites seeing a 1.6 percentage point increase and Hispanic households a 3.9 percentage point increase (Goodman, McCargo, and Zhu 2018). Further, any gains in housing wealth were completely erased during the recession. The black homeownership rate decreased by 5.6 percentage points between 2006 and 2016, the largest decrease of any racial and ethnic group (Goodman et al., 2018), placing the black homeownership rate at its 1970 level (Acolin, Lin, and Wachter 2019). As a result, black households are the only minority group whose homeownership remains lower than it was in 2000 (Landis and Reina 2019).

On the whole, black households rely on housing for a larger share of their wealth than white households do. Overall, 37 percent of black household wealth is from housing, whereas that number is 32 percent for white households (Dettling et al. 2017). Equity in owner-occupied homes accounts for somewhere between 53 percent (Shapiro, Meschede, and Osoro 2013) and 58 percent (Zonta 2019) of total wealth for the average black homeowner. In contrast, home equity represents only about 40 percent of the net worth for the average white homeowner (Shapiro, Meschede, and Osoro 2013; Zonta 2019). Despite the fact that housing wealth is a larger share of black households' wealth portfolio, the actual value of their housing wealth is much lower relative to white households. As of 2016, white households had an average housing wealth of $215,800, whereas black households had only $94,400 and Hispanic households had $129,800 in housing wealth (Dettling et al. 2017). Taken together, these statistics suggest that an important factor restricting African American households' wealth is lack of access to their most important wealth-building tool, homeownership. However, even when homeownership is attained, it does not serve as the same wealth-building engine for an African American house-hold as for a white household.

Economic Disparities: The Role of Geographic Separation

In this section, we draw a link between the disparities just highlighted and geographic separation, which is the main concern of fair housing efforts. We show that key factors contributing to disparities in economic outcomes—including school quality, incarceration, social capital, and access to neigh-borhood amenities—have important geographic dimensions, so that racial and ethnic minorities and those belonging to other protected classes are sys-tematically disadvantaged. We then close by discussing fair housing efforts in this context and note that a central goal of such efforts is to reduce these geographic disparities. If successful in that pursuit, fair housing efforts should, by extension, lead to the reduction of economic disparities as well.

Economic segregation is increasing across the United States. For exam-ple, a study by Bischoff and Reardon (2014) finds that economic segregation increased in the United States between 1970 and 2009. Economic segrega-tion is "the increasing geographic isolation of affluent families" such that "a significant proportion of society's resources are concentrated in a smaller and smaller proportion of neighborhoods." The authors argue that "this has con-sequences for low- and middle-income families: the isolation of the rich may lead to lower public and private investments in resources, services, and ame-nities that benefit large shares of the population, such as schools, parks, and public services" (Bischoff and Reardon 2014: 226). The phenomenon of eco-nomic segregation plays out both within and across racial and ethnic groups. Through their analysis, and a review of literature by Sharkey (2014) and Lo-gan (2011), Bischoff and Reardon find that Black and Hispanic households have significant within-group economic segregation. In particular, when the authors compare the within-race spatial isolation of low-income and middle-income households, they find that low-income black and Hispanics house-holds are more isolated from middle-income households of the same race or ethnicity than are low-income white households. In addition, they find that black households are more likely not to live near economic peers than are households of other races or ethnicities. Middle-income black households, for example, are more likely to live in neighborhoods with low-income whites than they are to live in those with middle-income whites. This finding raises the question whether reductions in segregation in some areas have merely been the product of black households' accessing lower-income white neighborhoods, rather than black households' accessing middle- or upper-income white neighborhoods. Such inequities are particularly present for households with children, which raises concerns about compounding economic segregation (Owens 2016). Reardon et al. (2018) take another look at economic segregation using methods to address any possible bias in the samples used in these previous studies and find that, while some of the magnitudes change, the overall story of increasing income segregation remains the same.

A number of factors shape individual economic performance. Perhaps most significant among these is the human capital that individuals accumulate in the years leading up to their employment and as they progress in their careers. In this context, schooling is quite important. Research has shown that school quality plays an important role in student achievement (Deming et al. 2014; Konstantopoulos and Borman 2011; and others). In most communities, school assignment is tied explicitly to where one lives. Schools typically belong to systems that are defined by jurisdictional boundaries, and, within school systems, each school is typically assigned a spatial catchment area defined by proximity (Church and Schoepfle 1993; Chubb and Moe 2011). Thus, to the extent that protected classes live in segregated neighborhoods, their children will go to different schools than the children of families in the racial or ethnic majority. Further, if school quality is correlated with segregation patterns, then the children of protected classes will be worse off. Research suggests that such a school quality–segregation pattern relationship does in fact exist (Fryer and Levitt 2004).

Abstracting from the issue of school quality, we know that a student's performance is influenced by a host of environmental factors. For example, housing stability can significantly affect student performance. Housing instability can trigger midyear moves that force a student to change schools, and research has shown that such moves are quite disruptive and harm student performance along many dimensions (Cohen and Wardrip 2011; National Research Council 2010; Kutty 2008). To the extent that factors such as housing instability have a geographic component—if instability, say, is more common in some neighborhoods than others—it reinforces the relationship between residential segregation and economic inequality. Evidence on the distribution of lower-income persons, whose families have the greatest degree of housing instability, suggests instability is in fact a geographically segregated reality (Bischoff and Reardon 2014). And given that low-income status is correlated with being in many protected classes (U.S. Department of Commerce 2017; Brucker et al. 2015; Sampson 2012; Sampson and Morenoff 2006; Kasarda 1993), it is straightforward to draw a link to fair housing issues.

A person's employability, which is key to their economic success, is determined by more than their educational attainment. Incarceration is a salient example. Those who have been incarcerated are ineligible for some jobs and disadvantaged when applying for many others. Ample evidence has shown that the incidence of incarceration falls more heavily on members of some protected classes (Western and Wildeman 2009). Moreover, incarceration is geographically concentrated, such that families living in some neighborhoods—mainly minority and lower- income—are much more likely to be touched by incarceration than families living in other areas. The geographic concentration of incarceration can contribute to an increase in family stress, which adversely affects labor market outcomes and reinforces economic isolation (Massoglia and Pridemore 2015).

Neighborhoods also influence whether and how households access professional networks, information about employment, and access to jobs (for a review of this neighborhood-based connection, see Ellen and Turner 1997). A person's economic potential is closely linked to the kinds of connections he or she is able to form with the broader economy. Workers benefit from the professional and personal networks they establish, as these networks transmit information that can lead to employment opportunities (Beaman 2012; Bayer, Ross, and Topa 2008; Lin 1999). Workers often learn of job opportunities through referrals that occur in informal settings (Faberman et al. 2017; Ioannides and Loury 2004; Addison and Portugal 2002; Granovetter 1995). Yet the ability of these local networks to provide access to more and better-paying economic opportunities is limited if they are segregated to one economic stratum. Research has noted a spatial mismatch between many of the jobs created since the 1960s and the places where lower-income and minority families live (Raphael and Stoll 2002; Kain 1968). Such a mismatch only exacerbates economic segregation.

Recognizing the relationship between geography and economic success, many researchers have sought to characterize neighborhoods as "high-opportunity" or "low-opportunity" based on the presence or absence of neighborhood qualities that tend to correlate with better economic outcomes, such as high-quality schools, safety, and connectedness with the broader economy. While the terminologies and indicators differ, all neighborhood opportunity indices assume that neighborhoods that perform strongly across

multiple indicators will generally provide their residents with a greater opportunity to succeed economically. As one example, after defining some
neighborhoods as "opportunity neighborhoods," Chetty, Hendren, and Katz
(2016) find that families who live in such neighborhoods have better economic
outcomes. Access to opportunity neighborhoods differs across race and income. Evidence suggests that in the United States, race is the more significant indicator of opportunity isolation (Fischer 2003). Almost two-thirds of
African Americans are concentrated in low-opportunity communities (Sharkey 2013). More strikingly, research that analyzed the nation's one hundred
largest metro areas found that roughly 40 percent of black children live in
the lowest-opportunity neighborhoods, compared with just 9 percent of white
children (Acevedo-Garcia 2014).

Geographic separation means that some groups are more likely to be exposed to positive or negative neighborhood features. We know that minority households are more likely to live in lower-cost neighborhoods (Reina,
Wegmann, and Guerra 2019) and that these housing cost levels in part reflect fewer neighborhood amenities (Ioannides 2011). Research shows that
levels of neighborhood investment directly affect the daily stress levels of
neighborhood residents (South et al. 2015), which then have implications for
residents' health. Low-income and minority households are more likely to live
in less healthy neighborhoods, and so are more likely to have ailments and
related costs that influence immediate spending and may hamper long-term
economic prospects (Taylor 2014; Brulle and Pellow 2004). In addition, minority households are more likely to live in housing that is less energy-efficient,
leaving them with less control over utility costs and more exposure to the
economic and physical implications of energy insecurity (Kontokosta, Reina,
and Bonczak 2019; Hernández 2016; Hernández and Bird 2010).[2] Similarly,
minorities are more likely to live in areas with high crime rates, with negative implications for their economic and overall well-being (Friedson and
Sharkey 2015; Logan and Stults 2006; Buka et al. 2001; Crouch et al. 2000).

Possibly one of the most significant ways that geographic separation
affects economic outcomes is through the compounding logic that governs
our society's wealth accrual mechanisms. We have shown that, for many
households, housing is a major contributor to wealth-building. An important additional fact is that value trajectories for housing vary geographically. Neighborhood amenities are capitalized in rents and housing values,
which means that higher-amenity neighborhoods have higher house values
(Ioannides 2011). We know that if two assets appreciate at the same rate

but one has a higher initial value, the value gap between the two assets will actually *grow* over time. But appreciation rates in high-opportunity neighborhoods tend to exceed those in other neighborhoods, which exacerbates the increase in the value differential caused by baseline compounding.

From the get-go, households belonging to racial and ethnic minorities face barriers to accessing the housing wealth accumulation mechanism. Whites are more likely to be homeowners than members of other races or ethnicities, as the data we have cited thus far have shown. Such inequities are closely tied to historic, and current, barriers that minority households face when accessing credit that are tied to their race or ethnicity rather than any actual risk factor (Hillier 2003). These inequities are also tied to historic zoning practices that were initially explicitly defined based on race, but still exist in more subtle ways that are just as limiting (Orfield 2006). Research has also shown that black homeowners are more likely to purchase less expensive homes than White homeowners and that they are more likely to purchase their homes later in life, which diminishes the potential wealth creation power of this mechanism (Choi et al. 2019). Exacerbating this inequity is the geographically compounding dynamic described earlier. If whites are more likely to purchase homes in higher-opportunity neighborhoods with higher initial values, then the housing wealth of white households will grow ever larger than that of nonwhite households. As Mehrsa Baradaran argues in her book *The Color of Money: Black Banks and the Racial Wealth Gap* (2017), such differences create a compounding legacy of racial inequality over time. Of particular concern is that such compounding inequities become costlier and more difficult to reconcile through policies and programs as time passes.

Inequities in wealth accrual also arise if the same engine for success works differently in different contexts. Evidence suggests that the value-compounding dynamic observed for high-opportunity neighborhoods also operates in a directly racial dimension. There appear to be unequal returns to investments in housing by race. Nationwide, between 1990 and 2013, the value of homes occupied by white families rose faster than those occupied by Black families, and in many markets capital gains from homeownership were consistently lower for minority homeowners than for nonminority households (Mayock and Malacrida 2018). A study analyzing the Panel Study of Income Dynamics (PSID) from 2003 to 2015 finds that average housing wealth for a first-time black homeowner who purchased their home prior to turning thirty-five is less than 60 percent of a similarly aged first-time white homeowner's housing wealth. The same ratio is 39 percent for those who purchased their first home between 35 and 44, and roughly 25 percent for those who purchase their home at 45 or older (Choi, McCargo, and Goodman 2019). Socioeconomic factors drive the majority of differences in home price appreciation, but even when we control for those factors, minority households still see lower returns to housing investments (Flippen 2004; Krivo and Kaufman 2004).

The differential in housing returns existed prior to the recent boom and bust, but the Great Recession greatly increased these differences. An abundance of research shows that minority households and neighborhoods were disproportionately targeted with predatory loan products during the housing boom of the 2000s and so were more likely to experience foreclosure and the overall downside of the subsequent bust (Hall, Crowder, and Spring 2015; Rugh and Massey 2010). Between 2007 and 2010, the average black household lost 28 percent of its housing equity wealth, whereas the average white household lost 24 percent of its housing equity wealth (McKernan et al. 2013). These differences become more profound when we look at overall wealth, with the average black household losing 31 percent of its overall wealth during this time, and the average white household losing only 11 percent (McKernan et al. 2013). The disparities in overall wealth are larger because black households invest a larger share of their overall wealth in housing (Grinstein-Weiss, Key, and Carrillo 2015). Black households have not recouped what they lost during the Great Recession. As one example, Raymond, Kyungsoon, and Immergluck (2016) find that, after controlling for age, type of housing, and poverty rates, zip codes in Atlanta with larger black populations were more likely to suffer steep declines in home values during the recession and have experienced little recovery.

The housing wealth creation mechanism features a self-reinforcing feedback loop. Increases in home equity are associated with human capital investments, mainly in the form of education. There is a direct positive relationship between increasing home equity and college enrollment, and the relationship is particularly strong for low-income households. A $10,000 increase in home equity is associated with a 5.7 percentage point increase in college enrollment for low-income families, according to one study (Lovenheim 2011). And because college completion is associated with higher odds of owning a home (Myers et al. 2019), increases in housing equity for existing low-income households could have important housing-related wealth creation benefits across generations. An obvious question is, How does all of this relate to fair housing? The preamble to the Affirmatively Furthering Fair

Housing regulation revision enacted recently by the U.S. Department of Housing and Urban Development (HUD), which defines HUD's approach to fair housing, provides a clear link between combating geographic separation and improving economic outcomes. The rule states: "Affirmatively furthering fair housing means taking meaningful actions, in addition to combating discrimination, that overcome patterns of segregation and foster inclusive communities free from barriers that restrict access to opportunity based on protected characteristics." More specifically, affirmatively furthering fair housing means "taking meaningful actions that, taken together, address significant disparities in housing needs and in access to opportunity, replacing segregated living patterns with truly integrated and balanced living patterns, transforming racially and ethnically concentrated areas of poverty into areas of opportunity, and fostering and maintaining compliance with civil rights and fair housing laws" (24 C.F.R. § 5.152). The emphasis this preamble places on inclusive communities and access to opportunity directly aligns with the goal of improving economic outcomes for those who have been geographically, and therefore economically, marginalized.

The Economic Case for Fair Housing

In this section, we argue that there is an equivalence between the pursuit of fair housing objectives and the goal of reducing disparities in economic outcomes based on status as a protected class. We also identify, to the extent possible, strategies that might be adopted in a fair housing context to weaken those factors that have acted as barriers to equitable access to opportunity in the past. We make an economic case for fair housing along the three dimensions highlighted earlier: its direct impact on income and employment, its direct impact on wealth and entrepreneurship, and its indirect impact on neighborhood stability and resilience.

Fair Housing and Income and Employment

While not explicitly framed as fair housing efforts, several federal programs have pursued goals that align with fair housing objectives. Each of these programs has generated improvements in economic equity that suggest that similar fair housing efforts could do the same.

One such effort, the Moving to Opportunity (MTO) demonstration, aimed to reduce geographic disparities and increase access to opportunity neighborhoods with low poverty rates by providing incentives and support for lower-income people to move to such neighborhoods. MTO was a controlled experiment with random assignment that was designed to test whether access to lower-poverty neighborhoods is sufficient to reduce socioeconomic disparities. The demonstration was implemented precisely because of concerns that economic isolation and segregation introduced barriers that lower-income families could not overcome. It is important to note that MTO was not a race-based policy intervention; it was an income-based one. However, the experiment's opportunity neighborhoods were largely exclusionary, majority white neighborhoods, while its participants were largely Black or Hispanic. Thus, racial integration was implicit in the economic integration of MTO families into high-cost areas. Early evaluations of MTO found few economic effects, though evaluators did note significant health and wellness benefits for those households who moved to neighborhoods with better amenities and greater access to opportunity, which might ultimately translate into better economic outcomes (U.S. Department of Housing and Urban Development 2011; Ludwig et al. 2008). Later studies with longer time horizons did, however, find that access to opportunity neighborhoods was associated with improvements in economic outcomes. Interestingly, the greatest beneficiaries of the increased access to opportunity neighborhoods were the children of the families that moved (Chetty, Hendren, and Katz 2016). The economic benefits were significant, with low-income children who grew up in opportunity neighborhoods ultimately garnering annual earnings more than $20,000 higher than those of low-income children who grew up in opportunity-poor neighborhoods.

The 1976 *Hills v. Gautreaux* Supreme Court decision provided the foundation for a race- based precursor to the MTO demonstration. The Court found that the Chicago Housing Authority (CHA) was steering public housing development into high-minority areas, which furthered racial segregation. The ruling required CHA to offer vouchers to public housing residents to deconcentrate racial segregation in its public housing. There is associative evidence that those households that used their vouchers were able to access predominately white suburbs and that these households experienced improved educational and employment outcomes (Rosenbaum 1995; Rubinowitz and Rosenbaum 2000).

The approach showcased in MTO and Gautreaux, which is often called a "mobility solution," has been applied in other contexts, though not with the MTO program's analytical rigor, which had permitted such straightforward conclusions about the effects of accessing opportunity neighborhoods. The city of Baltimore, in response to a consent decree, established a mobility program to make it easier for families with housing choice vouchers to choose housing units located in low-poverty and nonsegregated neighborhoods (Baltimore Regional Housing Partnership 2018). One study that followed 1,800 participating families for up to nine years found that the families moved to more integrated neighborhoods and that most remained in that neighborhood after initial lease-up. Those who later moved again usually moved to neighborhoods with lower poverty rates and higher median household incomes than those they had lived in prior to entering the program (DeLuca and Rosenblatt 2017).

Another recent program that has affected the mobility of low-income households is the Small Area Fair Market Rent (SAFMR) demonstration. This program modifies how fair market rents, which is the maximum rent HUD is willing to subsidize, are determined. Rather than conforming to the usual method, which is to set a county-wide fair market rent (FMR), jurisdictions participating in the SAFMR demonstration set different FMRs for individual zip codes. This approach increases housing voucher recipients' access to higher-income neighborhoods, which are also higher-opportunity neighborhoods, because the narrower geographic frame reduces the overall variation in rents in a given area and increases the likelihood that the FMR will be close to the local market rent. The initial impetus for this program came from a lawsuit, *The Inclusive Communities Project v. HUD*, in which the plaintiff claimed that the way HUD established its rent limits furthered the concentration of minority households in predominantly minority and/or lower-opportunity neighborhoods (Reina 2019). This claim is not surprising when we consider that the average black voucher household in a place like Cook County, Illinois, lives in a neighborhood with a poverty rate that is nine percentage points higher than the neighborhood where a similar white voucher household lives. Research also finds that households who use their voucher to move to another neighborhood tend to move to lower-poverty areas, but that such neighborhood gains are lower for Black households using a voucher (Reina and Winter 2019). Early evidence suggests that the use of small-area fair market rents results in a greater share of low-income households accessing higher-income neighborhoods (Reina, Bostic, and Acolin 2018; Collinson and Ganong 2018). Preliminary research also shows that such improvements in neighborhood access are particularly likely to accrue to minority households; still, the SAFMR program comes nowhere close to equalizing racial disparities in neighborhood outcomes in the voucher program (Reina 2019). With the passage of time, we will be better able to conclude whether this greater access has translated into improved economic outcomes for low-income households, minority households, or both. Increasing mobility is not the only approach to improving access to opportunity for families who lack such access. Another approach is to reduce the disparities in amenities across neighborhoods and communities, with the goal being to increase the degree of opportunity that previously distressed places can offer their residents. As with mobility strategies, neighborhood redevelopment strategies have already been pursued, though not in the context of fair housing.

One effort in this vein was HUD's HOPE VI program. The premise of HOPE VI was that the way many traditional public housing projects concentrated poverty in certain neighborhoods was an insurmountable barrier preventing those neighborhoods from receiving significant private investment and, ultimately, high-quality amenities (Popkin, Levy, and Buron 2009). Program participants used funds to demolish troubled projects and replace them with mixed-income developments that reduced poverty concentrations. Residents living in the troubled projects were displaced while the newer housing was being built. They were given housing vouchers to live elsewhere and retained a first right of return to the new HOPE VI property. But because the newer developments sometimes had fewer units than the original ones, not all were able to return. Thus, the HOPE VI program generated three categories of residents: (1) those who left and returned; (2) those who left, never returned, and lived in a higher-opportunity neighborhood; and (3) those who left, never returned, and lived in a neighborhood comparable to the one in which the original project was located.

The HOPE VI program was followed by Choice Neighborhoods, which broadened the programmatic mandate by allowing funds to be used for nonhousing purposes (S. HRG. 112–515, 2012). As documented in S. HRG. 112–515 (2012), the program grew out of a recognition that many of HUD's previous investments in housing resulted in high-quality housing located in the midst of a significant amount of distress, including unsafe streets, poor schools, and limited economic connectedness. Despite measurable improvements in the quality of their housing, residents of those upgraded developments were still unlikely to see major improvements in their economic outcomes. Choice Neighborhoods program funds could be used to augment school quality, retail offerings, and businesses in the neighborhood proximate to the public housing project that was being redeveloped. The Choice Neighborhoods program used the same displacement and return approach as HOPE VI.

In terms of impact, the evaluations of HOPE VI show at best mixed results, with those who were displaced and did not return to the public housing being the main beneficiaries. For example, Popkin, Levy, and Buron (2009) found that improvements to economic outcomes were largely limited to those public housing residents who moved away from the public housing project site and relocated to higher-opportunity neighborhoods. Using administrative records to track HOPE VI residents in Chicago and compare them with similar residents not in HOPE VI developments, Chyn (2018) finds that three years after demolition, households who were displaced lived in neighborhoods with lower poverty and crime rates. Chyn also finds that children who are displaced from public housing at any age have higher earnings in their early adulthood. The other group of interest is made up of the households who return to the redeveloped public housing. Popkin, Levy, and Buron (2009) find that this group experienced few economic gains. However, it could be that more time is needed to see measurable improvements—this was, after all, the case for MTO—but as of now, there is little to show for the efficacy of neighborhood redevelopment strategies.

Fair Housing, Wealth, and Entrepreneurship

Aside from establishing and building home equity, households can also build economic affluence and wealth through success in business and entrepreneurship. Small businesses are often cited as drivers of economic growth in the United States (Mills and McCarthy 2014; Acs and Armingon 2006), have been the primary source of new jobs over extended periods (Mills and McCarthy 2014), and are viewed as essential to the innovation that fuels economic growth (Acs and Armingon 2006).

Financing small business enterprises is challenging because they often carry elevated risks; they have limited balance sheets and short or nonexistent track records. Thus, a potential entrepreneur's personal assets become critical to determining a small business's viability, particularly in early years of operation. Housing, because of the significant contribution to family wealth that it represents, is therefore important for small business creation and growth. Potential entrepreneurs can extract their home equity via either a home equity line of credit or a small business loan that uses the home as collateral, and use the proceeds to open, expand, and adapt small businesses and build additional wealth. Thus one might say there is an economic multiplier associated with housing wealth.

It is not only the existence of home equity that is important for small business creation and growth. The amount of housing equity and how equity grows over time affect entrepreneurship rates as well. Research suggests that an increase in home equity increases the likelihood that a person becomes self-employed (Corradin and Popov 2015); a 20 percent increase in home value increases the likelihood of self-employment by 1.5 percentage points (Harding and Rosenthal 2017). This is a significant shift when we consider that the 2013 self- employment rate is estimated to be somewhere between 13.2 percent and 15.7 percent, depending on the source of data. With regard to business growth, higher levels of home equity enable households to make larger investments, and those households who enjoy growth in their home values can continue to extract equity from their home over time in order to grow their business.

It is important to note that the link between housing and business success is stronger for small businesses than for other business enterprises. Small businesses in areas with housing price appreciation actually increase their employment more than large firms in the same markets, and this link is particularly strong for small businesses that are more reliant on housing collateral (Adelino, Schoar, and Severino 2015). In addition, there is evidence that the recent economic recession created a significant constraint on small businesses owners because they had limited ability to access capital or credit from housing (Schweitzer and Shane 2018).

As difficult as it is to finance and support small businesses generally, minority households face additional barriers to accessing small business financing. There is less small business lending in urban and higher-minority areas (Bostic and Lee 2017; Bates and Robb 2016). Further, discrimination in small business lending practices has limited the ability of minority households to obtain small business loans (Bates and Robb 2016; Blanchflower, Levine, and Zimmerman 2003). These discriminatory practices have adversely affected the pricing of loans for minority small business enterprises, with lenders raising interest rates based on perceived, as opposed to actual, race-based risk (Blanchard, Zhao, and Yinger 2008). Though research suggests that the Community Reinvestment Act, which requires banks to reinvest in communities where they receive deposits, has positively impacted loan access (Bates and Robb 2015) and small business development and growth (Rupasingha and Wang 2017) in urban areas, the CRA's positive effects do not fully counterbalance the race-based inequality in small business lending arising from discriminatory practices (Bates and Robb 2015).

The presence of these additional barriers means that, for minorities and members of other protected classes, housing and housing wealth play an outsized role in the ability to start and sustain a small business. But minority households have less housing wealth and see lower gains from investments in housing, which in turn limits their ability to both create and grow small businesses. In short, absent a nondiscriminatory and fair housing market, minorities and other disadvantaged groups will be less able to benefit from the housing wealth multiplier for small business development and other economic investments. Effective fair housing efforts can reduce the extent of discrimination and the disparities that prevail in housing and increase the ability of those who have been historically unable to fully benefit from the housing wealth multiplier to do so. The result should be smaller disparities in minority households' propensity to start, and grow, a small business, which can contribute to the narrowing of income and wealth disparities in the United States.

Fair Housing and Macroeconomic Growth

Much of the preceding discussion has focused on implications of fair housing for household- and family-level economics. But there are good reasons to expect that efforts to promote fair housing will have positive macroeconomic effects. Success in achieving fair housing goals should result in a broader set of strong and resilient households and families, translating into a stronger and more resilient microeconomy. This improved economic strength and resilience at a microeconomic level should translate into improved macroeconomic performance.

To the extent that fair housing efforts are effective at increasing the wealth and income of low-income minority households, these efforts could have a positive impact on macroeconomic growth. Household consumption is a key contributor to macroeconomic growth, and there is a large literature that shows that consumption rises with household wealth (Iacoviello 2011). Moreover, research has found that the propensity to consume in response to increases in housing wealth is greater than the propensity to consume when financial wealth increases (see, for example, Bostic, Gabriel, and Painter 2009). As a result, the growth in housing wealth that can be a by-product of fair housing efforts could be particularly simulative.

A similar logic applies to income gains. On a dollar-for-dollar basis, the macroeconomic impact of increases in consumption is likely to be greater for lower-income families than for others. Because they will have more unmet needs generally, lower-income households have a higher propensity to spend any additional dollars they earn or accrue. Thus, a greater share of the additional money they have at their disposal is quickly recycled into the economy. One note of caution regarding this macroeconomic channel is that a reliance on housing wealth necessarily involves monetizing the equity in one's home. Recent experience leading up to the Great Recession suggests that there are significant risks associated with approach. Many homeowners borrowed against their housing wealth gains during this period. While evidence shows that much of this wealth extraction was used for consumption, as one might expect, such borrowing also was a significant contributor to the increased volume of mortgage defaults between 2006 and 2008 (Mian and Sufi 2011). The stability of local housing markets and the quality of loan underwriting thus become important factors for determining whether such a consumption strategy will be sound.

Fair housing efforts also seek to reduce the extent of segregation experienced by members of protected classes, and evidence is clear that this kind of segregation reduces income, wealth, and access to economic opportunities. For example, Acs et al. (2017) find that higher levels of racial segregation in Chicago are associated with lower income for blacks. Acs and colleagues (2017) also find that this segregation depressed property values, which the authors argue lowers property tax revenues and promotes sprawling, inefficient land use patterns that make public service provision more costly.

We see similar relationships when one considers business formation. A study by Samila and Sorenson (2017) focused on whether there was a relationship between segregation and entrepreneurship, and finds that metropolitan areas that are less racially segregated are better able to leverage venture capital to promote innovation entrepreneurship and increase wealth and employment. The authors argue that racially integrated regions likely produce ideas that attract venture capital investment, that the social cohesion produced through integration can allow for easier recruitment of employees with varied skills, and that greater exposure to a diverse set of people increases the likelihood one will be exposed to entrepreneurs and ideas that produce entrepreneurship.

Some have examined whether there is a link between segregation and aggregate economic performance more directly, and the evidence is consistent with theory that there is a clear negative relationship between the two. For example, Li, Campbell, and Fernandez (2013) explore the impact of racial segregation and skill segregation on economic growth and find that they each have both short- and long-term impacts on economic growth in U.S. metropolitan areas. Beyond these direct effects, a number of additional factors highlight the macroeconomic challenge posed by segregation. First, as already noted, segregation can lead to inefficient and high-cost public service provision. Localities in this circumstance are at a competitive macroeconomic disadvantage, because the inefficiencies make it costlier and more difficult to deliver high-quality services. A good example can be seen when we look at schools. There is clear evidence that high-quality schools are linked to higher growth in gross domestic product (Hanushek, Ruhose, and Woessmann 2016; Hanushek and Woessman 2015). Those regions that cannot provide good quality schooling are affecting local education levels and larger economic growth. Combined, this evidence suggests that those living in segregated communities are adversely affected by these higher costs, which affect their communities and the broader economy.

Second, spatial growth trajectories are increasingly systematically divergent. A 2018 report by the Brookings Institution showed that large metropolitan areas are drivers of macroeconomic growth, but that there is a growing divergence in growth rates (Muro and Whiton 2018). If segregation has a negative impact on local and regional development, it could throw communities and regions into the lower-growth group, with long-run implications for macroeconomic prosperity.

Similar studies have been conducted within metropolitan areas. Sahasranaman and Jensen (2017) find that neighborhoods in a metropolitan area tend to be locked into a particular income category. Thus, the richest neighborhoods and poorest neighborhoods both stay that way, implying that those living in the poorest neighborhoods are unlikely to make significant progress. Pendal and Hedman (2015) similarly show that, within a commuting zone, the top-performing census tracts are more likely to be locked into a positive cycle than low-performing tracts. Although these studies focused on income distribution, because of the high negative correlation between income and membership in a protected class, many people who are the focus of fair housing efforts are likely to live in these income-segregated communities. This likelihood makes these dynamics relevant in the current context.

On balance, existing theory and evidence suggest that inequality is putting neighborhoods and regions on divergent paths. As long as wealth and income continue to diverge, macroeconomic separation will continue or even worsen. Research suggests such long-run divergence is not good for macroeconomic performance. Benabou (1994) shows that in the short term, economic stratification can allow the rich to see gains that exceed the losses of the poor and result in aggregate growth, but that these divergent experiences will over the longer term have an opposite effect and ultimately hurt growth. A key goal of fair housing is to ensure that members of protected classes are not locked into poor neighborhoods plagued with persistently weak economic performance. Moreover, fair housing efforts aim to ensure that the existing compounding dynamic for income and wealth that perpetuates inequities does not lock members of protected classes out of markets or exacerbate regional economic divergence. If successful, fair housing efforts will ensure that members of protected classes are not bound to the negative economic trajectories associated with racial and economic segregation, in turn helping the economic growth of communities, regions, and the larger macroeconomy.

Conclusion

Fair housing seeks to ensure that people's zip codes do not determine their life's path, including their economic success. Within this context, we identify three economic cases for fair housing. The first two cases are direct. First, we argue that if fair housing enables all people to live in communities that have a full range of higher-quality amenities and services, it will exert a positive influence on individual economic outcomes. Second, we emphasize how fair housing is essential for individuals to build wealth and pursue entrepreneurial opportunities. The third case is indirect. We assert that when fair housing succeeds, wealth in disadvantaged communities grows, resulting in a more even distribution of wealth that can potentially elevate the rate of macroeconomic growth. Combined, these arguments establish the foundation for fair housing as both a micro- and macroeconomic concern.

Policies aimed at eliminating race-based barriers to accessing opportunity are essential not only to the long-term economic prosperity of individual households, but also to the national economy more broadly. Such policies should involve increasing access to capital and down payment assistance for minority households purchasing a home. Policies should also focus on actively using the legal strength of the Fair Housing Act to prosecute discrimination by lenders, real estate agents, and tech companies. We can also improve the operations of some of our existing programs, such as adopting SAFMR rents in the voucher program and providing financial and housing search support for household using the subsidy. Finally, it is important to acknowledge that these solutions need to go beyond household-level interventions and improve some of the structural factors limiting the economic prosperity of protected classes. A prime example is the need to acknowledge how zoning has been used as a means to exclude protected classes from homeownership opportunities, wealth accrual, and access to neighborhood opportunity. Ensuring that single-family zoning is not used as a tool to promote and enshrine racial and ethnic segregation, and that local land use and zoning rules promote the development of a diverse housing stock so that renters and individuals with disabilities can access a broad set of neighborhood amenities, is essential to ensuring that past inequities do not continue to compound.

Notes

1. Here unemployment is defined as the fraction of men not employed; the authors use two different measures. For more, see Bayer and Charles (2017).

2. This topic is a core component of the larger environmental justice movement.

References

Acevedo-Garcia, Dolores, Nancy McArdle, Erin F. Hardy, Unda Ioana Crisan, Bethany Romano, David Norris, Mikyung Baek, and Jason Reece. "The Child Opportunity Index: Improving Collaboration Between Community Development and Public Health." *Health Affairs* 33, no. 11 (2014): 1948–57.

Acolin, Arthur, Desen Lin, and Susan Wachter. "Endowments and Minority Homeownership." *Cityscape: A Journal of Policy Development and Research* 21, no. 1 (2019): 5–62.

Acs, Gregory, et al. *The Cost of Segregation: National Trends and the Case of Chicago, 1990–2010.* Washington, D.C.: Urban Institute, 2017.

Acs, Zoltan J., and Catherine Armington. *Entrepreneurship, Geography, and American Economic Growth.* Cambridge: Cambridge University Press, 2006.

Addison, John T., and Pedro Portugal. "Job Search Methods and Outcomes." *Oxford Economic Papers* 54, no. 3 (2002): 505–33.

Adelino, Manuel, Antoinette Schoar, and Felipe Severino. "House Prices, Collateral, and Self-Employment." *Journal of Financial Economics* 117, no. 2 (2015): 288–306.

Baltimore Regional Housing Partnership. *Baltimore Housing Mobility Program.* Accessed June 18, 2018. http://www.brhp.org/.

Baradaran, Mehrsa. *The Color of Money: Black Banks and the Racial Wealth Gap.* Cambridge, MA: Harvard University Press, 2017.

Bates, Timothy, and Alicia Robb. "Has the Community Reinvestment Act Increased Loan Availability Among Small Businesses Operating in Minority Neighbourhoods?" *Urban Studies* 52, no. 9 (2015): 1702–21.

———. "Impacts of Owner Race and Geographic Context on Access to Small-Business Financing." *Economic Development Quarterly* 30, no. 2 (2016): 159–70.

Bayer, Patrick, and Kerwin Kofi Charles. *Divergent Paths: Structural Change, Economic Rank, and the Evolution of Black-White Earnings Differences, 1940–2014.* No. w22797. Cambridge, MA: National Bureau of Economic Research, 2016.

Bayer, Patrick, Stephen L. Ross, and Giorgio Topa. "Place of Work and Place of Residence: Informal Hiring Networks and Labor Market Outcomes." *Journal of Political Economy* 116, no. 6 (2008): 1150–96.

Beaman, Lori A. "Social Networks and the Dynamics of Labour Market Outcomes: Evidence from Refugees Resettled in the US." *Review of Economic Studies* 79, no. 1 (2011): 128–61.

Benabou, Roland. "Human Capital, Inequality, and Growth: A Local Perspective." *European Economic Review* 38, no. 3–4 (1994): 817–26.

Bischoff, K., and S. F. Reardon. "Residential Segregation by Income, 1970–2009." In *Diversity and Disparities: America Enters a New Century*, edited by J. Logan, 208–33. New York: Russell Sage Foundation, 2014.

Blanchard, Lloyd, Bo Zhao, and John Yinger. "Do Lenders Discriminate Against Minority and Woman Entrepreneurs?" *Journal of Urban Economics* 63, no. 2 (2008): 467–97.

Blanchflower, David G., Phillip B. Levine, and David J. Zimmerman. "Discrimination in the Small-Business Credit Market." *Review of Economics and Statistics* 85, no. 4 (2003): 930–43.

Bostic, Raphael, Stuart Gabriel, and Gary Painter. "Housing Wealth, Financial Wealth, and Consumption: New Evidence from Micro Data." *Regional Science and Urban Economics* 39, no. 1 (2009): 79–89.

Bostic, Raphael W., and Hyojung Lee. "Small Business Lending Under the Community Reinvestment Act." *Cityscape* 19, no. 2 (2017): 63.

Brucker, Debra L., Sophie Mitra, Navena Chaitoo, and Joseph Mauro. "More Likely to Be Poor Whatever the Measure: Working-Age Persons with Disabilities in the United States." *Social Science Quarterly* 96, no. 1 (2015): 273–96.

Brulle, Robert J., and David N. Pellow. "Environmental Justice: Human Health and Environmental Inequalities." *Annual Review of Public Health* 27 (2006): 103–24.

Buka, Stephen L., Theresa L. Stichick, Isolde Birdthistle, and Felton J. Earls. "Youth Exposure to Violence: Prevalence, Risks, and Consequences." *American Journal of Orthopsychiatry* 71, no. 3 (2001): 298.

Card, David, and Alan B. Krueger. "School Quality and Black-White Relative Earnings: A Direct Assessment." *Quarterly Journal of Economics* 107, no. 1 (1992): 151–200.

———. "Trends in Relative Black-White Earnings Revisited." *American Economic Review* 83, no. 2 (1993): 85–91.

Chetty, Raj, Nathaniel Hendren, and Lawrence F. Katz. "The Effects of Exposure to Better Neighborhoods on Children: New Evidence from the Moving to Opportunity Experiment." *American Economic Review* 106, no. 4 (2016): 855–902.

Choi, Jung Hyun, Alanna McCargo, and Lauri Goodman. *Three Differences Between Black And White Homeownership Rate that Add to the Housing Wealth Gap.* Washington, D.C.: Urban Institute, February 28, 2019.

Chubb, John E., and Terry M. Moe. *Politics, Markets, and America's Schools.* Washington, D.C.: Brookings Institution Press, 2011.

Church, R. L., and O. B. Schoepfle. "The Choice Alternative to School Assignment." *Environment and Planning B: Planning and Design* 20, no. 4 (1993): 447–57.

Chyn, Eric. "Moved to Opportunity: The Long-Run Effects of Public Housing Demolition on Children." *American Economic Review* 108, no. 10 (2018): 3028–56.

Cohen, Rebecca, and Keith Wardrip. *Should I Stay or Should I Go?: Exploring the Effects of Housing Instability and Mobility on Children.* Washington, D.C.: Center for Housing Policy, 2011.

Collinson, Robert, and Peter Ganong. "How Do Changes in Housing Voucher Design Affect Rent and Neighborhood Quality?" *American Economic Journal: Economic Policy* 10, no. 2 (2018): 62–89.

Corradin, Stefano, and Alexander Popov. "House Prices, Home Equity Borrowing, and Entrepreneurship." *The Review of Financial Studies* 28, no. 8 (August 2015): 2399–428.

Crouch, Julie L., Rochelle F. Hanson, Benjamin E. Saunders, Dean G. Kilpatrick, and Heidi S. Resnick. "Income, Race/Ethnicity, and Exposure to Violence in Youth: Results from the National Survey of Adolescents." *Journal of Community Psychology* 28, no. 6 (2000): 625–41.

DeLuca, Stefanie, and Peter Rosenblatt. "Walking Away from the Wire: Housing Mobility and Neighborhood Opportunity in Baltimore." *Housing Policy Debate* 27, no. 4 (2017): 519–46.

Deming, David J., Justine S. Hastings, Thomas J. Kane, and Douglas O. Staiger. "School Choice, School Quality, and Postsecondary Attainment." *American Economic Review* 104, no. 3 (2014): 991–1013.

Dettling, Lisa J., Joanne W. Hsu, Lindsay Jacobs, Kevin B. Moore, and Jeffrey P. Thompson. *Recent Trends in Wealth-Holding by Race and Ethnicity: Evidence from the Survey of Consumer Finances.* Washington, D.C.: Board of Governors of the Federal Reserve System, 2017.

Ellen, Ingrid Gould, and Margery Austin Turner. "Does Neighborhood Matter? Assessing Recent Evidence." *Housing Policy Debate* 8, no. 4 (1997): 833–66.

Faberman, R. J., A. I. Mueller, A. Sahin, R. Shuh, and G. Topa. "How Do People Find Jobs?" *Liberty Street Economics*, Federal Reserve Bank of New York, 2017. http://libertystreeteconomics.newyorkfed.org/2017/04/how-do-people-find-jobs.html.

Fischer, Mary J. "The Relative Importance of Income and Race in Determining Residential Outcomes in US Urban Areas, 1970–2000." *Urban Affairs Review* 38, no. 5 (2003): 669–96.

Flippen, Chenoa. "Unequal Returns to Housing Investments? A Study of Real Housing Appreciation Among Black, White, and Hispanic Households." *Social Forces* 82, no. 4 (2004): 1523–51.

Friedson, Michael, and Patrick Sharkey. "Violence and Neighborhood Disadvantage After the Crime Decline." *Annals of the American Academy of Political and Social Science* 660, no. 1 (2015): 341–58.

Fryer Jr., Roland G., and Steven D. Levitt. "Understanding the Black-White Test Score Gap in the First Two Years of School." *Review of Economics and Statistics* 86, no. 2 (2004): 447–64.

Goodman, Laurie, Alanna McCargo, and Jun Zhu. *A Closer Look at the Fifteen-Year Drop in Black Homeownership*. Washington, D.C.: Urban Institute, February 13, 2018.

Granovetter, Mark. *Getting a Job: A Study of Contacts and Careers*. Chicago: University of Chicago Press, 1995.

Grinstein-Weiss, Michal, Clinton Key, and Shannon Carrillo. "Homeownership, the Great Recession, and Wealth: Evidence from the Survey of Consumer Finances." *Housing Policy Debate* 25, no. 3 (2015): 419–45.

Hall, Matthew, Kyle Crowder, and Amy Spring. "Variations in Housing Foreclosures by Race and Place, 2005–2012." *Annals of the American Academy of Political and Social Science* 660, no. 1 (2015): 217–37.

Hanushek, Eric A., Jens Ruhose, and Ludger Woessmann. "It Pays to Improve School Quality: States That Boost Student Achievement Could Reap Large Economic Gains." *Education Next* 16, no. 3 (2016): 52.

Hanushek, Eric A., and Ludger Woessmann. "Do Better Schools Lead to More Growth? Cognitive Skills, Economic Outcomes, and Causation." *Journal of Economic Growth* 17, no. 4 (2012): 267–321.

Harding, John, and Stuart Rosenthal. "Homeownership, Housing Capital Gains and Self-Employment." *Journal of Urban Economics* 99 (2017): 120–35.

Hernández, Diana. "Understanding 'Energy Insecurity' and Why It Matters to Health." *Social Science & Medicine* 167 (2016): 1–10.

Hernández, Diana, and Stephen Bird. "Energy Burden and the Need for Integrated Low-Income Housing and Energy Policy." *Poverty & Public Policy* 2, no. 4 (2010): 5–25.

Hillier, Amy E. "Redlining and the Home Owners' Loan Corporation." *Journal of Urban History* 29, no. 4 (2003): 394–420.

Iacoviello, Matteo M. "Housing Wealth and Consumption." Washington, D.C.: Federal Reserve Board International Finance Discussion Paper 1027, 2011.

Institute for Policy Studies. "Facts: Wealth Inequality in the US." *Inequality.org*. Accessed August 6, 2019. https://inequality.org/facts/wealth-inequality/.

Ioannides, Yannis M. "Neighborhood Effects and Housing." *Handbook of Social Economics* 1 (2011): 1281–340.

Ioannides, Yannis M., and Linda Datcher Loury. "Job Information Networks, Neighborhood Effects, and Inequality." *Journal of Economic Literature* 42, no. 4 (2004): 1056–93.

Kain, John F. "Housing Segregation, Negro Employment, and Metropolitan Decentralization." *Quarterly Journal of Economics* 82, no. 2 (1968): 175–97.

Kasarda, John D. "Inner-City Concentrated Poverty and Neighborhood Distress: 1970 to 1990." *Housing Policy Debate* 4, no. 3 (1993): 253–302.

Kijakazi, Kilolo, Rachel Marie Brooks Atkins, Mark Paul, Anne E. Price, Darrick Hamilton, and William A. Darity Jr. *The Color of Wealth in the Nation's Capital.* Durham, NC: Duke University, 2016.

Konstantopoulos, Spyros, and Geoffrey Borman. "Family Background and School Effects on Student Achievement: A Multilevel Analysis of the Coleman Data." *Teachers College Record* 113, no. 1 (2011): 97–132.

Kontokosta, Constantine E., Vincent Reina, and Bartosz Bonczak. "Energy Cost Burdens for Low-Income and Minority Households in Five U.S. Cities: Evidence from Energy Benchmarking and Audit Data." *Journal of the American Planning Association* (published online September 17, 2019). https://doi.org/10.1080/01944363.2019.1647446.

Krivo, Lauren J., and Robert L. Kaufman. "Housing and Wealth Inequality: Racial-Ethnic Differences in Home Equity in the United States." *Demography* 41, no. 3 (2004): 585–605.

Kutty, Nandinee K. "Using the Making Connections Survey Data to Analyze Housing Mobility and Child Outcomes Among Low-Income Families." Washington, D.C.: Center for Housing Policy, 2008.

Landis, John, and Vincent Reina. "Eleven Ways Demographic and Economic Change Is Reframing American Housing Policy." *Housing Policy Debate* 29, no. 1 (2019): 4–21.

Li, Huiping, Harrison Campbell, and Steven Fernandez. "Residential Segregation, Spatial Mismatch and Economic Growth Across US Metropolitan Areas." *Urban Studies* 50, no. 13 (2013): 2642–60.

Li, Jing. "Economic Segregation and Urban Growth." 2012. Available at SSRN 2149654.

Lin, Nan. "Social Networks and Status Attainment." *Annual Review of Sociology* 25, no. 1 (1999): 467–87.

Logan, John R. "Separate and Unequal: The Neighborhood Gap for Blacks, Hispanics, and Asians in Metropolitan America." *US2010 Project*, July 2011. Accessed August 10, 2019. www.s4.brown.edu/us2010/Data/Report/report0727.pdf.

Logan, John R., and Brian J. Stults. "Racial Differences in Exposure to Crime: The City and Suburbs of Cleveland in 1990." *Criminology* 37, no. 2 (1999): 251–76.

Lovenheim, Michael. "The Effect of Liquid Housing Wealth on College Enrollment." *Journal of Labor Economics* 29, no. 4 (2011): 741–71.

Ludwig, Jens, Jeffrey B. Liebman, Jeffrey R. Kling, Greg J. Duncan, Lawrence F. Katz, Ronald C. Kessler, and Lisa Sanbonmatsu. "What Can We Learn About Neighborhood Effects from the Moving to Opportunity Experiment?" *American Journal of Sociology* 114, no. 1 (2008): 144–88.

Massoglia, Michael, and William Alex Pridemore. "Incarceration and Health." *Annual Review of Sociology* 41 (2015): 291–310.

Mayock, Tom, and Rachel Spritzer Malacrida. "Socioeconomic and Racial Disparities in the Financial Returns to Homeownership." *Regional Science and Urban Economics* 70 (2018): 80–96.

McKernan, Signe-Mary, Caroline Ratcliffe, C. Eugene Steuerle, and Sisi Zhang. *Less than Equal: Racial Disparities in Wealth Accumulation.* Washington, D.C.: Urban Institute, 2013.

Mian, Atif, and Amir Sufi. "House Prices, Home Equity-Based Borrowing, and the US Household Leverage Crisis." *American Economic Review* 101, no. 5 (2011): 2132–56.

Mills, Karen, and Brayden McCarthy. "The State of Small Business Lending: Credit Access during the Recovery and How Technology May Change the Game." Harvard Business School General Management Unit Working Paper 15-004, 2014.

Muro, Mark, and Jacob Whiton. *Geographic Gaps Are Widening While U.S. Economic Growth Increases.* Washington, D.C.: Brookings Institution, January 23, 2018.

Myers, Dowell, Gary D. Painter, Julie Zissimopoulos, Hyojung Lee, and Johanna Thunell. "Simulating the Change in Young Adult Homeownership Through 2035: Effects of Growing Diversity and Rising Educational Attainment." *Housing Policy Debate* 29, no. 1 (2019): 126–42.

National Research Council. *Student Mobility: Exploring the Impacts of Frequent Moves on Achievement: Summary of a Workshop.* Washington, D.C.: National Academies Press, 2010.

Orfield, Myron. "Land Use and Housing Policies to Reduce Concentrated Poverty and Racial Segregation." *Fordham Urban Law Journal* 33 (2005): 877.

Owens, Ann. "Inequality in Children's Contexts: Income Segregation of Households with and Without Children." *American Sociological Review* 81, no. 3 (2016): 549–74.

Pendall, Rolf, and Carl Hedman. *Worlds Apart: Inequality Between America's Most and Least Affluent Neighborhoods.* Washington, D.C.: Urban Institute, 2015.

Popkin, Susan J., Diane K. Levy, and Larry Buron. "Has HOPE VI Transformed Residents' Lives? New Evidence from the HOPE VI Panel Study." *Housing Studies* 24, no. 4 (2009): 477–502.

Raphael, Steven, and Michael A. Stoll. *Modest Progress: The Narrowing Spatial Mismatch Between Blacks and Jobs in the 1990s.* Washington, D.C.: Brookings Institution Center on Urban and Metropolitan Policy, 2002.

Raymond, Elora, Kyungsoon Wang, and Dan Immergluck. "Race and Uneven Recovery: Neighborhood Home Value Trajectories in Atlanta Before and After the Housing Crisis." *Housing Studies* 31, no. 3 (2016): 324–39.

Reardon, Sean F., Kendra Bischoff, Ann Owens, and Joseph B. Townsend. "Has Income Segregation Really Increased? Bias and Bias Correction in Sample-Based Segregation Estimates." *Demography* 55, no. 6 (2018): 2129–60.

Reina, Vincent J. "Do Small Area Fair Market Rents Reduce Racial Disparities in the Voucher Program?" *Housing Policy Debate* (2019): 1–15.

Reina, Vincent, Raphael Bostic, and Arthur Acolin. "Section 8 Vouchers and Rent Limits: Do Small Area Fair Market Rent Limits Increase Access to Opportunity Neighborhoods?" *Housing Policy Debate* 29, no. 1 (2019): 44–61.

Reina, Vincent J., Jake Wegmann, and Erick Guerra. "Are Location Affordability and Fair Housing on a Collision Course? Race, Transportation Costs, and the Siting of Subsidized Housing." *Cityscape* 21, no. 1 (2019): 125–42.

Reina, Vincent J., and Ben Winter. "Safety Net? The Use of Vouchers When a Place-Based Rental Subsidy Ends." *Urban Studies* 56, no. 10 (2019): 2092–111.

Rosenbaum, James E. "Changing the Geography of Opportunity by Expanding Residential Choice: Lessons from the Gautreaux Program." *Housing Policy Debate* 6, no. 1 (1995): 231–69.

Rubinowitz, Leonard S., and James E. Rosenbaum. *Crossing the Class and Color Lines: From Public Housing to White Suburbia.* Chicago: University of Chicago Press, 2000.

Rugh, Jacob S., and Douglas S. Massey. "Racial Segregation and the American Foreclosure Crisis." *American Sociological Review* 75, no. 5 (2010): 629–51.

Rupasingha, Anil, and Kyungsoon Wang. "Access to Capital and Small Business Growth: Evidence from CRA Loans Data." *Annals of Regional Science* 59, no. 1 (2017): 15–41.

Sahasranaman, Anand, and Henrik Jensen. "Cooperative Dynamics of Neighborhood Economic Status in Cities." *PLOS One* 12, no. 8 (2017): 1–15.

Samila, Sampsa, and Olav Sorenson. "Community and Capital in Entrepreneurship and Economic Growth." *American Sociological Review* 82, no. 4 (2017): 770–95.

Sampson, Robert J. *Great American City: Chicago and the Enduring Neighborhood Effect.* Chicago: University of Chicago Press, 2012.

Sampson, Robert J., and Jeffrey D. Morenoff. "Durable Inequality: Spatial Dynamics, Social Processes and the Persistence of Poverty in Chicago Neighborhoods." In *Poverty Traps,* edited by Samuel Bowles, Steve Durlauf, and Karla Hoff, 176–203. Princeton, NJ: Princeton University Press, 2006.

Shapiro, Thomas, Tatjana Meschede, and Sam Osoro. "The Roots of the Widening Racial Wealth Gap: Explaining the Black-White Economic Divide." Waltham, MA: The Institute on Asseta and Social Policy Research and Policy Brief, 2013.

Sharkey, Patrick. "Spatial Segmentation and the Black Middle Class." *American Journal of Sociology* 119, no. 4 (2014): 903–54.

———. *Stuck in Place: Urban Neighborhoods and the End of Progress Toward Racial Equality.* Chicago: University of Chicago Press, 2013.

South, Eugenia C., Michelle C. Kondo, Rose A. Cheney, and Charles C. Branas. "Neighborhood Blight, Stress, and Health: A Walking Trial of Urban Greening and Ambulatory Heart Rate." *American Journal of Public Health* 105, no. 5 (2015): 909–13.

Taylor, Dorceta. *Toxic Communities: Environmental Racism, Industrial Pollution, and Residential Mobility.* New York: New York University Press, 2014.

Western, Bruce, and Christopher Wildeman. "The Black Family and Mass Incarceration." *Annals of the American Academy of Political and Social Science* 621, no. 1 (2009): 221–42.

Urban Institute. "Nine Charts about Wealth Inequality in America (Updated)." Accessed August 6, 2019. http://apps.urban.org/features/wealth-inequality-charts/.

U.S. Bureau of Labor Statistics. *The Employment Situation—May 2018.* Press release, 2018. https://www.bls.gov/news.release/archives/empsit_06012018.pdf.

U.S. Department of Commerce. *Income and Poverty in the United States: 2016.* Current Population Report, September 2017. https://census.gov/content/dam/Census/library/publications/2017/demo/P60-259.pdf.

U.S. Department of Housing and Urban Development. *Moving to Opportunity for Fair Housing Demonstration Program: Final Impacts Evaluation.* Office of Policy Development and Research, November 2011. https://www.huduser.gov/publications/pdf/MTOFHD_fullreport_v2.pdf.

———. *U.S. Housing Market Conditions: 1st Quarter 2018 National Housing Market Summary.* Office of Policy Development and Research, June 2018. https://www.huduser.gov/portal/ushmc/quarterly_commentary.html#undefined.

Zonta, Michela. *Racial Disparities in Home Appreciation Implications of the Racially Segmented Housing Market for African Americans' Equity Building and the Enforcement of Fair Housing Policies.* Washington, D.C.: Center for American Progress, 2019.

CHAPTER 5

The Fair Housing Act's Original Sin

Administrative Discretion and the Persistence of Segregation

Nestor M. Davidson and Eduardo M. Peñalver

Introduction

From the outset fifty years ago, the Fair Housing Act (FHA) has had a fundamental imbalance in its dual statutory missions. The FHA—enacted as Title VIII of the Civil Rights Act of 1968—familiarly bars discrimination in housing generally, as well as targeting lending, brokerage activities, and other aspects of the housing market that were particularly problematic at the time of the FHA's passage. Antidiscrimination was—and remains—crucial, but the Congress that enacted the FHA had broader ambition. That Congress sought to combat residential segregation and the dire concentration of poverty by race and ethnicity that was at the heart of the urban unrest of the 1960s. In the FHA, Congress recognized that the persistence of what people at the time called ghettos created distinct harms that required federal intervention to remedy, much as the federal government had long been intimately involved in the creation and isolation of these communities.

The FHA's integration mandate echoes in a sweeping purpose statement and in core liability provisions that courts have interpreted to apply not only to acts of discrimination but also to actions or policies that perpetuate segregation. Congress, however, delegated the FHA's integration mission most directly to the U.S. Department of Housing and Urban Development (HUD) and other federal agencies, charging them with the obligation to administer housing and urban development programs "in a manner affirmatively to further the purposes" of the FHA. Courts have made clear that this statutory language means that it is not enough to combat the pathologies of the private market or even for the federal government to refrain from actions that foster segregation. Rather, the FHA charges the federal government with the task of affirmatively bending its resources and regulatory power to "assist in ending . . . segregation, to the point where the supply of genuinely open housing increases."[1]

The challenge—also from the outset of the FHA—has been that the institutional structures and legal tools that Congress established to advance the FHA's affirmative integration mandate rely largely on a discretionary agency apparatus. As to antidiscrimination, the FHA and later amendments created mechanisms for individual redress and facilitated private litigation to combat discrimination—hamstrung originally and imperfect still, but ultimately not subject to agency control. By contrast, the FHA's mandate to directly advance integration and reduce racial concentrations of poverty were to be embodied in a panoply of grant conditions, delegated planning mechanisms, project siting factors, and the like—all within HUD's discretion as a functional matter. It was entirely predictable—perhaps inevitable—that this aspect of the FHA's legal commands would be inconsistently embraced as political priorities and perspectives shifted from administration to administration. Indeed, what is known as "affirmatively furthering fair housing" has been mostly ignored in the FHA's first fifty years. And recent attempts to give life to the mandate during the Obama administration are now being unwound by the Trump administration.

At the milestone half-century mark of the Fair Housing Act, is it possible to imagine an alternative path to make good on the FHA's directive that the federal government directly combat segregation and racially concentrated poverty? Certainly, the mixed history of judicially enforceable affirmative mandates in fair housing, which have been seen at the state level, albeit rarely, augur a note of caution about the comparative institutional competence of courts to manage complex systems. But more modestly opening up paths for engagement by advocates and the broader public in advancing the FHA's affirmative mandate—as HUD had begun to facilitate in recent years—as well as more tools of private enforcement could lessen the challenge posed by reliance on administrative discretion and the inconsistent commitment that attend the ever-fraught political economy of policies that address segregation and integration.

In short, deep institutional failures have marked the FHA's broadest ambitions in its first fifty years, even as the need for the FHA's affirmative integration mission remains urgent. It may be hard enough to preserve what progress has been made in advancing fair housing, with doctrinal challenges looming and a current administration that together warrant deep concern. Broader social trends only underscore the challenges facing fair housing, as widening economic inequality interacts with an increasing tendency among Americans to segregate by income.[2] Within the housing market, these trends combine with racial wealth and income disparities to further entrench our racially segregated residential landscape. A fundamental reckoning is needed if the FHA is finally to live up to its full meaning over its next fifty years.

The Imbalanced Institutional Structure of the FHA's Dual Missions

The Fair Housing Act's dual missions emerge clearly from the FHA's text, structure, context, and legislative history, all of which paint a consistent picture of ambitious aims and significantly imbalanced institutional means. The FHA, of course, instantiates well-known antidiscrimination mandates, but also has distinct, direct statutory focus on combating residential segregation and promoting integration. These goals intersect to the extent that creating a housing market free of invidious bias is a means to eroding segregation. But the FHA did not merely rely on the promise of housing choice to achieve its broader ambition.[3]

The FHA announces its sweep at the outset, declaring it "the policy of the United States to provide, within constitutional limitations, for fair housing throughout the United States,"[4] although the FHA did not actually define "fair housing." To understand what Congress meant by that, the context for the FHA, the last of the major federal civil rights acts of the 1960s to pass, is critical to remember. The period between 1964—when Congress began the Johnson-era project of transforming civil rights with the passage of the Civil Rights Act—and 1968 was a period of significant urban unrest. Riots in Los Angeles in 1965, Chicago in 1966, and Newark and Detroit in 1967 were only the most visible examples, and presaged the spasm of urban chaos that erupted in D.C., Chicago, Baltimore, and other cities across the country following the assassination of Martin Luther King Jr. on April 4, 1968. Members of Congress were painfully aware of this turmoil, the underlying segregation-focused causes of which had been laid out in the *Report of the National Advisory Commission on Civil Disorders*—the Kerner Report—in February 1968, while the FHA was making its way through Congress.[5] A fierce urgency and clear sense of crisis over the imperative to foster integration and eliminate racially concentrated areas of poverty faced the Congress that enacted the Fair Housing Act—indeed, it was arguably only that sense of crisis that finally broke determined, largely Southern, opposition (Massey 2015).

The FHA's legislative history reveals a correspondingly broad ambition, with the framers of the FHA making plain during legislative debates that it was not enough for the law to bar discrimination, as important as that was. As then-senator Walter F. Mondale, the FHA's cosponsor, put it, the FHA's ultimate intent was "to replace the ghettos 'by truly integrated and balanced living patterns.'"[6] This reflected the recognition that "where a family lives, where it is allowed to live, is inextricably bound up with better education, better jobs, economic motivation, and good living conditions."[7] Indeed, as the Second Circuit explained in an important early FHA case, *Otero v. New York City Housing Authority*, the FHA sought to achieve nothing less than "open, integrated residential housing patterns and [to] prevent the increase of segregation, in ghettos, of racial groups whose lack of opportunity the Act was designed to combat."[8]

The FHA's antidiscrimination mission is clear in its text, promising a transformation of the residential market. The FHA thus made it illegal to "refuse to sell or rent after the making of a bona fide offer, or to refuse to negotiate for the sale or rental of . . . a dwelling"[9] on the basis of a protected characteristic, and included a general prohibition against "otherwise mak[ing] unavailable or deny[ing]" housing,[10] or varying "terms, conditions, or privileges" or "the provision of services or facilities"[11] of housing. While this language sweeps remarkably broadly, the FHA also targeted specific activities, reflecting particular pathologies in the housing market at the time.[12]

Courts have interpreted the FHA's core liability provisions to advance the FHA's integration mandate as well. In a series of cases, courts have held that in addition to barring discrimination, the FHA distinctly targets practices or policies that cause "harm to the community generally by the perpetuation of segregation."[13] These cases have typically involved disparate impact claims—claims that rely on the discriminatory effects of seemingly neutral actions, rather than intentional discrimination—against local governments for exclusionary practices[14] (Schwemm 2017; Nier 1999: 647–52), and the Supreme Court recently acknowledged the continuing viability of this aspect of the FHA's antisegregation directives.[15]

Provisions in the FHA that address Congress's integration objectives most directly can be found largely in two sections.[16] The first directs the Secretary of Housing and Urban Development to "administer the programs and activities relating to housing and urban development in a manner affirmatively to further the policies of this subchapter."[17] A related provision that has been largely ignored over the past half-century[18] applied this same "affirmatively furthering fair housing" (or AFFH) mandate to *all* aspect of the federal government's housing and urban policy.[19]

While this text is spare, courts have made the import of the language clear: by 1968, members of Congress understood that it was not enough to bar discrimination or refrain from contributing to segregation—the federal government had an obligation to take affirmative steps to foster integration. As the Second Circuit in *Shannon v. HUD*[20] traced Congress's progression to fair housing, the 1949 Housing Act arguably gave HUD latitude to "act neutrally on the issue of racial segregation";[21] the Civil Rights Act of 1964 then required HUD "to prevent discrimination in housing resulting from" federal investments; but by 1968, Congress understood that HUD must "affirmatively promote fair housing."[22] These related directives mean that federal investments and other programs were to have been bent to the task of advancing fair housing beyond what antidiscrimination itself could accomplish.[23]

The FHA, at the structural level, however, created a stark institutional imbalance between the tools it set forth to implement each of its dual missions. The FHA and subsequent amendments created an elaborate—if often criticized—set of enforcement mechanisms for the act's antidiscrimination mandate.[24] Private parties can initiate administrative claims and pursue private litigation, as challenging as that can be in individual cases. But the FHA left it to HUD to determine how to deploy the apparatus of the federal government to affirmatively further fair housing. Courts have made clear that the FHA requires HUD, at a minimum, to consider the effects of federal investments on segregation and racial concentration of poverty.[25] HUD has, in very limited ways, tried to embody this requirement, for example by creating "site and neighborhood" standards for a handful of programs.[26] On the whole, however, HUD has taken few steps to embrace the FHA's affirmative mandate.

The fact that so much of the implementation of the AFFH mandate was left to HUD's discretion has over the history of the FHA's implementation unsurprisingly left a trail of great inconsistency, and mostly paths not pursued. When George Romney became HUD secretary in 1969, he advanced a program called "Open Communities" that would have conditioned HUD funding on increasing housing opportunity (Massey 2015: 577; Roisman

2007: 387). Romney's general counsel opined that "HUD had an obligation to consider the extent to which its every action 'will in fact open up new, non-segregated housing opportunities that will contribute to decreasing the effects of past housing discrimination'" (Roisman 2007: 387). A test case of this new policy came when Romney proposed to withhold a $3 million urban renewal grant from Warren, Michigan, a white suburb of Detroit, leading to a firestorm of protest (Roisman 2007: 387). The Nixon Administration refused to back Romney, effectively killing the program in 1970 (Massey 2015: 577). It would be decades before HUD would put any sustained effort into AFFH.

In the 1990s, HUD again tried to revive a comprehensive approach to the AFFH obligation, drafting a Fair Housing Planning Guide and requiring grantees to conduct an "analysis of impediments to fair housing choice." But, as the General Accountability Office found, this process proved ineffective, with HUD not reviewing most analyses and grantees rarely taking the obligation seriously.[27]

In 2015, after a seven-year process of development, HUD finalized a rule codifying a new approach to AFFH and attempting, for the first time since the earliest days of the FHA, to give real depth and consequences to the AFFH mandate. The rule required that HUD grantees, at the risk of losing funding, engage in a new planning process to understand and proactively address fair housing concerns, guided by a detailed HUD template and HUD-provided data.[28]

The new—and, as discussed later, perhaps stillborn in the current administration[29]—AFFH process sought to sidestep many of the most contentious issues that had hampered prior efforts to infuse federal housing and urban policy with an affirmative mandate to reduce segregation and combat racially concentrated areas of poverty. The rule's planning process mandated no specific outcomes, instead simply requiring grantees—cities, counties, states, public housing authorities, and others—to reflect on what the data reveal about historical patterns and barriers to fair housing choice. The rule then required a process of prioritization and grantee-driven decision-making to alleviate the fair housing conditions identified. The new process contained no obligation to prioritize, for example, mobility over community revitalization, nor any uniform metric of policy choices. To the extent possible, the AFFH planning framework was designed to surface information and facilitate an intentional discourse about solutions.

The Fair Housing Act set out to change the fundamental norms of the housing market, but members of the Congress that passed the FHA clearly understood that removing housing barriers would never be enough to over-come the bitter legacy of segregation and racially concentrated poverty. Congress, however, vested implementation of the FHA's broader ambitions in an agency that despite the clear direction of the early case law has rarely fully embraced this mission. For reasons explored in the next section, the FHA's affirmative imperative remains urgent at this milestone juncture.

The FHA's Continuing Integration Imperative

Fifty years after the FHA's passage, patterns of segregation, immigration, race and ethnicity have grown significantly more complex, for a variety of reasons, including the immigration reform that President Johnson ushered in in 1965, which contributed to creating a much more diverse country. But the basic challenges of racial segregation and racially concentrated poverty that animated Congress in 1968 have not abated. Arguably, there are fundamental structural reasons that suggest that mere neutrality—eliminating housing discrimination, if that could be done—is simply not enough to overcome generations of de jure segregationist policies at every level of government and ongoing dynamics that tend to overcome individual preferences for some level of integration.

Despite the dramatic legal changes ushered in by the enactment of the FHA, our residential landscape remains deeply divided along racial lines (Clark 2009). "Segregation of blacks from whites remains in the moderate to high range in most large metropolitan areas, and whites' levels of residential separation from fast-growing Asian and Latino populations have remained steady or increased in recent decades" (Crowder, Pais, and South 2012: 325). Although levels of segregation have broadly decreased since 1968, the progress has been slow and uneven, with many metropolitan areas seeing little or no improvement (Massey and Tannen 2015).

Social scientists have offered a number of hypotheses to explain this persistent segregation. Enduring racial disparities in income and wealth can help to explain some of the existing segregation, but the evidence suggests that economic inequality is a relatively small part of the story (Quillian 2002: 202; Jargowsky 2016: 21). Housing markets also tend to be relatively "sticky," with demographic patterns that can be very slow to overcome.

Discriminatory practices in the private housing market offer another explanation for continuing segregation. Notwithstanding the prohibition of discriminatory practices under the FHA, studies employing paired testers continue to find significant discrimination against African Americans, Latinos, and Asians in private housing markets (Dawkins 2004: 393; a study in 2000 found whites treated more favorably 22 percent of the time in rental market tests and 17 percent of the time in sales market tests). But the incidence of discrimination has declined over time, and the forms that disparate treatment tends to take today (practices like showing fewer units to people of color or steering renters and buyers to neighborhoods where their own race predominates) are less exclusionary than the practices that predominated prior to the FHA's enactment (Dawkins 2004). Some scholars estimate that discriminatory practices and economic inequality—combined—account for about half of observed residential segregation (Quillian 2002: 201).

A third theory for the persistence of racial segregation in housing looks to the preferences of housing market participants. First suggested by Nobel Prize–winning economist Thomas Schelling in a series of publications in the late 1960s, this approach posits that segregated housing patterns can emerge from the uncoordinated market activity of individual market participants with particular preferences about the racial composition of their neighborhoods. Indeed, Schelling provocatively suggested, stark segregation can result from decentralized market behavior even where no individual market participant prefers to live in a segregated neighborhood.

Schelling proposed two hypothetical models of participant preferences. In the so-called "checkerboard" model, Schelling compared a neighborhood to a checkerboard randomly populated with equal numbers of pennies and dimes, as well as some empty spaces. Each coin has up to eight neighbors. The coins have preferences to be surrounded by a minimum threshold of similar coins. Dimes want at least half (4) of their neighbors to be dimes. And pennies want at least a third (2) of their neighbors to be pennies. Coins surrounded by neighbors that violate that preference will move to a square that more closely matches their preferences. The coins will continue to move until no coin's neighbors exceed the threshold. Even in scenarios where coins have a preference (or tolerance) for some degree of integration (e.g., a preference not to have a majority of one's neighbors be of a different kind), Schelling found that the result of his model was a pattern of extreme segregation (Schelling 2006: 147–55).

In a second model, Schelling assumed two populations of different sizes, each composed of individuals with different preferences for neighborhood composition, ranging from more tolerant to less tolerant of neighborhood diversity. Schelling posited that under such circumstances, the only stable equilibria would be extreme segregation, even where very few individuals actually preferred that outcome (Schelling 2006: 157–66). As he put it, "the difficulty is that any such mixture attracts outsiders, more of one color or both colors, eventually more of just one color, so that one color begins to dominate numerically. A few individuals of the opposite color then leave; as they do, they further reduce the numerical status of those of their own color who stay behind. A few more are dissatisfied, and they leave; the minority becomes even smaller, and cumulatively the process causes evacuation of them all" (160–61).

Social scientists have studied both the robustness of Schelling's models—the range of conditions across which they would predict segregated outcomes—as well as their empirical validity. Schelling's models have proved to be powerful on both fronts. Scholars have found the preference-based model to predict extreme segregation even where residents have a strict preference for perfect integration, where all individuals prefer to live in mixed neighborhoods, where residents have heterogeneous preferences, and where neighborhoods take a wide variety of forms (Aydinonat 2007: 441).

Moreover, repeated surveys of market participants of various backgrounds have found widespread and persistent preferences regarding neighborhood racial composition. Summarizing the findings of several surveys, Lincoln Quillian says that "most Whites say they prefer neighborhoods that are less than 30% Black. African Americans, on the other hand, strongly prefer neighborhoods that are [at least] 50% Black" (2002: 199). Market behavior, rather than survey responses, evinces even lower thresholds of tolerance among white residents. Whites tend to search for housing in neighborhoods that are—on average—whiter than what their survey responses describe as their preferences (Havekes, Bader, and Krysan 2016: 115). Quillian observes that "Whites move out of tracts with more than 10% of their population Black at a very rapid pace" (Quillian 2002: 209).

Not all members of different racial and ethnic groups express the same preferences. African Americans with higher income and higher levels of education, for example, are more open to living in neighborhoods with a smaller percentage of residents of the same race. They also have greater residential mobility through which to express their preferences. Similarly, whites with higher levels of education are more tolerant of racial diversity in their neighborhoods. Whites who endorse negative stereotypes are "more likely to flee integrated neighborhoods and less likely to move into integrated neighborhoods." But Whites who have interacted with African Americans have a greater preference for neighborhood diversity (Dawkins 2004: 389; Clark 2009: 342–43).

Although there has been a significant increase in white tolerance for integration since the enactment of the FHA, the dynamics of Schelling's models—coupled with data on actual resident preferences not to be a minority in one's own neighborhood—support the conclusion that, in the absence of other factors, such as economic inequality and discrimination, segregated patterns are likely to be both pervasive and (once established) persistent. Considering the implications of Schelling's model, Quillian concludes that "fully curtailing segregation in housing . . . will require going beyond combating discriminatory housing market practices to somewhat check the collapse of White housing demand in neighborhoods with more than a few Blacks" (Quillian 2002: 222).

The Schelling preference model's prediction of the circumstances in which segregation will persist is consistent with empirical observations of actual preferences. And the forces described by the Schelling model are—in turn—additive to the other forces that contribute to segregated housing patterns, such as continued housing discrimination and widening economic inequality. The combined force of the complementary factors pushing in the direction of the segregated status quo confirms the wisdom of the FHA's endorsement of affirmative government action to combat residential segregation. As Schelling predicts, segregation emerges from the operation of hidden-hand forces that yield neighborhoods that embody almost no one's actual preferences. Racially segregated residential neighborhoods, therefore, reflect a kind of market failure that calls out for government intervention to foster a richer variety of neighborhood types, bringing the demographics of neighborhoods in America's metropolitan areas into closer alignment with the more integrated residential communities that most people say they would prefer. This, in fact, is exactly what the Fair Housing Act called for fifty years ago.

Administration and the Failure of Affirmatively Furthering

As urgent as it remains for the federal government to take robust affirmative steps to remedy the legacy and ongoing reality of segregation fifty years after Congress mandated such direct intervention, deep institutional challenges persist for this aspect of the FHA's mission. Ideally, HUD would embrace new technology and emerging data analytic capacities to revive in a more sophisticated way the early concept of evaluating all federal urban investments and policies in light of whether they will tend to increase or decrease segregation, foster or combat concentrated poverty on the basis of race (Davidson 2017). HUD—along with other federal agencies that have significant housing and urban development programs, such as the Internal Revenue Service in its oversight of the federal housing tax-credit program—relies on a network of tens of thousands of grantees, from states and local governments, to public housing authorities, to private developers. By and large, the overwhelming majority of these investments are made without adequate consideration of their effects or a long-term framework for evaluating their cumulative impacts. HUD's 2015 AFFH regulation would have created a planning proxy for this kind of focused, decisional analytical approach, and it held some promise as a first step back to the path that Governor Romney attempted to put the agency on so early in the life of the FHA.[30]

Perhaps the planning mandate HUD had developed in the Obama administration was the best the agency could have done politically, given widespread opposition to any federal step that hints at directly reducing segregation.[31] Even that mandate—seven years in the making—is now threatened. In early 2018 HUD first announced and then (facing litigation) withdrew a notice delaying implementation of the AFFH rule,[32] and later, again facing litigation, announced its intent to revisit the rule altogether.

In January 2020, HUD issued a proposed new rule for affirmatively furthering fair housing.[33] The proposed rule begins by stating that the 2015 approach was too onerous. It then goes on to offer an alternative that amounts to nothing less than a gutting of the mandate. One particularly notable change the proposed rule would make is to the definition of what it means "affirmatively to further" fair housing. The Obama administration rule defined that concept as "taking meaningful actions that, taken together, address significant disparities in housing needs and in access to opportunity, replacing segregated living patterns with truly integrated and balanced living patterns, transforming racially and ethnically concentrated areas of poverty into areas of opportunity, and fostering and maintaining compliance with civil rights and fair housing laws."[34] The proposed new rule would change that definition in a way that would collapse it into the FHA's nondiscrimination goal:

HUD proposes changing the definition of AFFH to "advancing fair housing choice within the program participant's control or influence." HUD is proposing a definition of "fair housing choice" to be allowing "individuals and families [to] have the opportunity and options to live where they choose, within their means, without unlawful discrimination related to race, color, religion, sex, familial status, national origin, or disability."[35]

In other words, whereas the Obama rule followed the FHA's original intention to affirmatively foster racially integrated neighborhoods as a policy goal, the proposed rule focuses on ensuring freedom of residential choice, without regard to the patterns that result. The proposed rule makes this intention clear when it says the following:

> The revised definition would make it clear that fair housing is based on fair housing choice. Fair housing involves combatting discrimination across all the classes protected by the Fair Housing Act: color, religion, sex, disability, familial status, and national origin. Finally, the revised AFFH definition would emphasize that a jurisdiction can AFFH in a variety of ways, according to the needs and means of the local community.[36]

This proposed shift again underscores what is so challenging about leaving the FHA's affirmative mandate to agency discretion.

At the fulcrum point of the FHA's fiftieth anniversary—as we look ahead to the FHA's next fifty years—it is worth considering paths not taken to advance the FHA's broader ambitions of affirmatively furthering integration and combating the racial concentration of poverty. Statutorily, more could have been done to set the institutional terms of and conditions for federal housing and urban development funding, in the form of explicit standards; mandatory processes; and, perhaps most important, some clear form of meaningful private right of action to enforce this crucial aspect of the FHA. There are obvious problems with relying on the judiciary to give content to an open-ended affirmative mandate—especially one that applies to literally tens of thousands of program participants in significantly different situations across the country. But Congress at a minimum could have provided mechanisms for advocates to ensure that it would not be left so open-endedly to the vicissitudes of administrative discretion to make AFFH work. It is admittedly a hard time to contemplate more creative approaches, given our current political environment, but without trying, we are likely to return the FHA's deepest ambitions to their long silence.

Legal Threats Looming at the Fair Housing Act's Anniversary

From a legal perspective, then, what lessons do the persistence of segregation and the underlying dynamics driving that persistence suggest at this anniversary moment for the next half-century of the FHA's implementation? Despite genuine progress on many fronts since 1968, deep challenges remain and, fundamentally, we need to match with much greater force the ongoing animating needs for the FHA to the legal tools the FHA and its implementing regulations make possible. At the same time, we also need to be wary of some jurisprudential developments that threaten to undermine the tentative progress made to date under the FHA.

Perhaps the most significant jurisprudential threat to a fully realized embrace of the FHA's dual missions is skepticism at the Supreme Court about the continued viability of race-conscious policymaking.[37] Although the Supreme Court affirmed the availability of disparate impact liability under the FHA in *Texas Department of Housing and Community Affairs v. Inclusive Communities Project, Inc.*,[38] the Court also signaled concern about approaches under the FHA that emphasize race. As the Court put it, "difficult questions might arise if disparate-impact liability under the FHA caused race to be used and considered in a pervasive and explicit manner to justify governmental or private actions that, in fact, tend to perpetuate race-based considerations rather than move beyond them."[39]

This is part of a larger trend across civil rights jurisprudence expressing doubt about the continued constitutional viability of race as a factor in policy, even when employed in a manner designed to combat private discrimination or its continuing impacts. As the Court has insisted in a broad range of legal contexts, *any* considerations of race must meet the most exacting standard of judicial review, "strict scrutiny," meaning that it must be shown to be strictly necessary to the achievement of a compelling government purpose.[40] The concern among some on the Court is that even well-intentioned use of racial categories perpetuates racial thinking. As Justice Roberts put it in one opinion for a plurality of the Court, "the way to stop discrimination on the basis of race is to stop discriminating on the basis of race."[41]

It is still not apparent how this shifting constitutional landscape will settle out, and much will depend on the Supreme Court in the near future. It seems clear that any kind of hard racial quota would not be acceptable to the current Supreme Court[42]—nor are they necessarily appealing.[43] Justice Kennedy, the author of the *Inclusive Communities* decision and a frequent swing voter on cases raising contentious civil rights issues, is no longer on the Supreme Court. Justice Kennedy's comfort with at least *some* race consciousness in policy-making in the context of higher education did seem to leave open the conceptual possibility that there might be room for policy-makers to take race into account in some ways to affirmatively promote residential integration, perhaps even by acting in ways that (if coupled with discriminatory intent) would violate the FHA.[44]

For instance, a developer or government entity might intentionally site low-income housing in an all-white neighborhood to foster racial integration. The use of amenities with racially disparate appeal presents another possible (race-conscious) tool for achieving targeted racial proportions (Strahilevitz 2006). As Lior Strahilevitz has provocatively suggested, locating a golf-course community in a predominantly African American community, might similarly be seen as promoting residential integration (2006: 486). A developer might consciously selectively advertise a development (using certain periodicals or using photos containing certain racial groups) to make it more likely to attract a more diverse and racially balanced pool of tenants even though doing so with an exclusionary purpose would violate the FHA. These sorts of indirect strategies fall short of quotas and yet involve the conscious use of race in order to achieve the FHA's goal of residential integration.

The constitutional justification for such race-conscious state action would proceed by way of an analogy to affirmative action in higher education. In the higher education context, the Supreme Court has repeatedly endorsed Justice Powell's conclusion in *Bakke* that "the attainment of a diverse student body . . . is a constitutionally permissible goal for an institution of higher education"[45] that would justify its use of race as a factor in admissions. The use of race is justified—not on the basis of abstract principles of racial justice, historical remediation, or balancing—but because of the instrumental value of a diverse student body to the institution's educational goals. As the Court has put it, enrolling a diverse student body "promotes cross-racial understanding, helps to break down racial stereotypes, and enables students to

better understand persons of different races. . . . Student body diversity promotes learning outcomes, and better prepares students for an increasingly
diverse workforce and society."[46] But, while acknowledging the value of diversity for schools, the Court has also said that the school's use of race must
not be the sole object of the school's attention but part of a holistic admissions process. Moreover, the use of race must be narrowly tailored to achieve
goals that could not otherwise be accomplished through means that do not
consider race.[47]

As the Supreme Court acknowledged in *Fisher II*, in a racially plural democracy, the learning outcomes made possible by student body diversity are
important for social stability and—for that reason—are a compelling interest for the state to pursue. In the housing context, the argument would be
that diverse neighborhoods are similarly instrumental to achieving goods
that are socially valuable. If, as the Schelling model and the other explanations
of segregation's persistence suggest, we cannot effectively counter existing
residential segregation without employing policies that take race into account,
an application of the *Fisher* rationale in the housing context might justify
narrowly targeted race-conscious policies aimed at nudging neighborhoods
in the direction of greater racial diversity.

One challenge for this approach in the housing context is marshalling evidence that residential integration generates the same sorts of social goods
that diversity helps to achieve in the context of higher education. Importantly,
the analogy to *Fisher* suggests that the kind of evidence that supporters of
race-conscious housing policy need is evidence of important social gains (e.g.,
for the city or broader polity as a whole) from neighborhood diversity, as opposed to improved outcomes for the specific beneficiaries of those policies.[48]
The social science on the broader social impacts of neighborhood diversity
is notoriously complex and conflicting. Robert Putnam has famously argued
that neighborhood diversity undermines social trust and civic engagement.[49]
But his work has been heartily criticized.[50] It is likely that neighborhood diversity is just one ingredient that affects residents' attitudes differently depending on a range of other contextual factors.[51] More research is needed.

We are not making a strong claim about the state of the social science or
the underlying social dynamics. Our point is simply that the use of narrowly
tailored race-conscious policies would seem to fall within the ambit of the
Supreme Court's reasoning in *Fisher*. But to fit within the *Fisher* paradigm,
the policies would need to be holistic in their approach and represent good-
faith efforts to achieve neighborhood diversity in pursuit of the sorts of broad

social goals (racial understanding, the breakdown of stereotypes) that the Court has already endorsed for institutions of higher learning.

Of course, Justice Kennedy's departure from the Supreme Court throws all of this into doubt. The remaining conservatives on the Court have been categorical in their rejection of race-conscious government action.[52] The balance of opinion rests on the views of the Court's newest justice, Brett Kavanaugh. As a judge on the Court of Appeals, Kavanaugh never had an opportunity to write an opinion addressing affirmative action. But public comments he has made over the years in speeches and writings suggest to some observers that his views are closer to those of Chief Justice Roberts than to Justice Kennedy's.[53] A rejection of Kennedy's nuanced approach in favor of a more categorical, color-blind approach to race under the Fourteenth Amendment could hobble attempts to reckon with the reality of segregation and the well-documented history of the government's role in creating current conditions (Rothstein 2017).

Conclusion

At the fiftieth anniversary of the FHA, fair housing law faces a nation that is more racially complex, with signs of progress that are undeniable. But it is increasingly clear that the national imperative to remedy the terrible legacy and continuing reality of segregation cannot be achieved without seriously reexamining the legal and institutional tools Congress created in the FHA. That reckoning is coming at a moment of political polarization and a retrenchment in the judiciary that may make even the limited promise of AFFH harder to accomplish—a sobering sentiment with which to mark such a significant milestone. It is more critical than ever to look ahead and seek change for the FHA's next fifty years.

Notes

1. *NAACP, Bos. Chapter v. HUD*, 817 F.2d 149, 154 (1st Cir. 1987).

2. See Rothwell and Massey (2010).

3. These overlapping goals have mostly been consonant in their implementation over the past fifty years, but at times internal tensions between these two aspects of the FHA have surfaced. This was perhaps most pronounced in the Second Circuit's two-to-one decision that the owners of Brooklyn's Starrett City, the largest housing development in the country, with forty-six high-rises containing nearly six thousand apartments, could not screen applicants

based on race in order to maintain an integrated community. See *United States v. Starrett City Assocs.*, 840 F.2d 1096 (2d Cir. 1988).

4. 42 U.S.C. § 3601.

5. As the Kerner Report concluded, in the language of its era, "what white Americans have never fully understood—but what the Negro can never forget—is that white society is deeply implicated in the ghetto. White institutions created it, white institutions maintain it, and white society condones it." United States National Advisory Commission on Civil Disorders, *Report of the National Advisory Commission on Civil Disorders* 2 (1968).

6. *Trafficante v. Metro. Life Ins. Co.*, 409 U.S. 205, 211 (1972) (quoting 114 Cong. Rec. 3422 (statement of Sen. Mondale)).

7. 114 Cong. Rec. 2276–2707 (1968); see also ibid. at 9616 (statement of Rep. McCormack) ("We must turn our face away from a course of segregation and separation").

8. 484 F.2d 1122, 1134 (2d Cir. 1973).

9. 42 U.S.C. § 3601(a).

10. Ibid. The FHA began with protections for race, color, religion, and national origin, but Congress has added new categories of protection in the intervening decades: sex in 1974, in the Housing and Community Development Act, P.L. 93-383, and disability and familial status in 1988, in the Fair Housing Amendments Act, P.L. 100-430.

11. § 3601(b).

12. These more targeted provisions include a prohibition on discriminatory communication or false statements about housing availability, ibid. at §§ 3601(c), (d); a provision to prevent blockbusting, the practice of real estate agents scaring white owners into selling by invoking the specter of minorities moving into the neighborhood, ibid. at § 3601(e); and separate sections barring discrimination in a range of services related to residential real estate, including lending, selling, brokering, and appraising. Ibid. at §§ 3605; 3606.

13. *Huntington Branch NAACP v. Town of Huntington*, 844 F.2d 926, 937 (2d Cir. 1988), aff'd per curiam, 488 U.S. 15 (1988) (citing *Metro. Hous. Dev. Corp. v. Village of Arlington Heights*, 558 F.2d 1283 (7th Cir. 1977)). *Arlington Heights* is generally understood to have set the framework for perpetuation of segregation claims, drawing on earlier cases such as *United States v. City of Black Jack*, 508 F.2d 1179 (8th Cir. 1974), and *Kennedy Park Homes Assoc., Inc. v. City of Lackawanna*, 436 F.2d 108 (2d Cir. 1970).

14. See *Tex. Dept. of Hous. & Cmty. Affairs v. Inclusive Communities Project, Inc.*, 135 S. Ct. 2507, 2522 (2015) ("The FHA is not an instrument to force housing authorities to reorder their priorities. Rather, the FHA aims to ensure that those priorities can be achieved without arbitrarily creating discriminatory effects or perpetuating segregation.").

15. See ibid. Relatedly, in the earliest FHA case that the Supreme Court decided, the Court held in 1972 that the consequences of segregation constituted an injury suffice to grant "standing" (the right to sue) to private parties under the FHA. The suit had been brought by white residents of an apartment complex who argued that a landlord's actions deprived them of the benefits of integrated living, and the Court agreed that this claim was cognizable under the FHA. *Trafficante v. Metro. Life Ins. Co.*, 409 U.S. 205, 209–10 (1972) (noting that "injury to existing [white] tenants by exclusion of minority persons from the apartment complex is the loss of important benefits from interracial associations").

16. Florence Roisman (2008) has noted that the FHA nowhere uses the word "integration," but it is commonly understood that that was Congress's focus at the time (509 n.8).

17. 42 U.S.C. § 3608(e).

18. One exception—which has required litigation to acknowledge; see *In re Adoption of 2003 Low Income Hous. Tax Credit Qualified Allocation Plan*, 848 A.2d 1 (N.J. Sup. Ct. App. Div. 2004)—is that the FHA's broad mandate to use *all* federal investments—not just those by HUD—to affirmatively further the purposes of the act has been applied to the federal Low-Income Housing Tax Credit (LIHTC) program. The LIHTC program is the most important source of federal funding for the new construction and rehabilitation of affordable housing and, because it is a tax subsidy, is administered by the Internal Revenue Service. The IRS has at least acknowledged that nothing in the legislation establishing the LIHTC program indicated that Congress intended to modify the Fair Housing Act's AFFH obligations (see Revenue Ruling 2016-29), but has not taken meaningful steps to ensure that the program more broadly fulfills the AFFH mandate.

19. As originally enacted, 42 U.S.C. § 3608(d) provided that "all executive departments and agencies shall administer their programs and activities relating to housing and urban development in a manner affirmatively to further the purposes of this subchapter and shall cooperate with the Secretary to further such purposes." In 1988, Congress added "(including any Federal agency having regulatory or supervisory authority over financial institutions)" after "urban development" to make clear that the provision really means *all* executive departments and agencies involved in housing and urban development.

20. 436 F.2d 809 (3d Cir. 1970).

21. Ibid. at 816.

22. Ibid. See also *Resident Advisory Bd. v. Rizzo*, 425 F. Supp. 987, 1014–15 (E.D. Pa. 1976), aff'd as modified, 564 F.2d 126 (3d Cir. 1977), cert. denied, 435 U.S. 908 (1978) (noting that "in an effort to end segregation . . . Congress enacted 3608(e)(5), requiring affirmative action . . . to cure this widespread problem.").

23. See, e.g., *NAACP v. Sec'y of Hous. & Urban Dev.*, 817 F.2d 149, 155 (1st Cir. 1987) (noting that "every court that has considered the question has held or stated that Title VIII imposes upon HUD an obligation to do more than simply refrain from discriminating (and from purposely aiding discrimination by others)"). Congress has reinforced the AFFH mandate through a number of subsequent statutes. The Housing and Community Development Act of 1974, the Cranston-Gonzalez National Affordable Housing Act, and the Quality Housing and Work Responsibility Act of 1998 each require that HUD grantees certify as a condition of receiving funds that they will affirmatively further fair housing. See AFFH Proposed Rule, 78 Fed. Reg. 43710, 43712 (July 19, 2013) (citing 42 U.S.C. 5304(b)(2), 5306(d)(7)(B), 12705(b)(15), 1437C–1(d)(16)).

24. As critics have noted, agency enforcement powers for discrimination under the FHA were quite limited from the start, and the FHA contained infamous carve-outs for single-family owner-occupied housing and for small-scale renters (Massey 2016). Other statutes, such as Section 1982 of the Civil Rights Act of 1866 and state and local civil rights laws, partly address these gaps, and Congress enhanced agency enforcement provisions in the Fair Housing Amendments Act of 1988.

25. See, e.g., *NAACP*, 817 F.2d at 156 (requiring HUD to "consider [the] effect [of a grant] on the racial and socio-economic composition of the surrounding area" and that "the need for such consideration itself implies, at a minimum, an obligation to assess negatively those aspects of a proposed course of action that would further limit the supply of genuinely open housing and to assess positively those aspects of a proposed course of action that would increase that supply."); *Otero v. N.Y.C. Hous. Auth.*, 484 F.2d 1122, 1133–34 (2d Cir. 1973).

26. See, e.g., 24 C.F.R. § 905.602(d); § 905.602(d)(2) (requiring a civil rights review for public housing development theoretically designed to include questions on the racial concentration of poverty and perpetuation of segregation).

27. See HUD Needs to Enhance Its Requirements and Oversight of Jurisdictions' Fair Housing Plans, GAO-10-905 (2010).

28. See generally 80 Fed. Reg. 42272 (July 16, 2015) (AFFH Final Rule).

29. Only the first round of analyses under this new process were completed, so it is difficult at this anniversary to speculate about whether the new process would live up to its promise, but complicating even that modest evaluation, the current administration has halted implementation of the rule.

30. See text accompanying notes 27–29.

31. Comments on the proposed AFFH rule—which, to the extent they were submitted electronically, are available on www.regulations.gov, under FR-5173-P-01—were rife with acrimony and often thinly veiled racial animus.

32. See Office of the Assistant Secretary for Fair Housing and Equal Opportunity, U.S. Department of Housing and Urban Development, Affirmatively Furthering Fair Housing: Withdrawal of Notice Extending the Deadline for Submission of Assessment of Fair Housing for Consolidated Plan Participants, 83 FR 23928-01 (May 23, 2018) (withdrawing an earlier notice extending the deadline for AFFH obligations by HUD program participants); Office of the Assistant Secretary for Fair Housing and Equal Opportunity, U.S. Department of Housing and Urban Development, Affirmatively Furthering Fair Housing: Streamlining and Enhancements, 83 Fed. Reg. 40713-01 (Aug. 16, 2018) (promulgating an advanced notice of proposed rulemaking soliciting public comments to create a new AFFH rule). HUD has also withdrawn a Local Government Assessment Tool designed to help grantees comply with the rule. See Office of the Assistant Secretary for Fair Housing and Equal Opportunity, U.S. Department of Housing and Urban Development, Affirmatively Furthering Fair Housing: Withdrawal of the Assessment Tool for Local Governments, 83 Fed. Reg. 23922-01 (May 23, 2018).

33. 85 Fed. Reg. 2041 (Jan. 14, 2020) (Affirmatively Furthering Fair Housing Proposed Rule).

34. 80 Fed. Reg. at 42353.

35. 85 Fed. Reg. at 2045.

36. Ibid.

37. A second, slightly more speculative concern that bears at least brief mention is a shifting First Amendment free speech and right of association jurisprudence that some courts have used to hint at limitations on important aspects of the FHA. See, e.g., *Fair Hous. Council of San Fernando Valley v. Roommate.com, LLC*, 666 F.3d 1216 (9th Cir. 2012) (interpreting the act not to apply to roommate situations partly out of constitutional avoidance concerns).

38. 135 S. Ct. 2507 (2015).

39. Ibid. at 2524. HUD recently proposed a rule that would significantly narrow disparate-impact liability, nominally to reflect the *Inclusive Communities* decision. See 84 Fed. Reg. 43854 (2020) (HUD's Implementation of the Fair Housing Act's Disparate Impact Standard Proposed Rule). The HUD rule, if finalized in the form the agency has proposed, would represent a break from FHA precedent, discouraging the collection of data, undermining the availability of punitive damages, seemingly eliminating the perpetuation of segregation as a basis for liability, raising significant barriers for plaintiffs, and creating significant new defenses for those facing charges of discrimination.

40. *Cooper v. Harris*, 137 S. Ct. 1455 (2017); *City of Richmond v. J.A. Croson Co.*, 488 U.S. 469 (1989); *Fisher v. Univ. of Tex.*, 570 U.S. 297 (2013).

41. *Parents Involved in Cmty. Schs. v. Seattle Sch. Dist. No. 1*, 551 U.S. 701 (2007) (Roberts, C.J.).

42. In *United States v. Starrett City*, 840 F.2d 1096 (2d Cir. 1988), a cooperative housing development sought to maintain a ratio of white to black to Hispanic residents of 64 percent, 22 percent, and 8 percent by maintaining separate waiting lists for each group. The developer said that it employed this strategy to maintain an integrated development by avoiding reaching a tipping point beyond which white residents would move out and prospective white residents would refuse to move in. The strategy was successful at maintaining a stable racial mix in the complex, but at the cost of significantly longer waiting lists for prospective black and Hispanic tenants. The U.S. Court of Appeals for the Second Circuit found the practice to be a plain violation of the antidiscrimination provisions of the Fair Housing Act, notwithstanding the pro-integration goals of the complex's managers. Ibid. Although the U.S. Supreme Court did not take up the case, there can be little doubt that the current Court would have agreed with the Second Circuit.

43. Indeed, we do not want to be understood as endorsing the *Starrett City* quota approach. Although the goal of residential integration requires at least some conception of what proportions of different groups constitute "integration," an overly rigid quota system (or fixed proportions) raises a host of problems. Among them are the changing demographics of the United States as a whole, not to mention of individual metropolitan communities. Moreover, the rigid use of quotas—as opposed to gentler, more indirect means of encouraging residential integration—runs the risk of creating significant misunderstanding. It is telling that the plaintiffs in the *Starrett City* case were members of minority groups subjected to long waiting lists necessitated by the desire to sustain the targeted racial quotas.

44. See 135 S. Ct. at 2525 ("While the automatic or pervasive injection of race into public and private transactions covered by the FHA has special dangers, it is also true that race may be considered in certain circumstances and in a proper fashion"); cf. *Parents Involved in Cmty. Schs.*, 551 U.S. at 789 (Kennedy, J., concurring in part and concurring in judgment) ("School boards may pursue the goal of bringing together students of diverse backgrounds and races through other means, including strategic site selection of new schools; [and] drawing attendance zones with general recognition of the demographics of neighborhoods").

45. *Regents of the Univ. of Cal. v. Bakke*, 483 U.S. 265, 311–12 (1978) (Powell, J.); *Gratz v. Bollinger*, 539 U.S. 244, 270–71 (2003); *Grutter v. Bollinger*, 539 U.S. 306, 325 (2003) ("We

endorse Justice Powell's view that student body diversity is a compelling state interest that can justify the use of race in university admissions.").

46. *Fisher v. Univ. of Tex.* ("*Fisher II*"), 136 S. Ct. 2198, 2210 (2016).

47. See ibid.

48. See, e.g., Chetty, Hendren, and Katz (2016) (finding significant benefits for young children who moved from high-poverty housing projects to lower poverty neighborhoods).

49. See Putnam (2007).

50. See, e.g., Abascal and Baldassarri (2015).

51. See ibid.

52. See *Inclusive Communities*, 135 S. Ct. at 2551 (Alito, J., dissenting, joined by Chief Justice Roberts, Justice Scalia, and Justice Thomas) (suggesting that allowing disparate impact claims under the FHA improperly opens the door to race-conscious policy-making); *Fisher v. Univ. of Tex.*, 570 U.S. 297, 315 (2013) (Thomas, J. dissenting) ("A State's use of race . . . is categorically prohibited by the Equal Protection Clause"); *Fisher v. Univ. of Tex.* ("Fisher II"), 136 S. Ct. 2198, 2220 (2016) (Alito, J. dissenting) ("UT's race-conscious admissions program cannot satisfy strict scrutiny").

53. See Ginger O'Donnell, *Brett Kavanaugh's Track Record Indicates a Threat to Affirmative Action*, Insight into Diversity (Sept. 5, 2018), http://www.insightintodiversity.com/brett-kavanaughs-track-record-indicates-a-threat-to-affirmative-action/.

References

Abascal, Maria, and Dalia Baldassarri. 2015. "Love Thy Neighbor? Ethnoracial Diversity and Trust Reexamined." *American Journal of Sociology* 121 (3): 722–82.

Aydinonat, N. Emrah. 2007. "Models, Conjectures, and Exploration: An Analysis of Schelling's Checkerboard Model of Residential Segregation." *Journal of Economic Methodology* 14 (4): 429–54.

Chetty, Raj, Nathaniel Hendren, and Lawrence F. Katz. 2016. "The Effects of Exposure to Better Neighborhoods on Children: New Evidence from the Moving to Opportunity Experiment." *American Economic Review* 106 (4): 855–902.

Clark, William A. V. 2009. "Changing Residential Preferences Across Income, Education and Age." *Urban Affairs Review* 44 (3): 334–55.

Crowder, Kyle, Jeremy Pais, and Scott South. 2012. "Neighborhood Diversity, Metropolitan Constraints, and Household Migration." *American Sociological Review* 77 (3): 325–53.

Davidson, Nestor D. 2017. "Affordable Housing Law and Policy in an Era of Big Data." *Fordham Urban Law Journal* 44 (2): 277–300.

Dawkins, Casey J. 2004. "Recent Evidence on the Continuing Causes of Black-White Residential Segregation." *Journal of Urban Affairs* 26 (3): 379–400.

Havekes, Esther, Michael Bader, and Maria Krysan. 2016. "Realizing Racial and Ethnic Neighborhood Preferences?" *Population Research and Policy Review* 35: 101–26.

Jargowsky, Paul. 2016. "Neighborhoods and Segregation." In *Shared Prosperity in America's Communities*, edited by Susan M. Wachter and Lei Ding, 20–40. Philadelphia: University of Pennsylvania Press.

Massey, Douglas S. 2015. "The Legacy of the 1968 Fair Housing Act." *Sociological Forum* 30 (SI): 571–88.

Massey, Douglas S., and Jonathan Tannen. 2015. "A Research Note on Trends in Black Hyper-segregation." *Demography* 52 (3): 1025–34.

Nier, Charles L. 1999. "Perpetuation of Segregation: Toward a New Historical and Legal Interpretation of Redlining Under the Fair Housing Act." *John Marshall Law Review* 31 (Spring): 617–65.

Putnam, Robert. 2007. "*E Pluribus Unum*, Diversity and Community in the Twenty-first Century." *Scandinavian Political Studies* 30 (2): 137.

Quillian, Lincoln. 2002. "Why Is Black-White Residential Segregation So Persistent?" *Social Science Research* 31 (2): 197–229.

Roisman, Florence W. 2008. "Living Together: Ending Racial Discrimination and Segregation in America." *Indiana Law Review* 41: 507–20.

———. 2007. "A Place to Call Home? Affordable Housing Issues in America." *Wake Forest Law Review* 42 (Summer): 333–91.

Rothstein, Richard. 2017. *The Color of Law: A Forgotten History of How Our Government Segregated America*. New York: Liveright.

Rothwell, Jonathan, and Douglas Massey. 2010. "Density Zoning and Class Segregation in U.S. Metropolitan Areas." *Social Science Quarterly* 91 (5): 1123–43.

Schelling, Thomas C. 2006. *MicroMotives and MacroBehavior*. New York: W. W. Norton & Company.

Schwemm, Robert G. 2017. "Segregative-Effect Claims Under the Fair Housing Act." *N.Y.U. Journal of Legislation and Public Policy* 20: 709–72.

Seicshnaydre, Stacy E. 2013. "Is Disparate Impact Having Any Impact? An Appellate Analysis of Forty Years of Disparate Impact Claims Under the Fair Housing Act." *American University Law Review* 65: 357–435.

Strahilevitz, Lior. 2006. "Exclusionary Amenities in Residential Communities." *Virginia Law Review* 92 (3): 437–99.

CHAPTER 6

A Queer and Intersectional
Approach to Fair Housing

Amy Hillier and Devin Michelle Bunten

Introduction

The Fair Housing Act of 1968 makes no reference to sexual orientation or gender identity. In 1974, the same year that Congress passed the Equal Credit Opportunity Act and established the Community Development Block Grant program, "sex" was added to the list of protected classes. While not explicitly defined, "sex" was understood to be determined fully by one's body and its capacity for sexual reproduction. The world was thus made of men and women, and women deserved explicit protection against housing discrimination.

The year 1988 brought further changes to the Fair Housing Act and the addition of two protected classes: families with children and persons with physical or mental disabilities. Families were understood to conform to heteronormative standards of mother, father, and children. It was within the debates about who warranted protection under the category of "persons with physical or mental disabilities" that discussion of gender identity was introduced—and with it the first explicit acknowledgment of trans people within fair housing legislation.

As these additions were being debated, Jesse Helms was afraid. A 1986 court opinion had found that trans status represents a handicap and that trans people are protected under antidiscrimination employment law as written (*Blackwell v. United States Department of the Treasury* 1986). Helms—who once said that "nothing positive happened to Sodom and Gomorrah and nothing positive is likely to happen to America if our people succumb to the drumbeats of support for the homosexual lifestyle"—

feared that trans people might sue for protection under the Fair Housing Act and win. He therefore put forward an amendment that made explicit that "individual with handicaps" in no way meant a person who was transgender. "I have no doubt that sometime, somewhere, another Federal court will be asked to revisit that issue—if not under the Rehabilitation Act, perhaps under the Fair Housing Act," explained Helms. "When that happens, it should be clear to the courts that Congress does not intend for transvestites to receive the benefits and protections that is [*sic*] provided for handicapped individuals."[1]

Senator Alan Cranston (D-CA) rose in opposition to Helms's amendment: "As a principal author of section 504 [of the Rehabilitation Act of 1973], I see this amendment as a direct attack on the heart and soul of antidiscrimination laws, which protect individuals against discrimination based on stereotypes," he insisted. "It is an appeal to our worst instincts—saying that we shouldn't have to associate with individuals who are different from ourselves because of the way they dress or their emotional problems," he argued further. "If we were to start excluding one category of individuals from coverage, we would be threatening to undermine the very essence of antidiscrimination laws." The amendment passed the Senate 89–2.

Three decades on from the explicit codification of antitrans discrimination in federal law, treatment of many queer and trans people has improved: health insurers will cover some components of transition, a small number of states have introduced an "X" marker for gender on identification cards, and a gay man runs one of the largest corporations in America. These improvements are unevenly distributed: most queer and trans people are not CEOs, most nonbinary people do not live in states with inclusive policies, and many trans people—particularly trans people of color—are uninsured. In this chapter, we interrogate the social worldview responsible for codifying antitrans legislation into fair housing legislation, focusing on ways that policy and law distinguish those deserving of fair housing from those who are not. In some cases, this distinction rests on singular aspects of identity: trans people are legally unworthy of protection. To that end, we interrogate the dominant framework for understanding fair housing over the past fifty years, a framework that also guides much of urban planning, zoning, and domestic housing policy writ large, more generally. This framework is heteronormative, privileging conceptions of family with two straight parents, and cisnormative, assuming that gender is fixed, falls neatly into a binary, and is consistent with the sex assigned to most babies at birth.

In other cases, the distinction of who deserves protections rests not on singular identities, but on intersections, as legal protections afforded in theory are not uniformly available to doubly (or triply, or . . .) marginalized persons. The dominant framework just described promotes a narrow way of understanding characteristics of individuals such as race, ethnicity, nationality, sex, ability, and religion as separate classes rather than offering an intersectional, holistic view of identity and centering poverty and issues of power. Together, these limitations have the effect of directing attention away from issues of poverty and power that arguably have the most significant impact on well-being and opportunity and of keeping us from focusing on the most marginalized communities.

In this article, we will use queer theory to interrogate existing laws, zoning regulations, and planning and real estate practices to better understand the limits of current understanding of fair housing. We will reconceptualize ideas about identity and "protected classes," adopting an intersectional lens; about "family" and "household," considering nontraditional families and households; and about "housing" as it incorporates neighborhood conditions, not simply shelter, and interactions outside the market. Through this reconceptualization, we will center the experiences of the most marginalized groups. First, however, we offer background on the concepts of "queering" and "intersectionality."

Queering Our Lens

We use the word "queer" throughout this chapter very deliberately, and depending upon the context, "queer" takes on different meanings. At a basic and literal level, this chapter is about people who identify as lesbian, gay, bisexual, pansexual, asexual, transgender, genderqueer, agender, and other gender and sexual identities that fall outside traditional heteronormative and cisnormative conventions. By queering our lens, we put these often marginalized communities into focus, making them visible and centering their varied histories and identities. We use "queer" to denote the collection of nonstraight sexualities, although we acknowledge that many or most people do not identify as queer. Similarly—and controversially—we use "trans" as an umbrella term for noncisgender people. People who identify as nonbinary or genderqueer or gender-fluid or agender may reject this umbrella term. Umbrella terms have a role, and that role is to encompass the constellation of identities while taking care not to center straightness or cisness.[2]

Our choice of "queer" to describe these communities reflects the political nature of the word and its connection to queer theory. Queer theory grew out of queer activism focused around HIV/AIDs and feminist, critical, and women's studies in the 1990s. Queering is the application of queer theory and the process of deconstructing, complicating, interrogating, disturbing, and resisting the gender, sexuality, and family norms and binaries associated with heteronormativity and cisnormativity (Oswald, Blume, and Marks 2005; Motta 2016). In the words of Hugh Lee, Mark Learmonth, and Nancy Harding (2008), queering involves "identification of the norms that govern identity, analysis of what is allowable within those norms, and exploration of what is unspeakable." The dominant regimes depend upon these nonnormative sexual and gender identities in order to "know and sustain themselves," to construct a "privileged 'inside,'" that "could not exist without a demeaned 'outside'" (Lugg and Murphy 2014).

Queering is typically a method for critical analysis and research, but it has been used in the context of public policy, public administration, institutions, and public space (Motta 2016; Lugg and Murphy 2014; Lee, Learmonth, and Harding 2008; Burgess 2005; Shipley 2004). Throughout this chapter, we explore what queering might mean in the context of fair housing.

Intersectionality

The concept of intersectionality emerged within the field of critical race theory, with the original reference in a 1989 essay by Columbia University scholar Kimberlé Crenshaw. She saw it as a way to recognize the multidimensional nature of Black women's experiences and a response to "single-axis analysis" that contributed to the marginalization of Black women. Crenshaw explained in a 2017 interview: "Intersectionality is a lens through which you can see where power comes and collides, where it interlocks and intersects. It's not simply that there's a race problem here, a gender problem here, and a class or LBGTQ problem there. Many times that framework erases what happens to people who are subject to all of these things" ("Kimberlé Crenshaw on Intersectionality" 2017). The most common interpretation of intersectionality considers how different identities interact, with an emphasis on cumulative disadvantage and the unique experiences of people with multiple marginalized identities. Valerie Purdie-Vaughns and Richard Eibach (2008) offer an alternative interpretation of intersectionality to what they call the traditional "score-keeping" mentality that focuses on intersectionality as being additive or interactional. Intersectional invisibility draws on the concepts of androcentrism, privileging men's experiences; ethnocentrism, privileging whiteness as the norm; and heterocentrism, privileging straightness as the normative sexuality. People with nonprototypical identities—women, nonwhite, queer—may experience a type of invisibility that may result in certain advantages and disadvantages relative to people with prototypical identities. Following this logic, the prototypical member of a subordinate ethnic or racial group will be defined as a straight man, the prototypical woman will be defined as straight and white, and the prototypical queer person will be defined as a white man.

Intersectional invisibility within politics means that advocacy groups will find it easier to frame issues around a single subordinate identity—white people as the ones with disabilities, Black men as victims of mass incarceration, white women as the face of women's rights. Legal invisibility means that people with multiply marginalized identities are less likely to be protected or seen as credible within the legal system. Crenshaw pointed to Anita Hill's testimony at the Clarence Thomas hearings as an example of legal invisibility.

America simply stumbled into the place where African American women live, a political vacuum of erasure and contradiction maintained by the almost routine polarization of "Blacks and women" into separate and competing camps. Existing within the overlapping margins of race and gender discourse and in the empty spaces between, it is a location whose very nature resists telling. This location contributes to Black women's ideological disempowerment in a way that tipped the scales against Anita Hill from the start (Crenshaw 1989: 403).

Similar legal logic stymied efforts by Black women to sue General Motors over employment discrimination in 1976. In *DeGraffenreid v. General Motors*, the court ruled that the plaintiffs could not combine their claims of discrimination on the basis of race and sex because this was beyond the scope of Title VII of the Civil Rights Act. Under this logic, the employment of Black men and white women rendered discrimination against Black women legally permissible.

Some of this existing research on queer and trans experiences of housing discrimination considers race or ethnicity and sexual orientation simultaneously. For example, Schwegman (2019) found that coupled nonwhite gay men received fewer responses to e-mail inquiries about apartment rentals than straight white couples. However, little attention has been given to the fact that the distinct classes protected by fair housing laws will always overlap in the form of individual identities. By queering our lens on fair housing, we can reconceptualize identity as inherently intersectional and consider who within queer and trans communities is most vulnerable to discrimination. This does not mean establishing a "hierarchy of oppressions" (Lorde 1983) but rather recognizing that aspects of identity interact in meaningful ways that must be acknowledged in order to address all forms of discrimination.

Heteronormativity and Cisnormativity in Urban Policy

Urban planning, the project of organizing our cities, has long privileged those with power. Most notably in the American context, as Steil and Charles describe in Chapter 2 of this book, this has meant that planning is a white supremacist project. Planning has similarly privileged other power structures. Michael Frisch (2002) described urban planning as a "heterosexist project," because planning discourses reinforce assumptions about heterosexuality— that it is necessary for procreation, is based on natural sex differences, and has the potential for pleasure. Heterosexuality is reinforced as the norm while queer and trans people are rendered invisible through violence and the destruction of records of their existence. "Zoning, housing rights, and our sense of the public realm are built around heterosexual constructs of family, work, and community life," he argued. "Planning reproduces structures of heterosexual domination" (256). In a more recent piece, Frisch (2015) explained that gender and sexual orientation have been "problematic" for urban planning because planning and zoning systems and suburban subdivisions that developed alongside one another during the twentieth century reinforced conventional norms around gender and sexuality. "Gender norms, especially in the post–World War II era, connected women to home space and men to the work world" (133–34). Frisch cited Foucault in linking the "categories of pathologies" and the "capitalist production of identities as commodities" (Frisch 2002: 256). In the 2011 volume *Queerying Planning*, Petra Doan asked whether planning practice constrains the evolution of queer communities—or whether they seek to commercialize such spaces to the benefit of large developers and the detriment of marginalized members of the community (Doan 2011). To improve the lives of the most marginalized, the capitalist underpinnings of planning may also need to be considered.

We argue that urban policy, including fair housing policy, is not just antiqueer but antitrans. It is both heteronormative and cisnormative, privileging

notions about gender and sexuality that fail to recognize the distinction between them, variations within them, and their fluid natures. The normative
American house is a single-family home, occupied by a straight cis couple
who have or will have children. This norm has long been enforced by housing policy at both local and federal levels. In this section, we review this history to contextualize the (mis)treatment of queer and trans people by the
Federal Housing Administration (FHA) and the current struggle for queer
and trans housing fairness. Much of this history takes the form of protection of the normative American family, with regulations regarding housing
structures oriented around the families expected (or regulatorily allowed) to
occupy them.

The Edmunds Act of 1882 banned cohabitation by what might today be
called polyamorous households, in a move generally read as an attack on the
Church of Jesus Christ of Latter-Day Saints and some adherents' practices of
patriarchal polygamy (Phipps 2009). Since the early twentieth century, zoning and other local housing policies have enforced and otherwise favored
measures to "protect" the single-family nature of neighborhoods (Fischel
2004). Transportation technology changes threatened the ability of (single-
family) homeowners and home builders to control the makeup of their
neighborhoods. The perceived threats came not just from the commercial
sphere and its brickyards and livery stables, but also from apartments. By
1916, Berkeley, California, had gone beyond residential districts to establishing zones solely for the use of single-family houses (Hirt 2014). Today,
such districts have proliferated across the United States. Although the Edmunds Act was repealed in 1983, state laws that effectively outlaw polyamorous cohabitation remain on the books of all fifty states today (Brown
2008). Indeed, Michigan and Mississippi have bans on straight cohabitation
prior to marriage (Michigan Compiled Laws; *Davis v. Davis* 1996).

The threats these districts protected against were couched in the language of normative family and often focused on children in particular. The
early planner Edward Bassett argued that the "chaotic conditions of un-
zoned cities" were an especial threat to children, who would benefit from
the "light and air in greater abundance in suburban districts" (Bassett
1922: 323). As Sonia Hirt argues, the precise mechanisms by which nonnormative housing and commercial uses threatened home life were viewed
as nebulous, even by those tasked with justifying the regulations (Hirt 2014).
Regardless of the justification, the argument was the same: homes constructed for single occupancy by a family need (and are worthy of) defense,

along all three lines: from nonresidential uses, from multiple-unit uses, and from nonfamily uses.

Industrial uses were long suspect in residential areas, and nuisance case law underwent tremendous innovation through the nineteenth century (Rosen 2003, Pontin 2012). By the twentieth century, commercial uses were suspect, as evidenced by the rise of residential districts. These laws had particular effects on women. White women almost unanimously did not do market work outside the home after marriage—even immigrant women who may have done so in their previous countries (Goldin 2006, Foner 1999). Married women of color worked outside the home at higher rates than did white women, but the norm remained that married women did not undertake wage work. Many did, however, work within the home, by taking in piecework as seamstresses. Among their other ends, prohibitions on commercial enterprise within single-family neighborhoods constrained one route to economic independence (or even contribution) by women, reinforcing patriarchal and heteronormative family structures through housing policy.

Multiple-family occupancy was likewise regarded as a social threat. This threat was often sexual: the residential hotels that proliferated in growing downtown districts like Times Square (in New York) or Tower Town (in Chicago) were often home to roommates of the same gender. The existence of roommate households, combined with the relative anonymity of the large buildings, lent a plausible deniability to cohabitating queer partners that could provide some safety (Groth 1994). At the same time, residential hotels became sites of queer congregation, and the districts that grew around these hotels hosted establishments that catered to—or at least allowed—visibly queer customers (Meyerowitz 1990).

Beyond queer relationships, rooming houses were also home to the revolution in women's sexuality more generally (Meyerowitz 1990). The availability of space by the bed or room brought independent living within reach of unmarried working women. This space also opened up new work opportunities in a sexual economy: prostitution could be conducted indoors in residential hotels. Still more broadly, a rented room and a cafeteria meal alleviated the patriarchal burden of housework for women—or at least, redistributed the burden into the market. Collectively, these "hazards" of rooming houses made them the target of campaigns of eradication (Groth 1994). These campaigns ended in a rout. Boarding was prohibited by zoning or other ordinances in the early 1900s. These prohibitions remain largely in place. Los Angeles, which defines family in a broad fashion as a "single housekeeping unit," nevertheless prohibits boarding houses toward the dual ends of limiting "transient occupancy" and commercial uses (Los Angeles City Council 2012). Today, proposals for updated versions of these arrangements continue to be viewed with suspicion (Baca 2018).

Nonfamily uses are broader than just taking boarders, and most of them can be outlawed by municipal authorities. In the 1970s, two seminal cases bounded—slightly—municipalities' ability to define *family*. In the 1974 case *Village of Belle Terre v. Boraas*, the Supreme Court found that cities could restrict single-family districts to occupancy by "one or more people related by blood, adoption, or marriage, or not more than two unrelated people, living and cooking together as a single housekeeping unit" (1). The latter distinction makes room for a normative unmarried couple—even a pair of roommates, who cook independently, may not technically qualify. Three years later, in *Moore v. City of East Cleveland*, the Supreme Court placed a small limit on these powers. East Cleveland's ordinance, which restricted even some relationships by birth, was found unconstitutional. Together, these cases found that municipalities could broadly restrict the types of household arrangements permissible within their cities, so long as normative families—defined by birth, marriage, or adoption—were not excluded. This *formalism* in defining families under zoning law stands in contrast to the *functional* turn taken in family law. In a recent article, Kate Redburn argues that family law is concerned chiefly with distributing the "benefits and obligations of long term familial connections," and as such the functional family approach is "normatively desirable" because it encompasses the variety of existing kinship networks and intimate relationships (Redburn 2019: 2422, 2419). Applying this functional family approach to zoning would ensure that communities are able to support the intimate relationships that *are* in the world, rather than those that regulation drafters may wish *were* in the community. Failing to do so ensures that municipalities "inflict material and dignitary harms on functional families" in service of maintaining this normative formal family vision (Redburn 2019: 2467).

Heteronormative and cisnormative policy has also been constructed via omission. The Fair Housing Act is just such a case: in stating the right to nondiscrimination on the grounds of other characteristics, the law failed to protect queer and trans individuals from discrimination. Of course, straight and cis people are likewise not protected on those grounds. But this lack of protection is asymmetrical: those living on top of a particular power structure are not so likely to feel its weight pressing down upon them.

Existing Legal Protections

Queer and trans communities benefited little from any kind of legal protections until the past twenty years. Not only did legal protections not exist before then; states actively codified restrictions against queer and trans people and certain sexual acts through laws banning loitering, solicitation of sex in public places, "sodomy," and cross-dressing, starting soon after the American Revolution. In 1936, the ACLU unsuccessfully defended the producer of the critically acclaimed Lillian Hellman Broadway play, *The Children's Hour*, after it was banned in Boston because of its "lesbian content." In 1957, the ACLU successfully defended City Lights Books, which had been charged with obscenity under California law for publishing Allen Ginsberg's poem *Howl*, with its references to gay sex. Not until forty years later did the Supreme Court begin systematically striking down state laws prohibiting sexual minorities from protected class status (*Romer v. Evans*, 1996), prosecuting certain sexual acts under sodomy laws (*Lawrence v. Texas*, 2003), and restricting the right to marriage and the right to adoption to straight couples (*Obergefell v. Hodges*, 2015). The Matthew Shepard and James Byrd Jr. Hate Crimes Prevention Act of 2009 made hate crimes based on sexual orientation or gender identity punishable under federal law.

In the absence of a comprehensive federal antidiscrimination law, states are left to decide for themselves about whether and in what domains to offer protections against discrimination on the basis of sexual orientation and gender identity. Only fourteen states offer consistent protections on the basis of sexual orientation and gender identity. Fifteen states have no antidiscrimination laws that extend to queer and trans communities; ten additional states offer protection against discrimination on the basis of sexual orientation, gender identity, or gender expression only to state employees.

State and Federal Fair Housing Laws

Similarly, federal statutes do not explicitly protect against housing discrimination on the basis of sexual orientation and gender identity, leaving individual courts and states to decide what is and is not allowable under current law. With the 1974 amendments, the Fair Housing Act prohibits discrimination on the basis of sex, but it does not explicitly reference sexual orientation or gender identity and expression. Individual courts and states interpret "sex" differently, with some considering the protections to cover sexual orientation and gender identity, as well. In August 2018, the U.S. Court of Appeals for the Seventh Circuit reversed a lower court decision and ruled that a senior living community in Chicago could be held liable under the Fair Housing Act for failing to protect a resident from harassment and physical abuse on the basis of her sexual orientation. This ongoing legal debate mimics that involving the rights of transgender students under federal Title IX, which, like the Fair Housing Act, prohibits discrimination on the basis of sex but is silent on the issue of sexual orientation and gender identity. In May 2019, the Supreme Court agreed to hear two cases, *Altitude Express v. Zarda*, from New York, and *Bostock v. Clayton County, Georgia*, involving the application of civil rights law prohibiting discrimination on the basis of sex to alleged employment discrimination against two gay men.

In the absence of clear federal protections, some states offer protection against housing discrimination on the basis of sexual orientation, gender identity, or both. At present, twenty-one states and the District of Columbia explicitly prohibit housing discrimination on the basis of sexual orientation and gender identity. Two additional states interpret current state laws against sex discrimination as prohibiting discrimination based on sexual orientation and gender identity, and one state prohibits housing discrimination on the basis of sexual orientation only. Twenty-six states offer no state-level protections for queer and trans communities against housing discrimination.

In the ensuing sections of this chapter, we broaden our scope beyond the traditional focal point of fair housing: the private housing market. In doing so, we aim to queer fair housing by bringing into consideration any manner of policy or action whose execution entails unequal outcomes for queer and trans people with regard to shelter.

HUD's Equal Access Rule

Unlike the Fair Housing Act, HUD's 2012 Equal Access Rule explicitly prohibits discrimination on the basis of gender identity and sexual orientation in the process of securing HUD-financed or insured housing as well as within

HUD-supported housing and Community Planning and Development (CPD) programs. In addition to those seeking loans insured by the Federal Housing Administration (FHA), this rule offers protection to the nearly seven million people living in public and subsidized housing as well as those participating in programs funded through Community Development Block Grants (CDBG), HOME Investment Partnerships Program (HOME), Continuum of Care (CoC), Emergency Solutions Grants (ESG), Housing Opportunities for People with AIDS (HOPWA), Housing Trust Fund, and Rural Housing.

These legal protections on the basis of gender identity, in particular, inform a wide range of local practices at shelters, including intake forms, sleeping arrangements, restroom use, agency policies, and staff training. In particular, the Equal Access Rule addresses how and where to place transgender individuals within gender-segregated emergency shelters and other facilities. HUD has offered multiple updates since establishing the rule in order to provide guidance consistent with best practices and other federal guidelines. Largely in response to a report that documented widespread refusal to place transgender clients (Center for American Progress and Movement Advancement Project 2016), HUD offered revisions in 2016 making explicit that placement in single-sex facilities should be done based on a client's gender identity unless they request otherwise for their own safety. Providers are permitted to offer access to single-occupancy bathrooms and other accommodations when any client, including but not limited to transgender clients, request additional privacy. The nondiscrimination statements in the Violence Against Women Act (VAWA) and Family Violence Prevention and Services Act (FVPSA) further reinforce protections on the basis of gender identity within shelters.

Prison Rape Elimination Act

The U.S. Justice Department issued rules in 2012 that extended protections in the Prison Rape Elimination Act of 2003 (PREA) to transgender individuals confined to adult prisons and jails, community correctional facilities, and juvenile facilities. Specifically, PREA states inmates cannot automatically be housed on the basis of their sex assigned at birth alone and that placement decisions should be individualized. Like HUD, the Bureau of Prisons (BOP) provides additional details that translate these rules into practice, specifically through the "Transgender Offender Manual." In 2018, the BOP updated the manual to reflect concerns within the Trump administration on "maintaining security and good order." With these updates, BOP deleted a sentence to "recommend housing by gender identity when appropriate" and called for initial decisions about the assignment to single-sex correctional facilities to be made based on so-called "biological sex" rather than gender identity. Contrary to the Trump administration guidance on these issues, courts across the county have ruled that transgender inmates have the right to be placed in "sex-segregated" facilities based on their gender identity.

Evidence of Housing Discrimination within Queer and Trans Communities

Evidence of housing discrimination against queer and trans individuals and households comes from formal complaints, surveys, paired-tester audits, statistical analysis of Home Mortgage Discrimination Act (HMDA) data, and qualitative studies. The National Fair Housing Alliance (NFHA) collects data about complaints filed with public agencies and private nonprofit fair housing organizations across the country to produce an annual report. In 2017, NFHA documented a total of 28,843 complaints of housing discrimination. Disability (57 percent) and race (19 percent) accounted for the largest proportion of complaints. A relatively tiny number related to queer and trans communities—153 complaints on the basis of sexual orientation and 50 on the basis of gender identity or expression. Underreporting of housing discrimination based on sexual orientation and gender identity is probably particularly pervasive because of the lack of systematic legal protections; queer and trans people facing housing discrimination may expect little or no recourse. The Williams Institute analyzed complaint data filed with state enforcement agencies and concluded that, when the size of the queer and trans population is taken into consideration, fair housing complaints about discrimination on the basis of sexual orientation and gender identity happen at similar rates to complaints based on sex and race.

The 2015 U.S. Transgender Survey documented far higher rates of housing discrimination against transgender adults than NFHA analysis of formal complaints. Almost one-quarter of the 27,715 survey participants reported experiencing some form of housing discrimination in the previous year. In an internet survey with a national probability sample of 662, adults who identified as lesbian, gay, or bisexual about antigay violence and related experiences, more than one in ten respondents (11.2 percent) reported having experienced housing or employment discrimination because of their sexual orientation. Employment and housing discrimination were significantly more likely among gay men and lesbians (17.7 percent and 16.3 percent, respectively) than among bisexual men and women (3.7 percent and 6.8 percent, respectively) (Herek 2009).

Discrimination in housing within queer and trans households occurs at many different points of homeseeking within the private housing market, as it does with straight and cisgender households. Several paired-tester audits—both in person and based on e-mail correspondence—have revealed patterns of discrimination on the basis of sexual orientation during initial inquiries into rental housing. In 2017, the Urban Institute conducted 2,009 matched-pair tests involving in-person and remote tests in three major metropolitan areas to assess discrimination among gay and lesbian couples and transgender individuals. Lesbian testers received comparable treatment to women in straight couples, while gay men testers were told about fewer rental units than straight men and transgender testers were told about fewer rental units than cisgender testers.

Schwegman (2019) conducted a randomized matched-pair test involving e-mail correspondence with 6,490 rental property owners in ninety-four cities. A subset of the fictional couples seeking apartments were assigned stereotypical Black or Hispanic names, and all of the fictional apartment seekers were assigned strongly gendered names, allowing for assessment of discrimination based on perceived queer or racial minority status. Both gay men and straight nonwhite couples were less likely to receive a response to e-mails inquiring about rental properties. Schwegman also detected more subtle forms of discrimination against gay men, namely more negative language used in the e-mail responses. Similarly, Friedman et al. (2013) found that queer couples received fewer responses to their e-mail inquiries as part of a large-scale, matched-pair test involving e-mail correspondence with 6,833 property owners in fifty metropolitan markets.

In a smaller study of thirty-three sets of paired-tester audits in the Boston metropolitan area, Langowski et al. (2018) documented widespread discrimination against transgender renters. They found that transgender and gender-nonconforming people received differential and discriminatory treatment in 61 percent of inquiries—not being shown additional areas within the apartment complex (27 percent), not being offered a financial incentive to rent (21 percent), being told negative things about the apartment building and neighborhood (12 percent), and being quoted a higher rental price than cisgender individuals (9 percent).

Researchers have also documented discrimination in the mortgage lending process. Sun and Gao modeled their 2019 study of discrimination in mortgage approvals in part after the Boston Fed Study. Their analysis of HMDA data from 1990 to 2015 showed that gay and lesbian couples were 73 percent more likely to be denied a mortgage than straight couples with the same creditworthiness and were charged higher interest rates—0.2 percent on average (Sun and Gao 2019). Furthermore, Sun and Gao documented a spillover effect; as the gay and lesbian population in an area increased, so did mortgage rejection rates and fees.

Discrimination at other points of the process of securing housing through the private market has not received as much attention from fair housing researchers. Results of the 2015 U.S. Transgender Survey indicate that discrimination takes the form of being denied an apartment or home or being evicted because they were found to be transgender. Those survey results also point to employment discrimination on the basis of gender identity, including losing a job, as a factor in housing instability and eviction. Verbal and physical abuse by neighbors, such as that experienced by Marsha Wetzel, a lesbian living in an assisted living facility in Illinois, as well as harassment by police—particularly of transgender people—should also be thought of as forms of housing discrimination against queer and trans communities. More than half (58 percent) of transgender people who interacted with police who knew they were transgender reported experiencing some form of harassment, abuse, or mistreatment by police (Herman et al. 2016).

Clearly, queer and trans people face various forms of housing discrimination outside the private housing market and residential neighborhoods, as well. Gender identities and sexual orientations come bundled with social power structures within families. This places queer and trans children at risk of homelessness, as children are normatively provided housing out of familial obligation rather than market compensation or government intervention. Accordingly, the Federal Housing Administration has no provisions for protecting children when the discrimination is coming from inside the house. This shortcoming leaves queer youth unprotected. Queer and trans youth represent approximately 7 percent of the total youth population but an estimated 40 percent of the homeless youth population (Choi et al. 2015). In a 2012 report, service providers who work with queer and trans homeless youth indicated that nearly seven in ten of their clients had experienced family rejection based on their sexual orientation or gender identity, and more than five in ten had experienced abuse in their family (Durso and Gates 2012). According to the 2015 U.S. Transgender Survey, more than half of trans adults have experienced some form of interpersonal violence (IPV), including physical abuse and coercive control (Herman et al. 2016).

Downstream, these same people face elevated risk for housing discrimination in homeless and domestic violence shelters. A 2016 study by the Center for American Progress involving calls to one hundred shelters across four states (Rooney, Durso, and Gruberg 2016) documented discrimination against transgender women who were trying to access housing through a shelter. Specifically, tester callers who were transgender received less positive information, were told they would be isolated from other women in the shelter or placed in a men's facility, were misgendered, were told that housing assignments were based on genitalia or surgery requirements, or were told that they would make other residents unsafe or uncomfortable. Only a minority of facilities expressed a willingness to house the transgender tester.

Just as family rejection and interpersonal violence are associated with elevated risk for homelessness among youth and adult queer and trans individuals, they are also associated with high rates of incarceration. For example, the 2010 U.S. Transgender Survey found that almost a third (29 percent) of those who experienced domestic violence relating to family rejection reported having been incarcerated, compared with only 11 percent of those whose families were accepting (Grant et al. 2011). As with homeless shelter placements, decisions by staff around where to house transgender individuals within sex-segregated detention facilities has implications for these individuals' safety and well-being. Queer and trans-identified immigrants detained in Immigration and Customs Enforcement (ICE) facilities are often housed based on their sex assigned at birth rather than their gender despite PREA laws. Not being able to live and dress according to one's gender can also have implications for convincing judges of the need for asylum based on gender identity (Center for American Progress and Movement Advancement Project 2016).

Trans communities, in particular, face elevated risks of harassment and physical and sexual abuse in prison, something that high-profile trans women including Chelsea Manning, Janet Mock, and CeCe McDonald have helped to spotlight. The 2015 U.S. Transgender Survey documented that trans people are ten times more likely to be sexually assaulted by fellow inmates and five times more likely to be sexually assaulted by staff. Imprisoned trans people also faced medical care denials and long stays in solitary confinement that they perceived to be based on their gender identity. Queer and trans individuals also face barriers related to sexual orientation and gender identity during reentry after incarceration. Specifically, the lack of support from family and protection from discrimination, strict probation and parole, and difficulty obtaining identity documents that reflect one's gender identity can all influence the likelihood of recidivism (Center for American Progress and Movement Advancement Project 2016).

To summarize, queer and trans communities are vulnerable to housing discrimination at some of the same points in the homeseeking process as straight and cisgender peers—during initial inquiry, in regard to what they are told is available and how much it will cost, and in securing financing. Special vulnerabilities within the private housing market involve likelihood of harassment and discrimination by neighbors and police based on sexual orientation and gender identity. Queer and trans communities are more likely to be housed in shelters and prisons, in part because of family rejection and IPV related to sexual orientation and gender identity. Once in these facilities, they face barriers to placement in accordance with their gender identity and have elevated risk of harassment and discrimination.

Queering Fair Housing Policy, Practice, and Research

In this final section, we describe what queering fair housing must involve in order to address the widespread housing discrimination that exists in all these different aspects of public and private housing. We describe changes needed in federal antidiscrimination policy and data collection practices, the need for enforcement and training around existing policies, and the development of subsidized housing to address the unique challenges of queer and trans youth and older adults. Before addressing these specific recommendations, we take a closer look at what adopting an intersectional approach would mean in the context of queering the Fair Housing Act, specifically, and fair housing, more generally.

Adopting an Intersectional Approach

While national-level protections against housing discrimination for queer and trans communities are essential, neither a new federal law nor a Supreme Court decision can eradicate heteronormative, cisnormative, and binaristic practices embedded in housing policies, programs, and institutions. Adopting a queer and intersectional approach to fair housing research, policy, and advocacy holds the promise of uprooting oppressive housing practices.

At its most simple, an intersectional approach calls on us to recognize the multiple and intersecting identities that people who face housing discrimination hold. Traditionally, fair housing research and advocacy has focused on a single protected class as the basis for discrimination, and aggregate data on complaints of housing discrimination are organized in separate categories based on race, color, national origin, religion, familial status, sex, and handicap. The form HUD makes available for complaints of housing discrimination does not preclude more than one protected class from being listed as the basis of discrimination, allowing individuals to "list the factor(s) why someone feels they have been discriminated against." In bringing civil charges against property owners and managers, the U.S. Justice Department will cite more than one basis of discrimination. For example, in *United States v. Loki Properties* (2011, D. Minn.), involving an African American man as the complainant, sex and race are both cited.

But an intersectional lens requires more than allowing individuals to "select all that apply." It requires a reconceptualization that sees an African American man as having a unique experience, not separate experiences as African American and as a man. Even though the courts have acknowledged compound discrimination claims, typical legal processes still "flatten" intersectional identities and fail to make clear how to prove and remedy claims of discrimination (Remedios et al. 2016; Abrokwa 2018). By not making clear the standards for successful intersectional claims, the legal system "erases an important perspective on the complex nature of discrimination and threatens to lead to shallow or misinformed legal remedies" in the words of disability rights attorney Alice Abrokwa (Abrokwa 2018: 73).

Beyond the courts, we need fair housing researchers, advocates, and government officials to see people in all their identities—a challenge given our propensity for seeing policy issues and individuals through a single lens (Corus et al. 2016). A *Reveal* article published in 2018 based on research conducted by the Center for Investigative Reporting in 2018 profiled a college-educated Black woman from Philadelphia who, despite having a job and savings, was denied a mortgage. She literally became the face of contemporary mortgage discrimination, with her photo dramatically superimposed on a 1937 Home Owners Redlining Corporation residential security map with a bold title, "KEPT OUT." The story goes on to explain that the woman's biracial (white and Japanese) partner, also a woman, was approved for a mortgage, so the article focuses on race as the basis of their experience of mortgage discrimination. Seen through an intersectional lens, the experience of discrimination might be understood as relating to the couple's marginalized status as queer women of color, a combination of identities that would make them particularly vulnerable in the housing and financial marketplace.

An intersectional approach allows us to see layers and levels of marginalization and vulnerability and makes visible those who hold multiply marginalized identities. When we look beyond the queer "prototype" (Purdie-Vaughns and Eibach 2008)—young, gay, cisgender, white, man— we can see a host of communities who are vulnerable to housing discrimination. Queer couples with children, for example, make up a significant and growing population. Of the approximately 700,000 cohabitating queer couples in the United States, about 114,000 are raising children, and three-quarters of these couples are women (Goldberg and Conron 2018). Do these families face discrimination from realtors, rental agents, mortgage brokers, or neighbors? How would our legal system treat a housing discrimination complaint from queer Black women raising children? Fair housing research needs to consider such groups.

Older adults within the queer and trans communities are also at risk of being overlooked. "Aging with Pride," a longitudinal study funded by the National Institutes of Health, tracked 2,400 LGBTQ-identified adults and identified multiple points of vulnerability. These included applying to live in retirement communities or long-term care facilities where they feared, and sometimes experienced, bias and bullying. One gay man in his seventies described the questions he was asked when visiting retirement communities: Had he ever been married? Why not? Did he have grandchildren? Would he be inviting "guests" to visit? (Wax-Thibodeaux 2014). Housing services for older adults do not necessarily anticipate queer and trans people, while services for queer and trans people do not always anticipate older adults.

Failing to recognize the diversity of identities and experiences within those we categorize together—people who are incarcerated, people who are homeless, renters, homeowners, domestic violence survivors—risks ignoring their humanity and the unique pathways to their marginalization. A 2015 report from the Homeless Rights Advocacy Project at the University of Seattle Law School describes this risk: "Homogenizing the people who are homeless facilitates their dehumanization, erasing not only their diverse identities, but also obscuring the diverse causes of their homelessness" (Lurie, Schuster, and Rankin 2015: iv).

In addition to rendering visible the people within queer and trans communities who hold multiple marginalized identities, intersectionality focuses attention on the institutional and structural levels of power that create and reinforce inequality within and beyond housing (López and Gadsden 2017). Corus et al. (2016) offer a framework for analyzing policy through an intersectional lens "to conceptually 'envision' and 'identify' novel and previously veiled aspects of consumption in poverty" (MacInnis 2011: 138; Corus et al. 2016: 215). This framework focuses on overlapping categories (understanding how members of the same group have different experiences), structural forces (understanding the relationship across processes of inequality), and the role of power (how control over decision-making and resources is held by dominant social groups). In Table 6.1, we reconsider two examples through the Corus et al. (2016) framework.

An intersectional approach also calls for critical self-reflection among fair housing researchers and practitioners and for them to "continually and closely examine their own race, gender, class, sexual orientation, disability, language, nativity/citizenship and social position, and their relationship to systems of inequality as part of intersecting systems of oppression and privilege" (López and Gadsden 2017: 15). Recognizing one's own positionality is an essential part of the process of recognizing intersectionality and identifying power structures.

Establishing Explicit and Consistent
Federal Antidiscrimination Policy

Local, state, and federal laws have reinforced heteronormativity and cisnormativity for more than a century, so in this section we turn to recommendations regarding legal solutions to the problem of housing discrimination against queer and trans communities. In the absence of federal policy, states are left to decide for themselves—an untenable arrangement in regard to a fundamental civil rights issue like access to housing. The proposed National Equality Act would provide protection against discrimination nationally on the basis of sexual orientation or gender identity in the areas of employment,

Table 6.1. Reimagining Fair Housing Policies and Programs Through an Intersectional Lens

Housing issues	Overlapping categories	Structural forces	Role of power
Youth homelessness	*How do queer and trans identities interact with race, class, education, ability, history of behavioral health and substance abuse, and experiences of verbal, physical, and sexual abuse?*	*How do family structures keep parents from supporting their queer and trans children? What funding mechanisms (local, state, federal) make it difficult for programs to serve youth with these multiple identities?*	*What agency do youth, particularly those under 18, have in regard to their housing? How do neighborhoods use political and economic privilege to prevent homeless shelters in their homes (NIMBYism)? What role do elected officials and bureaucrats play in redesigning and enforcing rules around equity and inclusion?*
Incarceration and reentry for trans individuals	*How does trans or nonbinary status impact placement in gender-segregated facilities and experiences of verbal, physical, and sexual abuse? How do race/ethnicity and age affect access to support services upon reentry?*	*How do prison policies, practices, and physical structures embody and reinforce transphobia, misogyny, and racism? What role does state-sanctioned employment discrimination against trans individuals play in their elevated risk for imprisonment? How do family structures, lack of family support, and experiences of interpersonal violence impact risk for incarceration and challenges upon reentry?*	*How are prison staff held accountable for their role in abuse and harassment of trans people who are incarcerated? What role do private prisons and their profit motive play in perpetuating mass incarceration? How does white supremacy and settler colonialism reinforce mass incarceration as a form of social control?*

credit, education, public spaces and services, federally funded programs, jury service, and housing. The Trump administration has stated that, while it "absolutely opposes discrimination of any kind and supports the equal treatment of all," the bill as written is "filled with poison pills." Conservatives have objected to the inclusion of gender identity and the expansion of the definition of public accommodations to include retail stores, banks, transportation services, and health care services. Furthermore, the Equality Act would prevent the 1994 Religious Freedom Restoration Act from allowing discrimination on the basis of sexual orientation and gender identity as an exercise of religious freedom. The measure has broad political, public, and corporate support but is unlikely to pass in a Republican-controlled U.S. Senate.

The proposed Fair and Equal Housing Act would amend the Fair Housing Act to add sexual orientation and gender identity as protected classes but would not address areas other than housing. In the absence of new legislation, the Supreme Court could rule that legal protections against discrimination on the basis sex extend to sexual orientation and gender identity, with the understanding that stereotypes about people based on their sex assigned at birth are at the root of such discrimination. The legal debate is likely to hinge on whether language in laws—in this case the word "sex"—can reasonably be reinterpreted as circumstances and societal issues change—in this case, the emergence of gender identity as a civil rights issue. Justice Ruth Bader Ginsburg, for one, has stated clearly that "Congress may design legislation to govern changing times and circumstances" (Ginsburg 2019). The Supreme Court ruled in *West v. Gibson* (1999) that legislation does not freeze the scope of language: "Words in statutes can enlarge or contract their scope as other changes, in law or in the world, require their application to new instances or make old applications anachronistic" (5).

National policies and programs also need to use consistent and accurate language that clearly distinguishes sexual orientation and gender identity. Such language must plan ahead for the evolution of language by being both specific and flexible. For example, gender identity is an internal belief about oneself and can be distinguished from gender roles, which are social norms about how people of different genders ought to behave, and gender expression, which is the outward style and behavior a person enacts in relation to gender. A person's gender identity may vary from the person's expression, and both may vary from societal gender roles. National policy should protect individuals on all of these bases: internal feeling, outward expression, social expectation, and any alignments among these.

Promoting Implementation, Enforcement, and Training

While they are essential, clear and consistent federal policies are not enough by themselves. The high levels of documented housing discrimination since passage of the 1968 Fair Housing Act underscore that compliance with such policies require the additional steps of training and enforcement. Implementation requires very deliberate efforts to translate policy for the myriad of gatekeepers—from leasing agents, realtors, and loan officers within the private housing market to administrative staff, case managers, and security officers within subsidized and institutional settings—who control access to housing.

Efforts within HUD to ensure full compliance with the 2012 Equal Access Rule provide one example of concerted effort to translate policy to everyday practice. The 2012 Rule explicitly prohibited those operating federally funded or federally insured housing from discriminating on the basis of sexual orientation and gender identity, but it did not translate those rules into everyday practices in emergency shelters and other congregate housing facilities. Working closely with service providers and advocates across the country, HUD staff compiled a series of resources to help emergency shelters and other housing providers comply with the 2012 Equal Access Rule with particular attention to the safety of transgender people. Prior to publication of the 2016 Final Equal Access Rule, HUD also made publicly available through HUD Exchange: (1) a twenty-four-page guide to providing trans-inclusive language, which addresses facilities and confidentiality, with a glossary of terms and sample antidiscrimination policies for individual facilities including standards for staff and residents; (2) a self-assessment for individual facilities to identify priorities and next steps for full compliance; (3) a decision tree outlining practices to encourage and discourage relating to outreach and engagement, assessment, referral, enrollment, and unit and bed assignment; and (4) training scenarios for frontline staff and management formatted as role-plays with discussion questions relating to common situations. HUD staff promoted these materials through in-person trainings and developed a notice explaining the Equal Access Rule.

Nominally, HUD's Equal Access Rule protects some of the most vulnerable groups, including queer and trans homeless youth and transgender adults who have experienced domestic abuse. In practice, implementation and enforcement have been limited, in part because explicit protections on the basis of sexual orientation and gender identity are more recent and require agency staff to rethink long-standing practices. Furthermore, while the Trump administration has not repealed these legal protections, HUD has taken guidance and training materials off its website and has not moved forward with requiring HUD-funded shelters to post a notice about residents' rights. Advocacy organizations still make the materials available online, but the implementation process no longer has the weight of the federal government behind it.

Similarly, implementation of PREA—mandating that prison staff understand what "transgender" and "gender-nonconforming" mean and that trans people are provided with appropriate housing and are kept safe, among other things—has been very uneven. A study by Malkin and DeJong (2018) found that only ten states were in full compliance with all thirteen of the PREA regulations regarding transgender people, and 40 percent of states continued to have at least one policy in direct conflict with PREA protections for transgender individuals. In the absence of clear state policy, including a mandate around training, it is unlikely that prison staff will fully understand the concepts and legal protections in PREA or change their day-to-day practices. The changes Trump administration officials made to the "Transgender Offenders Manual" in May 2018 further jeopardize implementation of PREA regulations.

Collecting Housing Data on Queer and Trans People and Their Experiences

The recent increase in research focused on housing discrimination that queer and trans communities face has provided crucial evidence of the need for explicit protections within the private housing market as well as subsidized facilities. A logical next step is to further integrate questions about sexual orientation and gender identity (SOGI) into national surveys to allow more extensive monitoring of the health and well-being of queer and trans communities. Consistent data collection is an essential step toward ending the invisibility of queer and trans communities.

The LGBTQ Data Inclusion Act, introduced in the U.S. Congress in 2017, would mandate inclusion of SOGI questions in federal population studies and establish data standards and routine assessments of changes needed in survey methods to obtain such data. Having SOGI information in the American Community Survey and American Housing Survey, in particular, would greatly expand our understanding of the housing and economic conditions in which queer and trans communities live. As with the materials developed to help shelters implement the Equal Access Rule, SOGI questions have been removed from federal surveys under the Trump administration.

Creating Housing That Addresses the Unique Challenges of Queer and Trans Youth and Older Adults

In addition to working toward full understanding and compliance with antidiscrimination laws, affirmatively furthering fair housing for queer and trans communities also means developing new affordable housing options for some of the most vulnerable queer and trans populations, including older adults and homeless youth. Several queer and trans elder-living communities have been developed over the past decade, including Triangle Square in West Hollywood, John C. Anderson Apartments in Philadelphia, and Ingersoll Senior Residences in Brooklyn, all of which used federal tax credits in conjunction with other state and local financing mechanisms. Similarly, housing advocates and developers are building new facilities like Philadelphia's Gloria Casarez Residence aimed at queer and trans young adults who are or have been homeless. As with the developments focusing on older adults, the Gloria Casarez Residence markets itself as "LGBTQ-friendly" rather than "exclusive" in order to comply with the same federal fair housing laws that do not explicitly protect queer and trans communities. The demand for these types of facilities—demonstrated by long wait lists—reflects the need for subsidized housing that specifically serves these two vulnerable age groups.

In the meantime, marginalized queer communities are taking action: the Crystal House Project in East New York provides "transitional low-cost living space dedicated to supporting the growth and leadership of Black and Brown poor, working, and queer individuals." The Audre Lorde Project engages in a variety of organizing initiatives centered on building queer spaces for people and communities of color in New York City. Their Brick by Brick campaign aims to secure safe, long-term housing; their Safe Outside the System campaign "[challenges] hate and police violence by using community based strategies." Specifically, canvassers for the project focus on gathering stories about efforts to secure housing and educating neighbors about the housing needs of trans people (Joseph 2019).

Queering the Fair Housing Act's Interpretation of Family

The Fair Housing Act protects people from discrimination on the basis of *family status*. Interpreted broadly, this basis could cover most households, including the *chosen families* of many queer and trans individuals, who experience familial rejection at high rates (Pew Research Center 2013). In practice, the Fair Housing Act's family status provision protects only those potential renters or purchasers who have children (with legal custody), who are pregnant, or who pursuing legal custody. Indeed, most household structures are legally susceptible to discrimination—in particular, many queer households. The legality of private discrimination against most household structures mirrors the skepticism of nonnormative housing long espoused by public policy.

In place of this limited family status protection, we should work to establish an affirmative right of co-residence. While adopting a functional family approach within the Federal Housing Administration would improve the lives of many people, queering the notion of family in 2019 entails going beyond the most immediately family-like living arrangements. Indeed, Rigel C. Oliveri (2016) argues that any regulation of the "intimate association" of co-residence is "wholly incompatible" with modern views on privacy as interpreted by the Supreme Court. Instead, Oliveri argues that a right to privacy in intimate associations implies a right of co-residence that trumps a municipality's ability to precisely prescribe the allowable composition of its constituent households.

Queer individuals and households may be disproportionately helped by a right of co-residence. In cooperative housing, (typically) nonrelated individuals seek community and kinship in a single large residential home. Queer collective living was an important avenue for the development of alternative ways of living in the 1970s and explicitly turned away from childbearing straight household arrangements to a more communal lifestyle (Vider 2015).

Conclusion

The fight for fair housing continues. The power to decide who deserves protection follows similar lines as it did when the Fair Housing Act was written in 1968, amended in 1974 to include women and families with children, and amended again to include those with a handicap but to exclude trans people in 1988. Jesse Helms and Alan Cranston are long since deceased, replaced by a new generation of political actors promulgating the same ideologies. The questions they debated—Should the law protect transgender individuals?—and those they did not—Should the law protect queer people against housing and other forms of discrimination?—remain contested. Jesse Helms easily won the day in 1988, excluding trans people from protection under the Fair Housing Act's provisions for people with a handicap. Are we now ready to protect queer and trans people? Are we ready to adopt an intersectional lens that renders visible those marginalized by their racial, sexual, and gender identities? Are the gatekeepers to housing—realtors, mortgage brokers, rental agents, neighbors, parents, intake workers and case managers at shelters, and prison staff—ready to embrace the full humanity of people across sexual orientation and gender identity? We shall see.

Notes

1. Both Helms and the eventual legislation used the word "transvestite." The word is pathologizing and problematic, reflecting a history of language being used against trans people "by political, religious, legal, and medical cultural institutions for the purpose of normalizing their marginalization and discrimination against them" (Bouman et al. 2017). The context of the lawsuit and discussion in the congressional record suggests the amendment intends to apply to individuals with a gender identity and presentation that does not match the sex assigned to them at birth—a trans person.

2. In the interests of precision and harm reduction, we have made several other stylistic choices that we encourage others to adopt. We avoid words like "male" and "female," which reflect the binary roles in sexual reproduction. As such, the words are incomplete descriptors for the wide variety of biological sex differences observed in the world, leaving no room for intersex people. Further, these sex differences are merely one aspect of the social control and oppression felt by queer and trans people. We therefore use words like "man," "woman," and "nonbinary," which are specific to a person's gender and not to their body. Similarly, we avoid words like "same-sex" and "opposite-sex." Given the root word, as well as the clinical history of the word "homosexual," we avoid it—and "heterosexual," which implies the former. In their places, we use clear and straightforward words like "gay," "lesbian," and "straight." A person's gender is the relevant attribute in these contexts, not their body. Finally, when relevant for the discussion, we use the phrase "sex assigned at birth" to discuss sex. We aim to be inclusive of not just trans people but also intersex people whose bodies and experiences reflect an assignment by physicians or caregivers.

References

Abrokwa, Alice. "'When They Enter, We All Enter': Opening the Door to Intersectional Discrimination Claims Based on Race and Disability." *Michigan Journal of Race & Law* 24 (2018): 15–74.

Baca, Alex. "In Defense of Dorms for Grown-Ups." *Slate*, March 7, 2018. Accessed July 14, 2019. https://slate.com/technology/2018/03/dorms-for-grown-ups-are-good-even-in-san-francisco.html.

Bassett, Edward. *Zoning*. National Municipal League, Technical Pamphlet Series No. 5, 1922.

Blackwell v. United States Department of the Treasury. U.S. District Court, District of Columbia, 639 F. Supp. 289 (D.D.C. 1986), May 27, 1986.

Bouman, Walter Pierre, Amets Suess Schwend, Joz Motmans, Adam Smiley, Joshua D. Safer, Madeline B. Deutsch, Noah J. Adams, and Sam Winter. "Language and Trans Health." *International Journal of Transgenderism* 18, no. 1 (January 2, 2017): 1–6. https://doi.org/10.1080/15532739.2016.1262127.

Brown, Laura Elizabeth. "Regulating the Marrying Kind: The Constitutionality of Federal Regulation of Polygamy under the Mann Act." *McGeorge Law Review* 39, no. 1 (2008): 267–98.

Brown, Taylor N. T., and Jody L. Herman. *Intimate Partner Violence and Sexual Abuse Among LGBT People: A Review of Existing Research*. Los Angeles: Williams Institute, 2015. Accessed June 14, 2019. https://williamsinstitute.law.ucla.edu/wp-content/uploads/Intimate-Partner-Violence-and-Sexual-Abuse-among-LGBT-People.pdf.

Burgess, A. "Queering Heterosexual Spaces: Positive Space Campaigns Disrupting Campus Heteronormativity." *Canadian Woman Studies* 24, no. 2–3 (2005): 27–30.

Center for American Progress and Movement Advancement Project. *Unjust: How the Broken Criminal Justice System Fails Transgender People*. 2016. Accessed June 14, 2019. http://www.lgbtmap.org/file/lgbt-criminal-justice-trans.pdf.

Choi, S. K., B. D. M. Wilson, J. Shelton, and G. Gates. *Serving Our Youth 2015: The Needs and Experiences of Lesbian, Gay, Bisexual, Transgender, and Questioning Youth Experiencing Homelessness*. Los Angeles: Williams Institute with True Colors Fund, 2015.

Corus, Canon, Bige Saatcioglu, Carol Kaufman-Scarborough, Christopher P. Blocker, Shikha Upadhyaya, and Samuelson Appau. "Transforming Poverty-Related Policy with Intersectionality." *Journal of Public Policy & Marketing* 35, no. 2 (2016): 211–22.

Crenshaw, Kimberlé. "Demarginalizing the Intersection of Race and Sex: A Black Feminist Critique of Antidiscrimination Doctrine, Feminist Theory and Antiracist Politics." *University of Chicago Legal Forum*, issue 1, article 8 (1989).

Davis v. Davis, 643 So.2d 931 (Supreme Court of Mississippi, October 6, 1994).

DeGraffenreid v. Gender Motors Assembly Division, 413 F. Supp. 142 (U.S. District Court E.D. Mo. 1976).

Desmond, Matthew. *Evicted: Poverty and Profit in the American City*. New York: Crown Books, 2016.

Doan, Petra L. *Queering Planning: Challenging Heteronormative Assumptions and Reframing Planning Practice*. Burlington, VT: Ashgate, 2011.

Durso, L. E., and G. J. Gates. *Serving Our Youth: Findings from a National Survey of Service Providers Working with Lesbian, Gay, Bisexual, and Transgender Youth Who Are Homeless or at Risk of Becoming Homeless.* Los Angeles: Williams Institute with True Colors Fund and the Palette Fund, 2012.

Fischel, William A. "An Economic History of Zoning and a Cure for Its Exclusionary Effects." *Urban Studies* 41, no. 2 (February 2004): 317–40. https://doi.org/10.1080/0042098032000165271.

Foner, Nancy. "Immigrant Women and Work in New York City, Then and Now." *Journal of American Ethnic History* 18, no. 3 (1999): 95–113.

Friedman, Samantha, Angela Reynolds, Susan Scovill, Florence R. Brassier, Ron Campbell, and McKenzie Ballou. *An Estimate of Housing Discrimination Against Same-Sex Couples.* Washington, D.C.: Department of Housing and Urban Development, Office of Policy Development and Research, June 2013.

Frisch, Michael. "Finding Transformative Planning Practice in the Spaces of Intersectionality." In *Planning and LGBTQ Communities: The Need for Inclusive Queer Spaces*, edited by Petra L. Doan. New York: Routledge, 2015.

———. "Planning as a Heterosexist Project." *Journal of Planning Education and Research* 21, no. 3 (March 2002): 254–66. https://doi.org/10.1177/0739456X0202100303.

Giesking, J. J. "Crossing Over into Neighbourhoods of The Body: Urban Territories, Borders and Lesbian-Queer Bodies in New York City." *Area* 48, no. 3 (2016): 262–70.

Ginsburg, Ruth Bader. Concurring statement, Supreme Court of the United States No. 17–340 *New Prime Inc., Petitioner v. Dominic Oliveira*, 2019.

Glantz, Aaron, and Emmanuel Martinez. "Kept Out: For People of Color, Banks Are Shutting the Door to Homeownership." *Reveal*, February 15, 2018. Accessed March 3, 2019. https://www.revealnews.org/article/for-people-of-color-banks-are-shutting-the-door-to-homeownership/.

Goldberg, Shoshana K., and Kerith J. Conron. 2018. *How Many Same-Sex Couples in the U.S. Are Raising Children?* Williams Institute, UCLA School of Law. Accessed June 16, 2019. https://williamsinstitute.law.ucla.edu/research/parenting/how-many-same-sex-parents-in-us/.

Goldin, Claudia. "The Quiet Revolution That Transformed Women's Employment, Education, and Family." *American Economic Review* 96, no. 2 (2006): 21.

Grant, Jaime M., Lisa A. Mottet, Justin Tanis, Jack Harrison, Jody L. Herman, and Mara Keisling. *Injustice at Every Turn: A Report of the National Transgender Discrimination Survey.* Washington, D.C.: National Center for Transgender Equality and National Gay and Lesbian Task Force, 2011. Accessed June 14, 2019. https://transequality.org/sites/default/files/docs/resources/NTDS_Report.pdf.

Groth, Paul Erling. *Living Downtown: The History of Residential Hotels in the United States.* Berkeley: University of California Press, 1994.

Herek, Gregory M. "Hate Crimes and Stigma-Related Experiences Among Sexual Minority Adults in the United States: Prevalence Estimates From a National Probability Sample." *Journal of Interpersonal Violence* 24, no. 1 (January 2009): 54–74. https://doi.org/10.1177/0886260508316477.

Hirt, Sonia. *Zoned in the USA: The Origins and Implications of American Land-Use Regulation.* Ithaca, NY: Cornell University Press, 2014.

Hunt, Jerome, and Aisha Moodie-Mills. "The Unfair Criminalization of Gay and Transgender Youth." Center for American Progress, 2012, 12. https://cdn.americanprogress.org/wp -content/uploads/issues/2012/06/pdf/juvenile_justice.pdf.

James, S. E., J. L. Herman, S. Rankin, M. Keisling, L. Mottet, and M. Anafi. *The Report of the 2015 U.S. Transgender Survey*. Washington, D.C.: National Center for Transgender Equality, 2016. Accessed June 14, 2019. http://www.transequality.org/sites/default/files/docs /usts/USTS%20Full%20Report%20-%20FINAL%201.6.17.pdf.

Jan, Tracy. "Proposed HUD Rule Would Strip Transgender Protections at Homeless Shelters." *Washington Post*, May 22, 2019. Accessed June 24, 2019. https://www.washingtonpost.com /business/2019/05/22/proposed-hud-rule-would-strip-transgender-protections -homeless-shelters/.

Joseph, Kerbie. Telephone interview with Kerbie Joseph of the Audre Lorde Project, March 31, 2019.

"Kimberlé Crenshaw on Intersectionality, More than Two Decades Later." Interview with Columbia University Law School correspondent, June 8, 2017. Accessed March 19, 2019. https://www.law.columbia.edu/pt-br/news/2017/06/kimberle-crenshaw-intersectionality.

Langowski, Jamie, William L. Berman, Regina Holloway, and Cameron McGinn. "Transcending Prejudice: Gender Identity and Expression-Based Discrimination in the Metro Boston Rental Housing Market." *Yale Journal of Law & Feminism* 29, no. 2, article 2 (2018).

Lee, Hugh, Mark Learmonth, and Nancy Harding. "Queering Public Administration." *Public Administration* 86, no. 1 (2008): 149–67.

Levy, Diane K., Doug Wissoker, Claudia L. Aranda, Brent Howell, Rob Pitingol, Sarale Sewel, and Rob Santos. *A Paired-Testing Pilot Study of Housing Discrimination against Same-Sex Couples and Transgender Individuals*. Washington, D.C.: Urban Institute, June 2017.

Lipsitz, George. "'Living Downstream': The Fair Housing Act at Fifty." In *The Fight for Fair Housing: Causes, Consequences, and Future Implications of the 1968 Federal Fair Housing Act*, edited by Gregory Squires. New York: Routledge, 2017.

López, Nancy, and Vivian L. Gadsden. "Health Inequities, Social Determinants, and Intersectionality." In *Perspectives on Health Equity and Social Determinants of Health*, edited by Kimber Bogard, Velma McBride Murry, and Charlee Alexander. Washington, D.C.: National Academy of Medicine, 2017.

Lorde, Audre. "There Is No Hierarchy of Oppressions." *Bulletin: Homophobia and Education* 14, no. 3/4 (1983): 9.

Los Angeles City Council, Community Care Facilities Ordinance CF 11~0262, March 8, 2012. Accessed March 14, 2020. http://clkrep.lacity.org/onlinedocs/2011/11-0262_RPT_PLAN _3-08-2012.pdf.

Lugg, Catherine A., and Jason P. Murphy. "Thinking Whimsically: Queering the Study of Educational Policy-Making and Politics." *International Journal of Qualitative Studies in Education* 27, no. 9 (2014): 1183–204.

Lurie, Kaya, Breanne Schuster, and Sara Rankin. "Discrimination at the Margins: The Intersectionality of Homelessness & Other Marginalized Groups." *Homeless Rights Advocacy Project* 8, 2015. Accessed June 23, 2019.

MacInnis, Deborah J. "A Framework for Conceptual Contributions in Marketing." *Journal of Marketing* 75 (July 2011): 136–54.

Malkin, Michelle L., and Christina DeJong. "Protections for Transgender Inmates Under PREA: A Comparison of State Correctional Policies in the United States." *Sexuality Research and Social Policy* (August 15, 2018): 1–15.

Mallory, Christy, and Brad Sears. *Evidence of Housing Discrimination Based on Sexual Orientation and Gender Identity: An Analysis of Complaints Filed with State Enforcement Agencies, 2008–2014.* Los Angeles: Williams Institute, February 2016.

Meyerowitz, Joanne. "Sexual Geography and Gender Economy: The Furnished Room Districts of Chicago, 1890–1930." *Gender & History* 2, no. 3 (September 1990): 274–97. https://doi.org/10.1111/j.1468-0424.1990.tb00101.x.

Michigan Compiled Laws, Michigan Penal Code § 750.335. Lewd and Lascivious Cohabitation and Gross Lewdness. Act 328 of 1931. http://www.legislature.mi.gov/(S(ilgm04inxggauaenxge0f0uz))/documents/mcl/pdf/mcl-750-335.pdf.

Moore v. City of East Cleveland, No. 75-6289 (U.S. Supreme Court, May 31, 1977).

Moskowitz, P. "When It Comes to Gentrification, LGBTQ People Are Both Victim and Perpetrator." *Vice*, March 12, 2017. Accessed June 23, 2019. https://www.vice.com/en_us/article/nz5qwb/when-it-comes-to-gentrification-lgbtq-people-are-both-victim-and-perpetrator.

Motta, Jose Inacio Jardim. "Sexualities and Public Policies: A Queer Approach for Times of Democratic Crisis." *Saúde Debate* 40 (2016): 73–85.

National Fair Housing Alliance. *Making Every Neighborhood a Place of Opportunity: 2018 Fair Housing Trends Report.* Accessed February 17, 2019. https://nationalfairhousing.org/wp-content/uploads/2018/04/NFHA-2018-Fair-Housing-Trends-Report.pdf.

Oliveri, Rigel C. "Single-Family Zoning, Intimate Association, and the Right to Choose Household Companions." *Florida Law Review* 67 (2016): 55.

Oswald, Ramona Faith, Libby Balter Blume, and Stephen R. Marks. 2005. "Decentering Heteronormativity: A Model for Family Studies." In *Sourcebook of Family Theory and Research*, edited by Vern L. Bengtson, Alan C. Acock, Katherine R. Allen, Peggye Dilworth-Anderson, and David M. Klein, 143–66. Thousand Oaks, CA: Sage Publications, 2005.

Pew Research Center. *A Survey of LGBT Americans.* Washington, D.C.: Pew Research Center, June 13, 2013.

Philadelphia Commission on Human Relations. *Inform, Monitor and Enforce: Addressing Racism and Discrimination in Philadelphia's LGBTQ Community.* 2016. Accessed June 23, 2019. https://pchrlgbt.files.wordpress.com/2017/08/pchr-final-lgbtq-report-0617.pdf.

———. *Inform, Monitor and Enforce: Progress Report, Addressing Racism and Discrimination in Philadelphia's LGBTQ Community.* 2017. Accessed June 23, 2019. https://pchrlgbt.files.wordpress.com/2017/10/pchr-progress-report1.pdf.

Phipps, Kelly Elizabeth. "Marriage & Redemption: Mormon Polygamy in the Congressional Imagination, 1862–1887." *Virginia Law Review* 95, no. 2 (April 2009): 53.

Pontin, Ben. "Nuisance Law and the Industrial Revolution: A Reinterpretation of Doctrine and Institutional Competence: Nuisance Law and the Industrial Revolution." *Modern Law Review* 75, no. 6 (November 2012): 1010–36. https://doi.org/10.1111/j.1468-2230.2012.00935.x.

Purdie-Vaughns, Valerie, and Richard P. Eibach. "Intersectional Invisibility: The Distinctive Advantages and Disadvantages of Multiple Subordinate-Group Identities." *Sex Roles* 59 (2008): 377–91.

Redburn, Kate. "Zoned Out: How Zoning Law Undermines Family Law's Functional Turn." *Yale Law Journal* 128, no. 8 (2019): 2122–473.

Remedios, J. D., S. H. Synder, and C. A. Lizza. "Perceptions of Women of Color Who Claim Compound Discrimination: Interpersonal Judgments and Perceived Credibility." *Group Processes and Intergroup Relations* 9 (2016): 769–83.

Rooney, Caitlin, Laura E. Durso, and Sharita J. Gruberg. *Discrimination Against Transgender Women Seeking Access to Homeless Shelters*. Center for American Progress and the Equal Rights Center, January 7, 2016. https://cdn.americanprogress.org/wp-content/uploads /2016/01/06113001/HomelessTransgender.pdf.

Rosen, Christine Meisner. "'Knowing' Industrial Pollution: Nuisance Law and the Power of Tradition in a Time of Rapid Economic Change, 1840–1864." *Environmental History* 8, no. 4 (October 2003): 565.

Schwegman, David. "Rental Market Discrimination Against Same-Sex Couples: Evidence From a Pairwise-Matched Email Correspondence Test." *Housing Policy Debate* 29, no. 2 (2019): 250–72.

Shipley, H. "Queering Institutions?: Sexual Identity in Public Education in a Canadian Context." *Feminist Teacher* 23, no. 3 (2004): 196–210.

Smith, Amy Symens, Charles Holmberg, and Marcella Jones-Puthoff. *The Emergency and Transitional Shelter Population: 2010*. U.S. Census Bureau, September 2012.

Sun, Hua, and Lei Gao. "Lending Practices to Same-Sex Borrowers." *Proceedings of the National Academy of Sciences of the United States of America*, April 16, 2019. Accessed April 20, 2019. https://www.pnas.org/content/early/2019/04/15/1903592116.

Tester, Griff. "An Intersectional Analysis of Sexual Harassment in Housing." *Gender & Society* 22, no. 3 (2008): 349–66.

Vider, Stephen. "'The Ultimate Extension of Gay Community': Communal Living and Gay Liberation in the 1970s." *Gender & History* 27, no. 3 (November 2015): 865–81. https://doi .org/10.1111/1468-0424.12167.

Village of Belle Terre et al. v. Boraas et al., No. 73-191 (United States Court of Appeals for the Second Circuit, April 1, 1974).

Wax-Thibodeaux, Emily. "A Philadelphia Apartment Building May Be a National Model for Low-Income LGBT Seniors." *Washington Post*, September 12, 2014. Accessed March 9, 2019. https://www.washingtonpost.com/politics/a-philadelphia-apartment-building-may -be-a-national-model-for-low-income-lgbt-seniors/2014/09/12/f64e06bc-352d-11e4 -8f02-03c644b2d7d0_story.html.

Westbrook, Laurel, and Kristen Schilt. "Doing Gender, Determining Gender: Transgender People, Gender Panics, and the Maintenance of the Sex/Gender/Sexuality System." *Gender & Society* 28, no. 1 (2014): 32–57.

Zoukis, Christopher. "More Legal Cases Involving Transgender Prisoners in Multiple States." *Prison Legal News*, November 6, 2018. Accessed April 27, 2019. https://www.prisonlegalnews .org/news/2018/nov/6/more-legal-cases-involving-transgender-prisoners-multiple-states/.

CONTRIBUTORS

Francesca Russello Ammon is associate professor in the Departments of City and Regional Planning and Historic Preservation at the University of Pennsylvania. As a cultural historian of the built environment, her teaching, research, and writing focus on the changing shapes and spaces of the twentieth- and twenty-first-century American city.

Raphael Bostic is the president and chief executive officer of the Federal Reserve Bank of Atlanta. His work spans many fields, including home ownership, housing finance, neighborhood change, and the role of institutions in shaping policy effectiveness.

Devin Michelle Bunten is assistant professor of Urban Economics and Housing in the Department of Urban Studies and Planning at the Massachusetts Institute of Technology. She is a writer and economist, whose research uses economic theory and empirical tools to study a range of urban topics, including gentrification and neighborhood change, restrictive zoning, and racial housing disparities.

Camille Z. Charles is Walter H. and Leonore C. Annenberg Professor in the Social Sciences, Professor of Sociology, Africana Studies, and Education, and director of the Center for Africana Studies at the University of Pennsylvania. Her research interests are in the areas of urban inequality, racial attitudes and intergroup relations, racial residential segregation, minorities in higher education, and racial identity.

Nestor M. Davidson is Albert A. Walsh Chair in Real Estate, Land Use, and Property Law at Fordham University. He is an expert in property law, urban law, and affordable housing law and policy.

Amy Hillier is associate professor at the University of Pennsylvania School of Social Policy and Practice. Her research has focused largely on issues of geographic disparities and access to services and resources in disadvantaged communities.

Marc Morial is president and CEO of the National Urban League, the nation's largest historic civil rights and urban advocacy organization. As mayor of New Orleans from 1994 to 2002, Morial led New Orleans's renaissance and left office with a 70 percent approval rating.

Eduardo M. Peñalver is Allan R. Tessler Dean and Professor of Law at Cornell Law School. Previously, he served as the John P. Wilson Professor of Law at the University of Chicago Law School. His scholarship explores the way in which the law mediates the interests of individuals and communities, focusing on property and land use, as well as law and religion.

Wendell E. Pritchett is Provost and James S. Riepe Presidential Professor of Law and Education at the University of Pennsylvania. His research examines the development of postwar urban policy, in particular urban renewal, housing finance, and housing discrimination.

Rand Quinn is associate professor at the University of Pennsylvania Graduate School of Education. His research interests include the origins and political consequences of private sector engagement in public education, the politics of race and ethnicity in urban school reform, and the impact of community-based institutions, organizations, and action in education.

Vincent J. Reina is assistant professor of Urban Economics and Housing in the Department of City and Regional Planning at the University of Pennsylvania. His research focuses on urban economics, low-income housing policy, household mobility, and the role of housing in community and economic development.

Akira Drake Rodriguez is a lecturer at the University of Pennsylvania Stuart Weitzman School of Design. Her research examines the politics of urban planning, or the ways that disenfranchised groups reappropriate their marginalized spaces in the city to gain access to and sustain urban political power.

Justin P. Steil is associate professor of law and urban planning in the Department of Urban Studies and Planning at the Massachusetts Institute of Technology. His research focuses on the intersection of law and urban policy, particularly as they relate to social stratification and spatial dimensions of inequality.

Susan M. Wachter is Sussman professor and professor of real estate and finance at the Wharton School of the University of Pennsylvania. From 1998 to 2001, she served as assistant secretary for Policy Development and Research, U.S. Department of Housing and Urban Development, the senior urban policy official and principal advisor to the secretary. At the Wharton School, she was chairperson of the Real Estate Department and professor of real estate and finance from July 1997 until her 1998 appointment to HUD. At Penn, she co-founded and currently is co-director of the Penn Institute for Urban Research. She also founded and currently serves as director of Wharton's Geographical Information Systems Lab. She was the editor of *Real Estate Economics* from 1997 to 1999 and currently serves on the editorial boards of several real estate journals. She is the author of more than two hundred scholarly publications and the recipient of several awards for teaching excellence at the Wharton School. Her previous edited volumes include *Shared Prosperity in America's*

Communities and *Neighborhood and Life Chances.* She has served on multiple for-profit and not-for-profit boards and currently serves on the Affordable Housing Advisory Committee of Fannie Mae and the Office of Financial Research Advisory Committee of the U.S. Treasury. She frequently comments on national media and testifies to Congress on U.S. housing policy.

INDEX

Figures and tables are indicated by page numbers followed by (fig.) and (tab.) respectively.

unemployment rates, 105–6, 106(tab.)
United States v. Loki Properties, 171
United States v. Starrett City, 147n3, 151n42
University of Chicago, 49
Urban Planning and the African American Community (Ritzdorf and Thomas), 2
urban policy: affirmatively furthering fair housing (AFFH) and, 136–37; antitrans, 159; heteronormative framework of, 159–62; neoliberalism and, 90; nonfamily uses, 162; residential segregation and, 29; rooming houses and, 161–62
urban renewal, 23–24, 29
urban sociology, 45, 49–50, 53
urban space: color-line in, 3, 11, 47–48, 51; displacement and, 46, 64; goods and services in, 92; resegregation and, 46; structural inequalities in, 65
U.S. Department of Housing and Urban Development (HUD): AFFH and, 95, 114, 133, 136–37, 141–43; antidiscrimination law, 164–65; charge to reverse segregation, 5, 132, 136; discretionary agency and, 133, 136–37; disparate impact liability and, 151n39; Equal Access Rule, 164–65, 176–77; fair housing and, 79; fair market rent (FMR) and, 116; HOPE VI program and, 93, 117; lack of investment oversight, 142; protected classes and, 171; trans people and, 165

Vale, Lawrence, 62
Vaughn, Edward, 25(fig.)
veterans, 17–18
Veterans Administration (VA), 17
Vidgor, Jacob L., 3
Village of Belle Terre v. Boraas, 162
Violence Against Women Act (VAWA), 165
Voting Rights Act (1965), 53, 96
voucher systems: affordable housing and, 80, 90–92, 116–17; educational outcomes of, 92; public housing and, 117; publicly funded, 86; school tuition and, 86–87

Wang, Kyungsoon, 111
Warren, Earl, 75
Washington, Booker T., 49
Washington, D. C., 84, 87
Weaver, Robert, 28–30, 33, 39
West, 52, 76–77

West v. Gibson, 175
Wetzel, Marsha, 168
white neighborhoods: better schools in, 89; blockbusting and, 22–23; gentrification and, 62; public schools and, 19, 54; racial zoning in, 13; real estate codes of ethics and, 14–15, 16(fig.), 33; residential segregation and, 59–60; restrictive covenants and, 14, 15(fig.); white preference for, 59–61
white racism, 38, 51
white rage, 96
whites: attitudes towards fair housing, 64; homeownership and, 107; household wealth, 59, 106–7; housing wealth and, 107; income distribution, 105; neighborhood preferences and, 60–61, 140–41; preferences for social distance from nonwhites, 64; real estate investment and, 11; resistance to desegregation, 75–76; social order and, 48; suburbanization and, 52, 84; tolerance for integration, 141; unemployment rates of, 105–6
white supremacy: representation of Blacks and, 66; resistance to, 48, 54; state and collective enforcement of, 47; urban planning and, 159; violence against Black progress and, 96–97
white violence: African American homeownership and, 20, 20(fig.); collective resistance to, 48; against housing discrimination protestors, 36, 53–54; racial segregation and, 51; school desegregation and, 76
Williams, Rhonda, 57
Wilson, William Julius, 56
women: commercial enterprise and, 161; heteronormativity and, 154, 159; housing and patriarchal family structure, 161; intersectionality and, 157–58; public housing and, 57; rooming houses and, 161; transgender, 169. *See also* Black women

zoning: exclusionary, 11, 81, 84, 124; formalism in defining families, 162; functional family approach in, 162; heterosexism and, 159; low-density, 2; racial, 2, 11, 13; single-family, 2, 124, 160–62